Governing in the
Information Age

Public Policy and Management

Series Editor: Professor R.A.W. Rhodes, Department of Politics, University of Newcastle.

The effectiveness of public policies is a matter of public concern and the efficiency with which policies are put into practice is a continuing problem for governments of all political persuasions. This series contributes to these debates by publishing informed, in-depth and contemporary analyses of public administration, public policy and public management.

The intention is to go beyond the usual textbook approach to the analysis of public policy and management and to encourage authors to move debate about their issue forward. In this sense, each book both describes current thinking and research, and explores future policy directions. Accessibility is a key feature and, as a result, the series will appeal to academics and their students as well as to the informed practitioner.

Current titles include:

Governing in the Information Age

Christine Bellamy and
John A. Taylor

Open University Press
Buckingham · Philadelphia

Open University Press
Celtic Court
22 Ballmoor
Buckingham
MK18 1XW

and

1900 Frost Road, Suite 101
Bristol, PA 19007, USA

First Published 1998

A catalogue record of this book is available from the British Library.

ISBN   0 335 19450 8 (pb)   0 335 19451 6 (hb)

Library of Congress Cataloging-in-Publication Data
Bellamy, Christine.
    Governing in the information age / Christine Bellamy, John A.
Taylor.
        p.   cm.
    Includes bibliographical references and index.
    ISBN 0-335-19451-6. — ISBN 0-335-19450-8 (pbk.)
    1. Administrative agencies—Great Britain—Data processing.
2. Great Britain—Politics and government—1945–   3. Public
administration—Data processing.   I. Taylor, John A., 1944–
II. Title.
JN329.E4B45   1997
351.41'00285—dc21   97–23719
                                                    CIP

Typeset by Dorwyn Ltd, Rowlands Castle, Hants
Printed in Great Britain by Biddles Ltd, Guildford and King's Lynn

Contents

Preface

Many readers will interpret this book as one dealing with technological change, diffusion and impact, despite the protestations of its authors. After all, any book labelled *information age* must, *ipso facto*, be about that high tide of new information and communication technologies which threatens to engulf all in its wake. Two things follow. One is that many people will read the book from a perspective which assumes a determining role for the technologies. The technologies convey into government certain capabilities. They allow information to be handled in new ways; they permit new forms of communication around government and the wider polity. The technologies shape government and they do so in ways which are either breathtaking in their potential for progress and improvement, or which threaten the fabric of social and working life.

We have been at pains in writing this book to dispel this all too frequently held assumption. It is vital that we understand why and how these new technologies are diffusing into government. It is equally vital that the intellectual baggage of technological determinisms (for good or ill) be discarded. New technologies will not open society's door to a better future. Nor will they bring with them a frightening future of human despair. Utopian and dystopian imagery may be important for human discourse, benchmarking logical possibilities for our futures. Such imagery is not useful for academic research, however, if it serves to pre-form our scholarly thinking. Our concern here has been to break out of this oppositional determinism and to break into a social shaping perspective on new technologies in governance by exploring technological change in its institutional context.

The institutions of government, those longstanding values, norms and conventions which shape action and structure relationships and which are made manifest in organizations and processes, have always been informational in character. The so-called information technology (IT) revolution does not make them so. Institutions have determined the kind of information which governments collect, utilize and communicate for all the time we have had governments. What once went into the filing cabinet now goes into the computer. What was once transmitted by human courier in paper form is now sent at the speed of light along strands of glass from computer to computer. These technological transformations do not of themselves transform the content of the information gathered and transmitted, however. If changes occur in the information itself, in its specification, formatting and interpretation, then that is because of shifts within institutional structures.

Many of our assumptions are now fed by the prolific commentaries which herald the information revolution that is seen as coming upon us. Yet the vast uptake of new technologies, including the enormous IT budgets of governments, should not be seen as revolutionary. Those indicators of diffusion and expenditure tell us almost nothing about application and even less about content. In a polity with its myriad of interactions between the citizen and the state, for example, what is critical to our understanding of change is the information content of those interactions. Let us propose then a sequence of pertinent questions which take us away from this deterministic tendency. For example, how well informed are citizens in the information age? How much better informed are those citizens today than they were ten years ago, if at all? What is the prospect of citizens becoming better informed during the next ten years? How will new technologies be deployed within these relationships?

Though it is largely unrecognized in mainstream academic treatises on government and public administration, information is the key to understanding so much that we observe. To examine questions of structure, of process and of policy and decision-making is, in effect, to study information. Flows of information provide us with our government processes and, in turn, with our government structures. That is, they provide the dynamic ingredient within the polity that helps us to lay bare and understand its essential relationships, whether that between government and citizen, that between executive branch and legislature or that between bureaucracy and politician. Information is the lifeblood of public administration. Perhaps the most revolutionary aspect of these pervasive new technologies lies in their revelation of that simple fact.

The two-year period in which we have written this book has been a period of immense technological change. For that reason we urge readers to interpret the examples which we use and the technologies which we describe as transient in importance. While the empirical world will move on, in this field more than others, of more lasting value will be the analytical, conceptual and theoretical tools which we use. The debates which we open will be lasting debates, including those which will have immediate, practical implications for workers in the field and those of a more scholarly nature which will be taken up and dissected by our academic colleagues and their students. For both these sets of readers we hope to have provided the kind of intellectual nourishment which will ensure that questions are asked and debates engaged.

Debts

All authors are in debt. That could be a statement aimed at the publisher (it should be) or an employer (it must be). It is also, of course, a statement intended to recognize the social processes by which knowledge is acquired. While this book is authored by Bellamy and Taylor it has been influenced by many colleagues and friends who surround our work and infuse it with their wisdom. There are, for example, members of the former ESRC-supported UK study group on information, communication and new technologies in public administration, especially Justin Keen, Helen Margetts, Lawrence Pratchett and Charles Raab; members of the Permanent Study Group on Informatization in Public Administration of the European Group of Public Administration, most notably Paul Frissen, Klaus Lenk, Ig Snellen, Wim van de Donk, Victor Bekkers, Miriam Lips and Arre Zuurmond. There are, too, our colleagues, including our graduate students, in our own universities: particularly Ivan Horrocks and Neil Hambley at Nottingham Trent, and Barbara Bardski, Colin Smith and William Webster at Glasgow Caledonian. There are also high-value colleagues from the wider academic and practitioner milieux: Howard Williams from Strathclyde, Bill Dutton from Southern California, John Goddard from Newcastle, Nicki Gardner from Ulster, Colin Muid from CITU, David McLean previously from the CCTA and William Heath from Kable – good friends and supportive colleagues, all of them. Each has added enormously to our project to bring a fresh understanding of the world of government and public administration. Nevertheless, it goes without saying that we take full responsibility for the facts, errors and opinions that are contained in this book. We wish, too, to record our warm thanks to colleagues who made the process of producing this book easier than it would otherwise have been: the members of the Politics Division at Nottingham Trent University, especially Larry Wilde, colleagues in the Social Sciences Faculty, especially Sandra Odell, and colleagues in the Management Department at Glasgow Caledonian University, especially Lynn Whiteside, who all provided much valued moral and practical support. Lastly, we are pleased to record our thanks to the Nuffield Foundation for supporting our research on the coordination of computerization in the criminal justice system (grant number Soc 100/1065).

Each of these lists could, of course, be enlarged. There are many colleagues in whose debt we have written this book, but we should stop this preface at the wordcount instructed. Whatever the publisher's injunction, we cannot end, however, without finally recognizing where our accounts are deepest in the red, with David Orton and Helen McIntosh.

Christine Bellamy, The Nottingham Trent University
John A. Taylor, Glasgow Caledonian University

1

Contexts for governing in the information age

The prophetic hype and ideological manipulation characterizing most discourses on the information technology revolution should not mislead us into underestimating its truly fundamental significance.

(Castells 1996: 30)

Introduction

The view is now commonplace that industrial economy and society are receding as a new wave of economic and social activity flows in to replace them, a wave associated with profound technological change. The industrial age is being superseded by an 'information age' in which 'knowledge workers' and 'information labour' are coming to the fore, and service industries are of increasing economic significance. Here is a perspective on economic and social change which lays emphasis upon the idea that a new techno-economic paradigm is upon us, a new 'Kondratiev' or long-wave economic cycle (Freeman 1984). Information and communication technologies (ICTs) are perceived to be at the centre of this new economic revolution, bringing new flexibilities into the workplace, pushing aside the numerous dysfunctions associated with bureaucratic forms of organization and permitting a growing emphasis upon achieving economies of scope rather than economies of scale.

This interpretation of change in contemporary economies has been mirrored by analyses of the emerging 'information society' (Bell 1973; Nora and Minc 1980; Toffler 1980, 1990; Lyon 1988; Miles 1996). These authors have sought to track the *impact* of these new technologies upon social relationships, with heady images being called up of a more egalitarian society founded on the primacy of new forms of knowledge and vastly expanded opportunities for accessing and exchanging information. Crucially, however, some of this writing has also begun to identify the potential downsides of the information society: the emergence of new social divisions between the information rich and information poor and enhanced opportunities for more subtle forms of social control.

In contrast to these relatively well established analyses of the information economy and the information society, little has been written on the information age as it relates to governing. This book provides an opportunity to redress that lacuna. In so doing we will confront many of the all-too-easy assumptions that pervade much of the literature about the information age. For example, the assumption that the information age is being forged from a new techno-economic paradigm raises the question of whether these are, indeed, revolutionary technologies. Equally in need of being challenged is the casual assumption that these are technologies which will have a strong impact on society, whether for good or for ill. This is a book which, as Chapter 6 in particular makes clear, draws strongly on institutional analysis so as to counter this casual assumption by introducing a more balanced perspective. Indeed, institutionalism provides a core theme of this book, sensitizing us to the question of how amenable government organizations are to the proleptic visions of the information age.

In seeking to achieve this balance, particular emphasis will be placed upon the 'I' and the 'C' in the acronym ICT. While it is important to engage in close examination of changes in *technology*, it is equally important to understand the significance of technologically mediated changes in *information* and *communication*. For these reasons we have been inclined to move away from an interpretation of the information age which places technology to the fore, towards a view which is more like that of Dizard, who observes that: 'Of all the changes taking place in our time, none has more profound effect than the new ways in which we communicate with one another. For the first time in human history there is a realistic prospect of communication networks that will link everyone on earth' (Dizard 1989: 1). For this reason this book will examine the changing nature of information and communication in and around governance and government, exposing as it does so a profound paradox within the discourse of the information age. Despite the frequency with which the sobriquets information age, information economy and information society are applied, it has nevertheless been innovations in information *technology* which have dominated analysis of social change. Here we intend to rebalance that emphasis by focusing primarily upon information and communication, and upon their significance for the practices, processes and structures of contemporary governance.

The information society: an emerging field for public policy

Although there are numerous references to the 'information society', some dating from more than twenty years ago, it was the 1980s and, even more strongly, the 1990s which saw a huge upswell of official, academic and journalistic interest in this subject. Since 1993, many developed nations, including the USA, the G–7 Group of industrialized nations and the European Union, have published papers setting out their visions of the information age that would follow in the wake of the information superhighway (Information Infrastructure Task Force 1993; European Commission 1994a; Bangemann 1994). In Britain, these contributions have been joined by policy papers from individual ministries, from the local government community, from the Labour Party and from other bodies such as the National Consumer Council (Department for Education and Employment 1995; Department of Trade and Industry 1994, 1996; LGUA 1996; Labour Party 1996; NCC 1996). Furthermore, there is now an impressive array of Web sites and electronic bulletin boards covering this topic, some of the most useful of which are listed in Appendix II. The significance of this expanding interest is that a high-level policy agenda has now emerged within Western polities, with governments, oppositions and lobbies adopting both the rhetoric and the policy prescriptions which seem to them to be appropriate to the dawning of the information age.

The most visible British example of *academic* engagement with the information age came in 1986, when the Economic and Social Research Council launched its largest ever research programme, a programme devoted to the exploration, from a variety of social science perspectives, of issues relating to the origin, diffusion and application of ICTs. The Programme on Information and Communications Technologies (PICT) produced an enormous quantity of published outputs (Dutton 1996a) though it must be said that very few of them indeed focused specifically on government or politics. The research agenda which formed around the PICT continues to be a major source of academic analysis, and there is no doubt that, despite the termination of this particular programme of work in 1995, the large body of researchers who were associated with the programme will continue to take forward their ideas over many more years. We wish to acknowledge our own involvement in that programme and our debts to many of the scholars who participated in it.

The journalistic column count on information age topics also expanded enormously during the late 1980s and 1990s, with the result that most quality newspapers in Britain, for example, now have discrete sections devoted on a frequent basis to technological developments and applications. It is inevitable that many of the ICT-related stories carried by these newspapers are not only highly influenced by, but add their own force and authority to, heady images of the Internet, the information superhighway and the latest multimedia innovations. Popularization is spawning a new lexicon, a glossary of terms for the information age. Thus, the 'wired student' is familiar with hyperbolic terms such as cyberspace, cyberpunk and virtual reality, as well as with the more prosaic language of information systems, telecoms networks and information architecture. And as this discourse enters everyday language, so it excites the imagination, giving rise to powerful combinations of utopian and dystopian intepretations of the information age.

However, arraigned behind these broad gauge interpretations there are, too, complex sets of influential social, economic and political interests. The power of commercial forces to shape the information age should not be under-estimated. Despite occasional market downturns, the telecommunications and computing industries have grown to colossal proportions. It is important, too, to understand that these industries are in the throes of a convergence of interest, not only between themselves but also with an equally powerful giant, the electronic entertainments industry. For example, the media entertainment company BSkyB, the telecommunications operator BT and the software com-pany Microsoft are moving towards each other as competitors in what is in effect becoming a single digital communications industry.

The rhetoric of the information age is both forming around this new industrial complex and being formed by it. It is a powerful rhetoric, suffusing all sectors of society, economy and polity, as it promotes the uptake of the technologies. Inevitably it is bringing in its wake important new issues for social, economic and political behaviour and relationships. Governments can-not be immune from these issues. Indeed, they increasingly perceive tech-nological innovation to be central to their own 'reinvention'.

Reinventing government for the information age

It is remarkable how quickly, in the mid-1990s, most Western governments moved not only to adopt policy statements designed to promote the coming information age but, at the same time, to embrace the idea that new technol-ogy might be exploited to 'reinvent' their own activities. The force behind this newfound zeal was undoubtedly the increasing urgency with which this agenda was developed within the US federal government (US Congress Office of Technology Assessment 1993; Office of the Vice President 1993a, 1993b). The role of information and communications technology in the reinvention of government was explicitly recognized by the Clinton administration through the close political connection, personified by the twin responsibilities of Vice President Gore, between the National Performance Review (NPR), on the one hand, and the laying down of the National Information Infrastructure (NII), or information superhighway, on the other. The NPR's objectives in reinventing government were incorporated into the NII's *Agenda for Action*, alongside the latter's economic, industrial, educational and cultural policy ob-jectives. Moreover, the NII was recognized to have the potential to enrich and reinvigorate American political and civic life by exploiting new electronic facilities for American citizens to communicate with their governments, as well as with each other. Hence, the NII would, by design, provide the means to 'build a more open and participatory democracy at all levels of government' (Information Infrastructure Task Force 1993: 21). Indeed, the NII has become a focus for political lobbies who believe that the superhighway could liberate profoundly important opportunities for reinventing democracy, as well as mak-ing government services more accessible and responsive (Varn 1992; Alliance for Public Technology 1993; Civille *et al.* 1993). In short, the exploitation of ICTs is widely seen to be the key to striking a more effective accommodation

between efficiency, quality and democracy in governmental reform programmes.

The Clinton Administration's plans for developing the NII were quickly
followed by similar initiatives in many other developed countries. The years
1994 and 1995 saw a flurry of activity as governments throughout the developed world sought to ensure that their own nations would not be left
behind in the race to join the information age (e.g. Canada: Information
Highway Advisory Council 1994; Dybkjær and Christensen 1994; Japan: Telecommunications Council 1994; Australia: ASTEC 1995; Singapore: National
Computer Board 1995). At the same time, parallel initiatives at international
level have exposed the limits of national action in dealing with many of the
issues generated by this agenda. In December 1993, the European Commission
published a White Paper setting out the principles of a pan-European response
to the crucial economic and employment issues raised by the information
economy (European Commission 1993), and the European summit in Brussels
mandated Martin Bangemann, the Commissioner in charge of the Telecommunications Directorate, DG-XIII, to form a special High Level Group to
bring forward specific measures for carrying Europe into the information age.
The Bangemann Report of May 1994 focused on the 'information society', a
term specifically chosen in preference to the 'information superhighway' in
order to signal that the policy focus must be as much on wider social and
cultural issues, as on economic and technical development (Bangemann 1994).
Following endorsement of the report at the European summit at Corfu in June
1994, an action plan, *Europe's Way to the Information Society*, was published,
setting out the operational principles, policies and projects designed to secure
international cooperation in reaching the objectives of the information society
(European Commission 1994a). Heads of EU member states endorsed the
action plan in December 1994. In February 1995, the European Commission
established an Information Society Forum to bring together five main
stakeholder constituencies, representing users, social groups (including municipal representatives), service providers, network operators and European institutions, in order to provide advice on the development of the information
society (Information Society Forum 1995, 1996).

At around the same time, early July 1994, the G-7 industrialized nations
met to discuss American proposals for a Global Information Infrastructure
(GII). The plan was to develop a GII on the principles of open competition,
common technical standards and interoperability of systems. The most con-
crete outcome of this initiative to date has been the establishment of a G-7
Forum, which was also strongly backed by the EU. Formal representation is
confined to the G-7 nations (the USA, Japan, Canada, France, Italy, Germany
and the UK) but participation was not intended to be restricted and the Forum
expressed a positive wish to cooperate with the relevant international organizations, including UN agencies and the OECD. A set of eleven projects
were then brought forward to a joint G-7/EU ministerial conference on the
information society in February 1995, including a project to be known as

Government On-line (European Commission 1995a, b, c). The G-7 projects were designed explicitly to demonstrate the value of international cooperation, and were interpreted as being especially important in promoting the social and cultural objectives of what was now being referred to as the 'global information society'. They were formally adopted by G-7 heads of state in June 1995.

Each of these initiatives differed considerably in its emphasis and detail. For example, whereas US, Canadian, Australian and the Bangemann visions of the information superhighway all assumed a strong role for private companies, usually the privatized telecommunications operators, in laying down the infrastructure of the superhighway, the Nordic countries assumed a more direct role for the state. Many documents also reflected a set of wider concerns about the development of the information society, concerns which are likely to be of long-term political importance in shaping these initiatives. For example, there is, in many of the European national strategies, a strong awareness of a possible tension between the economic objectives of the GII and its potential for strengthening the practice of citizenship, for promoting social cohesion and social inclusion, and for enriching political participation and democracy. Furthermore, much attention is also being paid to protecting national values from the cultural imperialism associated with economic and social globalization. For example, in its report *Info-Soc 2000*, the Danish government expressly adopted the case for preserving 'Danish values' (Dybkjær and Christensen 1994). At the same time, the EU has also placed much emphasis on the significance of the information society both as an instrument for and as an outcome of the development of European consciousness and political cooperation. 'An Information Society is a means to achieve so many of the [European] Union's objectives. We have to get it right, and get it right now' (Bangemann 1994: 4).

For the purposes of this book, our interest lies primarily in understanding and dissecting visions of information age government which are, in varying degrees, explicit in all these commentaries and documents, particularly as they apply to British government. It should already be apparent that governments at international, national and municipal levels are seen as the key instruments through which the, not always compatible, social and economic objectives of the information society will be secured. Yet there is also an equally strong belief that the structures and processes of governance themselves will change. In other words, governments are seen not only as the facilitators of the information society, but also as major participants within it. As facilitators, governments are seen to have a key role in developing a partnership with high-tech industries: by establishing appropriate economic and legislative frameworks for the development of the technological infrastructure, products and services on which participation in the information society will depend; and by using their own economic power as technology procurers. Governments are also acquiring a role in *regulating* the development of superhighways, including the GII, in order to promote the social objectives of the information society, including the securing of universal access and preventing the emergence of a new underclass of the 'information poor'. However, many national governments have also

published proposals showing how, by becoming model users of ICTs themselves, governments could give a positive lead to other organizations, demonstrating both the means and value of conducting business electronically (e.g.
Treasury Board of Canada 1995; Information Technology Review Group
1995; Dybkjær and Christensen 1994).

Visions of information age governance and citizenship have also been
influential in shaping agendas at international level. Thus, among the 'themes'
identified for discussion within the European Society Forum are 'democratic
life in the "virtual community"' and 'towards more transparent and better
quality public services' (Information Society Forum 1995), while the G-7
initiative has spawned the Government On-line project (GOL), which will
promote electronic communication within and between governments, as well
as between government, businesses and citizens (Kerry and Harrop n.d.; European Commission 1995c).

British government and the information age

The involvement of the British government in this agenda is best described as
patchy and cautious. In part, this attitude reflects the relative underdevelopment of the computing base of governmental organizations, for which it was
severely rebuked in a stinging report on government computing by a Select
Committee of the House of Commons (1988–9). Although government was
among the first large-scale users of administrative computing in the late 1950s,
it has since been much slower in adopting ICTs than analogous businesses, such
as financial services, even though 'The nature of a government department in
which paper and people abound should particularly lend itself to the use of
information technology' (House of Commons 1988–9: para. 92). Whereas the
ratio of workstations to employees in IBM was 1:1 and that in the insurance
industry was 1:3, in central government it was 1:10, in local government 1:12;
and in the NHS 1:14. Nevertheless, the sheer scale of government means that it
constitutes an enormous market for ICTs. Total spending on IT at that time
was around £2 billion, with a growth rate of around 20 per cent *a year* (CCTA
1990; SOCITM 1988).

The data presented in Tables 1.1 and 1.2 capture key contemporary
trends in the adoption of these technologies in central and local government.
There are many reasons to be cautious about these data, not least the trend
towards distributed control over computing and IT budgets. This process

Table 1.1   IT spend in UK central and local government (£ million)

	1993–4	1994–5	1995–6
Central government	2315	2361	2311
Local government	1100	1064	1040

Source: Compiled from Kable (1995), SOCITM (1994, 1995, 1996).

almost certainly means that some expenditure is hidden in other operational or administration budget heads. It is also the case that rather more of the effort devoted in government to information systems is now invested in broader 'business development' and not simply in hardware or software. For both these reasons, these figures probably underestimate, rather than overestimate, the resources devoted to developing ICTs. While the data demonstrate the immense strategic importance of IT in both central and local government, what is also striking is the flattening of the IT spend in the early to mid-1990s. Compared to the steady growth in IT-related expenditure in the late 1980s, the 1990s showed a trend towards a diminishing investment in IT, a trend which was almost certainly associated with financial pressures on departmental running costs and capital spending.

The data also mask significant differences in the IT spend within and between governmental organizations. In local government, for example, the largest IT spend as a percentage of total budget has, historically, been undertaken by district, rather than by county, councils. In 1993–4, for example, English and Welsh district councils spent an average of 9 per cent of their total budget on IT, whereas counties spent about 1.5 per cent, a gap which was

Table 1.2   IT expenditure by government department 1993–4 to 1995–6 (£m)

Department	IT spend 1993–4	% of total IT spend	IT spend 1994–5	% of total IT spend	IT spend 1995–6	% of total IT spend	Total budget of dept. 1995–6	IT as % of total 1995–6
MAFF	65.9	2.8	66.7	2.8	60.1	2.6	860	7
Cabinet Office	36.9	1.6	32.6	1.4	33	1.4	3,915	0.8
Ministry of Defence	699.8	30.2	722	30.6	748	32.4	22,559	3.3
Dept. of Education	10.1	0.4	9.6	0.4	9	0.4	11,680	.07
Employment	89.6	3.9	89.9	3.8	136	5.9	3,231	4.2
DOE	36.9	1.6	47	2	38.9	1.7	39,060	0.1
HM Treasury	52.8	2.3	61.1	2.6	54.1	2.3	3,668	1.5
Customs	69.4	3	69.6	2.9	69	3	850	8.1
Inland Revenue	257	11	269	11.4	247	11	1,928	12.8
FCO	66.1	2.8	73.4	3.1	71	3.1	3,091	2.3
Health	110	4.8	127	5.4	94.1	4.1	32,957	0.3
Home Office	74.7	3.2	65.8	2.8	72.9	3.2	6,305	1.15
Lord Chancellor	40	1.7	41.5	1.8	48.1	2.1	2,733	1.75
Heritage	3.6	0.15	3.5	0.13	3.2	0.1	2,857	0.1
N. Ireland	50.9	2.2	54	2.3	51.9	2.2	2,889	1.8
Scotland	40.1	1.7	70.3	3	65	2.8	13,302	0.5
Wales	6.1	0.26	6.4	0.3	7	0.3	6,080	0.1
DSS	477	20.6	422	17.9	370	16	72,798	0.5
DTI	75.2	3.2	75.6	3.2	83.9	3.6	1,762	4.8
Transport	52.3	2.3	50	2.1	47	2	5,815	0.8

Source: Compiled from Kable (1995), SOCITM (1994, 1995, 1996).

substantially reduced by 1995–6. In central government, total spending declined from 1.7 per cent of overall expenditure in 1988–9 to 1.0 per cent in 1995–6, although again this global figure masks significant differences in the IT spend between departments. Thus, in the mid-1990s Defence commanded almost one-third of Whitehall's total IT spend, a figure which was rising year-on-year, while spending in Social Security fell in the two years between 1993–4 and 1995–6 from 20 per cent of Whitehall's total spend on IT to 16 per cent. The final column of Table 1.2 shows that, as a percentage of their total budget, these two departments appear to spend relatively small amounts on IT: however, this spend represents a substantial proportion of departmental administrative (or running) costs, as opposed to the spending on departmental policies and programmes. The Inland Revenue (12.8 per cent), Customs and Excise (8.1 per cent) and the Ministry of Agriculture (MAFF, 7 per cent) are also relatively intensive users of IT.

This distribution reflects the relatively high concentration of IT in departments and authorities which engage in large-scale data processing, where computers are used extensively, for example, to support the conduct of high-volume financial transactions. As we will see in Chapter 2, automatic data processing (ADP) has provided the mainstay of government computing for over three decades, but it represents a significantly restricted approach to the use of ICT in government, one which is now coming under serious challenge from information age agendas. The fundamental, even paradigmatic, nature of the shift which these agendas appear to demand, and the difficulties of bringing it about in a period of sustained and significant financial retrenchment, account, no doubt at least in part, for the vigour, indeed the almost evangelical fervour, with which its champions are promoting these agendas, as well as for the noticeably uneven manner in which they are being pursued.

Certainly, the British government has been more hesitant than many others in embracing the notion that governments should reinvent themselves for the information age. Although it has a longstanding policy interest in the 'wired society', this interest did not extend to its own operations until late 1993, when the publication of the American plans for the NII stimulated political pressure in Parliament and in the British media for a commensurate British response. The opportunity was seized by CCTA, which had been originally set up in the Treasury as the Central Computing and Telecommunications Agency with a brief to supervise IT procurement in government, and was then known as the Government Centre for Information Systems, working out of the Office of Public Service and Science. CCTA proposed to develop a programme which would not only encourage the development of a British superhighway but elevate government itself to be a model user of ICTs. The upshot was a consultation paper on the information superhighway (CCTA 1994a), which was subsequently endorsed at a major national conference in November 1994. This paper was followed a year later by two further documents: a progress report on the development of government's on-line information services (CCTA 1995a) and an update on the somewhat uneven application of the information superhighway to public services (CCTA 1995b). It was not until the autumn of 1995 that the British government established CITU, the Cabinet Office's Central IT Unit, to coordinate the strategic development of ICTs across government, and to stimulate active collaboration with the private IT industry. This initiative was followed in February 1996 by the creation of a new ministerial group specially charged with identifying and taking forward cross-departmental IT projects. The result was the publication in November 1996 of *government.direct*, a Green Paper billed as a 'prospectus for the electronic delivery of government services'. This prospectus was said by ministers to herald a new phase of public service reform. Just as Britain had claimed to be at the forefront of public service reform with the creation of 'Next Steps' agencies, the Citizen's Charter and the Deregulation Initiative, so it was now claimed that the Green Paper 'marks the beginning of a new phase of equally radical and wide ranging reform which will build on the existing programmes' (Office of Public Service 1996b: 1). Following public consultation, the principles of *government.direct* were formally accepted by the government in March 1997, when a series of pilot projects were launched.

One important aim of this book is to explore in detail the implications of the ideas which are set out in *government.direct*, and other such prospectuses. Before we undertake this task, however, we propose in the present chapter to explore the climate in which such ideas are brought forward, by identifying the important, generic aspects of the technological environment within which prevailing attitudes to the information society are being shaped. We will explore, too, the intellectual context for understanding interpretations of the information age by examining, in some detail, two potent elements in the rhetoric of the information age: technological utopianism and technological determinism.

The digital revolution

Unquestionably, some of the most powerful technological advances of the twentieth century are those associated with information and communications technologies. Particularly during the past fifty years, the development of both computing and telecommunications has been extraordinarily rapid, and has resulted in a technological *convergence* whose significance it seems almost impossible to overstate. Governments have been deeply involved in these advances, partly through support for research and development and partly through policy and procurement initiatives designed to support the equipment industry and its diffusion of the technologies. Paradoxically, where they have, until recently, been much less heavily involved is in their own uptake of the technologies, as we have already begun to see.

The development of computing

The breakthroughs in computing, paradigmatic at first then technical in orientation, saw the emergence in the 1940s and 1950s of the first modern computers. These computers were the predecessors of the 'mainframe' machines which were to dominate the computing industry from the late 1950s to the 1980s. The emergence of the mainframe machine signalled that two major barriers to the development of modern computing had been overcome: first, developing the capability of the machine to undertake large-scale numerical processing tasks rapidly; second, developing its capability to be programmed. The latter was particularly important because it removed the critical mismatch between the rapidity of electronic numerical processing, on the one hand, and laborious set-up times, on the other. The new mainframe machines were taken gradually into business use during the 1950s and 1960s, so that by the end of the 1960s most large-scale organizations, including many governmental organizations, were applying the technologies to their internal business processes. Mainframe computing was well adapted to the fundamental requirement of many governmental organizations to store and manage very large quantities of data, and was rapidly integrated into their administrative functions (Fulton Report 1968: Vol. 5). For example, the National Savings Department used mainframe computing facilities from the 1960s onwards to record all repayment transactions to its six million savers, and the computerization of the basic transactions involved in collecting value added tax was crucial to its introduction into Britain in 1972. From this relatively early period, therefore, computers were being employed by government organizations for large-scale ADP. Here, in these early days of government computing, was affirmation by machine of the centralized forms of bureaucratic organization which prevailed at the time. The mainframe computer was being used to process data which had central, corporate functionality. It offered no challenge to the hierarchical and centralized structures by which it was surrounded. Indeed its effect was to sustain and even to reinforce those features of large-scale bureaucracy. Its reason for being was simple automation; the accomplishment of large-scale data processing tasks at lower cost than hitherto.

Towards microprocessing
Since those early years, the technological development of computing proceeded in two highly significant ways. The first of these centred upon developments in integrated circuitry, the 'brain' of the computer. Here the breakthrough came with the realization that a single microprocessor could be used to handle all the tasks to which the computer was applied. The general purpose computer could, therefore, be driven from a single integrated circuit which was capable of responding to different programs stored on memory chips. This development meant that it did not require separate circuits for each of its major functions. The significance of these developments was that the physical size, and the costs in proportion to processing power, of the general purpose computer fell rapidly from the 1980s onwards.

The second highly significant development since the 1980s has been the growth of the software industry and the delivery of increasingly user-friendly products, particularly in business applications. Specifically with the launch of the Apple Macintosh microcomputer in 1984, the software industry began to attach much more importance to the 'useability' of computers. In consequence, microcomputing was rapidly developed and diffused, moving into all parts of the office environment as well as into the home. By the end of the 1980s the personal computer (PC) and equivalent machines were becoming ubiquitous throughout governmental organizations, just as they were throughout the world of work. The significance of this process is that, unlike the first main era of business computing, the 'micro revolution' permits challenges to be mounted to the very organization of government. The microcomputer is bringing new information resources to the desktop of every government official, and is thereby delivering the potential for far-reaching changes in business and labour processes.

Developments in telecommunications

Before this last point can be further developed, we should also consider a further set of technological advances which have occurred during the past thirty years, advances which have, in effect, consummated the 'digital revolution'. They involve the technological sibling of the computer, telecommunications. Half a century ago, at about the same time that the modern computer was being developed, experiments were beginning to be designed to permit remote control of the calculating devices which were the predecessor of the computer. The underlying idea of this early work was that co-location, the physical propinquity of the human operator and the electronic device, would no longer be necessary to effect a task. By using ordinary telecommunications lines the remote operator could 'instruct' the machine to set about its work. By the 1960s the impetus behind developments of this kind was primarily to gain economic advantage rather than to secure operational enhancements. Specifically, the main thrust of business computing lay in exploiting fully the economies of scale which appeared to be offered by mainframe computers. Thus, accessing the machine from remote locations was being developed, on the one hand, to apportion the high costs of computing more widely across large, geographically distributed organizations and, on the other, to enable those organizations to gain additional economies, including those which derived from the relocation of data-inputting functions to low-cost labour markets. However, it was not until the mid-1970s that British central government developed projects, such as the Department of Health and Social Security's Operational Strategy, which exploited these sorts of possibilities for its own organizational arrangements.

Digitalizing telecommunications
The telecommunications technology which was facilitating these data transfers was still, however, fundamentally different from computing technology. Whereas the computer stored and managed data in the form of binary code, the telecommunications lines still used analogue signalling systems which were

routed through electro-mechanical switching devices or exchanges. However, between the 1960s and the early 1980s a number of innovations occurred in signalling systems, switches and exchanges, and, from the 1980s onwards, these innovations paved the way for the advent of full-blown digital telecommunications. Thus, two revolutionary technologies were, in two senses, converging towards each other. First, the advent of the microcomputer coincided broadly with the development of fully digitalized telecommunications. This was a purely temporal, historically accidental, convergence of associated technologies. However, a second, and more profound, form of convergence lay in the fully digital form of electronic data transmission which now became possible. Thus voice, data, text and pictures carried over digital telecommunications could now be converted into the same binary language used by computers, with the consequence that the quality, reliability, speed and volume of transmissions became the subjects of step improvements. These historical and technological convergences, which amount to the advent of *telematics*, by which we mean the conjoined use of computers and telecommunications, have opened the way for strong forms of distributed intelligence to be introduced into organizations. They thereby facilitate important challenges to existing ways of organizing.

Transmitting information
The final highly significant technological development in the digital revolution concerns developments in the *means* of digital transmission. Historically, telecommunications have been run over twisted-pair copper wires with narrow bandwidth; that is, with relatively limited capacity for carrying signals. In the era of POTS (plain old telephone service) copper wire was largely adequate for the purpose. In most geographical areas within developed economies, copper still remains, therefore, the core transmission technology for telecommunications. As one commentary has recently put it, 'much of our IT has changed little since it was originally introduced . . . a telephone still has more or less the same bandwidth as it did in 1876' (P. Cochrane 1994: 11). The technologies whose development we have traced here have, however, begun to make possible new sets of potentialities and therefore new demands for higher bandwidth, or broadband, telecommunications. The era of POTS is giving way to the era of PANS: pretty amazing new services. But whereas POTS required no more than narrow bandwidth twisted pairs, PANS demands increasing bandwidth, especially for the delivery of multimedia services. Technological developments are therefore proceeding in three main directions in order to fulfil requirements for greater bandwidth at affordable costs: first, developments in the compression of data carried over copper, which allow more data to be transmitted over the existing copper investment; second, developments in satellite technology; third, developments in optical fibre switching and transmission.

Huge amounts of sunk investment in copper wire mean that the prospect of 'making copper sweat' — that is, deriving more bandwidth from copper through data compression techniques – is highly attractive for the public telephone operators. While this approach is undoubtedly favoured for accommodating contemporary demands for enhanced telecommunications (Valdar *et al.* 1992), the professional judgement is that copper is ultimately limited in the services it can deliver. Moreover, it is believed that the use of copper will not eliminate switching and maintenance costs from the network to anything like the same degree as could optical fibres, for example (Hawker *et al.* 1994).

Satellite technology is a second field where there is considerable research and development. At present its application in developed economies for point to point communications (for example, telephones), rather than for mass communication, is likely to be most favoured for reaching remote or topographically difficult locations. In other places, the signal delays and interference associated with satellite communications render it second best to optical fibre. Nevertheless, some UK public authorities, most notably the more remote Scottish local authorities, are building satellite communications into their communications strategies (Taylor *et al.* 1995a).

Optical fibres, the third area in which major research and development activities are occurring, undoubtedly represent a major breakthrough in telecommunications technologies. There are two basic reasons for making this claim. First, optical fibre technology overcomes the problems of bandwidth, which is the most significant problem of copper transmission. Second, optical fibre transmission removes massive switching costs from telecommunications networks, because, unlike copper, the signal carried on optical fibres does not degrade over distance. Here, then, is a technology which, once the massive costs of initial investment have been met, will not only produce lower operating costs but also result in more reliable services. It is not surprising that many public sector organizations have incorporated fibre into their private circuits, although usually only as a small proportion of the total circuit length (Taylor and Williams 1989).

Contemporary developments in information systems and applications

The digitalization of telecommunications, together with the advent of user-friendly, desktop computing, has enabled important innovations to occur in both computing architecture and information systems. It is these technical innovations which are the source of so much of the 'impact' which is claimed for ICTs. In particular, these innovations are creating new, and still expanding, capabilities for computers to communicate with computers, and therefore for wired-up businesses, governments and individuals to communicate with each other, instantaneously and independently of geographical distance. In the next section we will look briefly at some of the most important technical innovations which underpin new ways of conducting business and relating to suppliers, consumers and citizens in information age government.

Changing systems architecture: 'logical' databases

Accessing, sharing and cross-matching data between computer systems has become much more flexible because of the shift from networks built around central mainframe computers to networks which link decentralized systems. Until the early 1980s, large organizations such as government departments assumed, for example, that the construction of an operational database of clients or customer records implied its physical concentration into a huge mainframe computer, to which remote 'dumb' terminals, terminals which are incapable of independent processing, would then be connected. More recently, the advent of 'client–server' architecture has enabled datalinks to be constructed in the 'logical' or 'virtual' sense: that is, independently of the computers which host the data. Internet, intranet and extranet 'browsers' are the most visible contemporary examples of this facility. Client–server architecture is supporting the growth of these 'nets', each of which currently uses html (hypertext markup language) protocols to link data held in separate systems within and between organizations, sometimes bringing data together from all over the world. The significance of this architecture for public administration is that, in contrast to the centralized and compartmentalized approach to the management of data, it permits much more flexible and inclusive datasets to be made available, in a much wider range of locations. This flexibility permits the design of radically different 'distribution networks' for public services, and also facilitates the capture of richer operational data for management or policy purposes. For example, contemporary thinking within the English police service suggests that a national criminal intelligence service might most effectively be developed, not by physically concentrating criminal records within Phoenix, the national criminal records system, but by establishing access to the intelligence which resides within all forty-three police forces through a virtual database. The primary purpose of such an extensive virtual database is operational, to support the investigation of crime, though it would also enable more powerful criminological analysis to be made available throughout the criminal justice system.

Knowledge-based systems (KBS)

The proliferation of connections on the electronic networks which are developing within and between organizations places a potentially enormous strain on the cognitive faculties of human beings who wish to manage and exploit this new connectivity. Knowledge-based systems, or 'expert systems', are, therefore, becoming increasingly important in data management. KBS are systems which apply complex rules to complex datasets, in order to arrive at decisions. Thus, KBS can be used within complex electronic networks to locate automatically the customer files which are needed to conduct specific transactions, or they can be called up by front-office staff to navigate elaborate operational codes and complex records. For example, the social security Benefits Agency has developed a system known as IBIS (the Integrated Benefits Information System), which enables a customer's details to be run through the codes governing eight complex social security benefits in order to arrive at an optimal claiming strategy for that particular customer (Benefits Agency 1993b). The use of diagnostic KBS in primary care units can permit paramedical staff to arrive at a provisional assessment of a patient so that they can offer first-line care and define the priority of access to specialist services. For such reasons, KBS are often associated with the assumption that ICTs can support the distribution of much more of the intelligence possessed by organizations to front-line staff, underpinning an apparent shift towards decentralized organizational forms (Bench-Capon 1991).

Multimedia applications
The digitalization of telecommunications permits the transmission of information in both visual and aural form, including voice, music, text, images and graphics. The term 'multimedia' refers, therefore, to the simultaneous transmission, processing and display of information in these various forms. The main significance which is attached to multimedia in government derives from its capacity to render information much more accessible and useable. For example, multimedia screens can support the provision of 'direct' transactions with public services: to pay fines or taxes, to claim welfare benefits, to apply for licences or, to apply for a job. Or they can provide electronic access to officials, politicians or community groups. Multimedia applications can be accessed from the home using a TV set-top box or a PC linked to a telecommunications line, or they can be accessed through community access terminals (CATs) located in public places such as shopping malls, hospitals, colleges or community centres. CATs are therefore much favoured as a way to widen access to public services in geographically or economically marginalized areas, or for providing services that are adapted to the needs of disadvantaged groups, such as the physically disabled or minority language users. Indeed, the G-7 GOP has identified multimedia kiosks as the 'leading opportunity' to improve accessibility to public services (G-7 Government On-line Project 1995).

Swipe card and smart card technology
As these brief forays into the world of technological innovations should now be making abundantly clear, most information age scenarios assume that new information systems will be used to support an ever increasing range of electronic transactions between businesses, governments and their customers. Plastic card technology is deeply implicated in these scenarios. 'Swipe cards' which allow remote access to personal, computerized records, especially bank statements, are now a familiar part of everyday life in Western economies, as are commercial transactions using such devices as electronic funds transfer at point of sale (EFTPOS), and automated teller machines, known more familiarly as 'holes in the wall'. Apart from saving labour and other costs, plastic cards offer a relatively fraud-proof way of conducting financial transactions: for example, swipe cards are coming into widespread use for the payment of social security benefits.

'Smart cards', or cards capable of storing and processing data, are less widely used as yet. Nevertheless, they have enormous potential for changing the way organizations conduct business, because of their capability to record and process a wide variety of transactions on a single card. For example, smart cards may eventually allow customers to do business with a wide range of public services, including renewing driving and television licences or paying National Insurance contributions, child maintenance or fines. Indeed, smart cards could ultimately demolish the case for dedicated public service outlets, by permitting transactions to occur through electronic networks run by, or shared with, private commerce. For example, it might become possible to apply and pay for a passport in a travel agent's office using a smart card which both identifies its holder and permits a financial transaction to occur.

One of the most obvious and controversial uses of smart card technology in government lies in the development of plastic 'identity cards'. The core purpose of an identity card is to provide official confirmation of the true identity of its holder. However, it is also clear that the main practical application of contemporary identity cards would be to permit access to myriad computer systems on which personal details are held. For example, the British government has floated a number of options for a 'voluntary' plastic identity card which could also serve as a gateway to on-line public services and could eventually supersede official documents such as passports and driving licences (Home Office 1995b). In other words, contemporary debates about identity cards reflect the increasingly obvious fact that it is, in practice, becoming progressively more difficult to function as a citizen, consumer or customer without the means of accessing computerized information systems (Lyon 1994). However, the notion of a single identity card also makes tangible the dangers and opportunities that arise from the possibility that computerized systems can exchange and share information.

Exchanging information between computers
The significance of the applications which we have now reviewed is that, particularly when used in combination, they offer enormous potential for a massive increase in the electronic exchange of information between computers. The electronic interchange of data has, in principle, many applications in public administration. It can permit faster, more accurate and more efficient flows of data between government departments and their clients: for example, for direct filing of tax returns or welfare claims; between governments and businesses, for submitting tenders for public contracts; and between governments, for exchanging data on expatriate retirement pensioners or for customs or criminal justice purposes. It can be expected, therefore, to give rise to a vast range of new information flows around and between information age governments. It is the potential of these new information flows to reshape the processes and institutions of government – for example, by establishing 'direct' transactions between governments and citizens, by rendering boundaries between organizations much less significant and by breaking down the formal

barriers between national jurisdictions – which lends such enormous force and plausibility to radical scenarios for information-age government.

Perspectives on the information age

It can be seen from this brief review of computing, telecommunications and information systems that, at least in a technological sense, the digital revolution has already occurred. In principle, computers and telecommunications are fully conjoined, providing the infrastructure for digital information flows. The translation of this technological revolution into the realm of government is, of course, the subject of this book. What is clear, however, is that it is this technological conjunction which has stimulated the powerful notion that there is, or soon will be, an 'information society'.

Technological determinism versus social shaping

There is, however, considerable divergence in interpreting the nature and implications of the information society. On the one hand the rhetoric of the information society is heady with golden age visions. On the other, far bleaker images are purveyed, though usually with less force, as images are conjured of the societal panopticon, of the all-seeing state. However, at the centre of these images lies a casual technicism, a simple-minded approach to socio-technical analysis which assumes a unilinear technological 'impact'. As new technology is introduced, so it is assumed to bring with it a set of inescapable social, economic, political and managerial logics, with new forms of behaviour ineluctably in attendance. On this view, it is to the technology and its characteristics that we must look if we are fully to understand the social significance of the information age. In much of the contemporary rhetoric, therefore, we find an implicit belief in an unproblematic causal progression from technological innovations to social change, a belief which appears to find little room either for specific technological complexities or for independent human or social agency (Scarbrough and Corbett 1992).

Our own perspective on the advent and use of ICTs by government is not one which subscribes to this technicist account. As with the roads and the physical traffic management systems with which ICTs are often compared, we prefer to emphasize the social shaping of both the infrastructure and its exploitation. Just as both road developments and their subsequent use are the outcome of complex social processes, some in varying degrees promotional and others similarly demotional, so with electronic infrastructures. However, we must also accept that infrastructures, and the systems which depend upon them, do provide a set of possibilities as well as sets of constraints. The roads and the information superhighways bring new capabilities for social and economic activity, but equally they present restrictions and set limitations. Without further development of existing arrangements, existing infrastructures and information systems will undoubtedly have a strong shaping role, setting limits on what is attainable in the particular technological context. It is only in this latter and highly reduced sense that we consider technologies (or indeed, by analogy, roads) to be determinants of social and economic activity. Thus we emphasize that the social, political and cultural factors which shape the nature, even the existence, of technologies are also, in effect, defining the range of uses to which they can be put.

In particular, it is important to recognize that the information age is being shaped as much by the economic, social and political arrangements from which it has emerged, as it is by the technological innovations on which so much emphasis is placed. Even the brief history of business computing which we provided above shows how, for over three decades, computers were harnessed to, and reinforced, the organizational forms and business functions characteristic of the industrial age, and it is the legacies from those decades which continue powerfully to shape and constrain the exploitation of ICTs. Furthermore, a recurring theme throughout this book will be the complex ways in which information and communications infrastructures and systems not only reflect, but become embedded in, the institutions of governance as active agents in their maintenance and reproduction. Information systems, and the infrastructures on which they depend, give shape and material form to the routines of organizational and political life, as well as tangible expression to the cultural values on which they are based. It is hardly surprising, therefore, that information systems become highly visible symbols of organizational power and authority. Indeed, according to this analysis, the reconstruction of information systems, and the redirecting of information flows, that would inevitably accompany the radical reinvention of government would be acts of considerable political significance, as much for their symbolic as for their operational role.

One of the most important institutional dimensions of ICTs is that the way they are developed reflects and embeds dominant cultural assumptions about technologies. Just as the relatively large sums of money that were expended through the Economic and Social Research Council's PICT were a material reflection of widely held assumptions both in government and in the academic world about the relative importance of technological change, 1990s reinvention strategies give political force to assumptions about the role of technologies in forging an information age. However, as we will see throughout this book, these assumptions are being forced into confrontations with deeply rooted assumptions about the role of computer technologies, assumptions which are as much the legacy of earlier eras as are the mainframe-based ADP systems which are still widely used in governmental organizations. It is for these kinds of reasons that we choose to emphasize the importance of attitudes to the role of technology as a factor in social and organizational change. Thus, in choosing to confront stereotypical assumptions about the information age, we see ourselves not simply as engaging in academic debate but also as exploring an important factor in the social shaping of technologically mediated change. In other words, we are interested in mapping the controversies which are forming around the notion of an information age, not least for their part in its social construction.

Utopian perspectives on the information age

The introduction of new technologies of all kinds into social, economic and political life has invariably excited controversy, especially among those who believe in the power of technology to drive social change. ICTs are no exception to this general rule. Indeed, they are a prime exemplar of it, particularly for the way in which they have provoked fierce debate around polarized opinions, represented by utopian and dystopian perspectives on social change. Tom Stonier provides one such example of the broad-brush utopianism frequently associated with the uptake of ICTs in society:

> In late industrial society, we stopped worrying about food. In late communicative society we will stop worrying about material resources. And just as the industrial economy eliminated slavery, famine and pestilence, so will post-industrial economy eliminate authoritarianism, war, and strife. For the first time in history the rate at which we solve problems will exceed the rate at which they appear. This will leave us to get on with the real business of the next century. To take care of each other. To fathom what it means to be human. To explore human intelligence. To move out into space.
>
> (Stonier 1983: 214)

Commentators in this tradition believe that ICTs ineluctably promote desirable values in society and organization, and typically lay emphasis upon certain features of their utopian edifice. First, they stress the role of ICTs in promoting harmony in the political system through the raised social awareness which derives from enhancing access to common information (Masuda 1990; Toffler 1980). Closely linked to this first point is a second, which stresses the development of desirable communitarian values around the adoption and diffusion of ICTs. Here, the media of the information age are seen as acting at a number of levels in society, stimulating local political debates through events on cable TV, for example, or promoting new national and international communities of interest or of cultural identity through the development of the Internet. Third, utopian writers celebrate the opportunities for self-actualization which they perceive to be promoted by new ICTs. Access to information of a myriad of kinds, 'surfing' on the Internet, teleshopping on the French minitel system, home banking from domestic or office computers, distance learning in 'virtual' universities and e-mailing the American President are all examples of the way in which the technologies appear to promote the exercise of choice by individuals at the push of a button, thus adding to opportunities for self-management and self-fulfilment. These examples suggest a fourth utopian value, that of equality. On this view, the wider access to information and electronic services provided by ICTs breaks down the power structures which are contiguous with the holding of information (Taylor and Williams 1994; Bellamy and Taylor 1994a). Thus the argument is that information holdings bestow power, whether at the social level or the organizational level, and, as the 'information commons' is developed, so greater equality ensues.

According to this line of utopian thinking, a fifth set of values advanced by new ICTs are those associated with 'open government' and with greater organizational and political 'transparency'. On this reading, ICTs can deliver greater levels of access to government for citizens, as well as enhanced involvement in the workplace for employees, making decision-making more open and engendering a stronger sense of ownership and engagement. Thus, one of the best examples of an explicit commitment to open government *via* the medium of ICTs is to be found in the USA, where the Clinton/Gore administration has strongly promoted citizenship with its open access programme. British central government too has developed opportunities for access to information by citizens *via* the on-line Government Information Service. Within organizations, it is claimed that new technologies can 'increase the intellectual content of work at virtually every organizational level, as the ability to decipher explicit information and make decisions informed by that understanding becomes broadly distributed among organizational members' (Zuboff 1988: 243). As one white collar worker in Zuboff's study put it: 'The best part about having this new (information) system is knowing what is in the unit and being able to feel like I have control over the work . . . Now that I can see the total functioning of the office, I feel more ownership towards all of the units, not just my own' (Zuboff 1988: 157).

Finally, there is a form of utopian thinking which derives largely from an economic 'regulationist' or 'post-Fordist' perspective (Lipietz 1987; Elam 1990). As the business firm takes on the widespread adoption and application of new ICTs, so it is enabled to do its business in new and innovative ways that move it away from a 'Fordist' reliance on the mass production of highly standardized goods for undifferentiated, mass markets. In particular, the firm becomes increasingly sensitive to the changing and distinctive needs of different customers, managing the range of its products or services by reference to consumer preferences. Firms may also come to trade with more suppliers than hitherto, establishing vertical integration; for example, between large retailers and small suppliers. In so doing they may promote the well-being of rural and local economies (Piore and Sabel 1984). This process may also contribute to what Toffler refers to as the 'de-massification' of the economy by allowing niche markets to be identified and catered for by a range of specialist skills (Toffler 1980). ICTs are identified as the crucial facilitators of new flows of information, enabling closer customer–buyer–supplier relationships to emerge, and linking design, production and distribution processes in new kinds of partnerships.

By this reading, the ICT-intensive business firm is moving from one in which products or services are designed for mass consumption, to one in which the product or service is designed and tailored for a particular market segment. Thus new kinds of information are enabling the shift from old Fordist methods of production and distribution to a post-Fordist regime characterized by 'flexible specialization' (Piore and Sabel 1984). Later in this book, we will be exploring the influence in government of the model of the 'networked firm', characterized as it is by its informational intensity. Governments, too, can trade electronically with their suppliers and their buyers, setting up new kinds of relationships with the businesses and individuals who are the main source of the information upon which government runs. They, too, can become more sensitive to specific 'customer' needs and requirements; they, too, can shape services to the specific circumstances of consumers; and they, too, can target their promotional activities more effectively. Equally, governments can seek to take advantage of the new transaction cost economies to be realized by 'out-sourcing' non-core functions and establishing internal trading relationships. Indeed, on this view, post-Fordist government has huge advantages over its Fordist forms, including: advantages for consumers through improved quality of service; advantages to taxpayers through cost reductions; and advantages to employees through their empowerment at work.

This celebration of the post-industrial information society is typical of a *genre* of academic thinking and journalistic commentary which interprets ICTs as a generally 'good thing'. In short, utopian thinking perceives ICTs as the means of realizing desirable citizenship and workplace values, such as access to information and managerial openness and transparency, a shift away from the 'authority of hierarchy' and an emphasis on the 'authority of knowledge'. These values are to be fostered and sustained by a wider distribution of infor-mation resources, as well as by the 'de-massification' of the scale of production and consumption (Toffler 1980) as organizations take on new networked forms (Taylor and Williams 1991b; Jarillo 1993; Davidow and Malone 1992). Open-ness and transparency are seen to follow from widespread access to high-level management information, so that the 'information commons' of the organiza-tion is greatly extended. The ascendancy of the 'authority of knowledge' presumes strong information resources at the disposal of individual knowledge workers, while the changing scale of organization is attendant on changes in transaction cost structures, thus allowing for strategic downsizing, internal disaggregation and extensive outsourcing.

Heralding dystopia: the control society

Contending with these optimistic views of the information society is a range of counter-arguments which stress that, far from importing desirable values into society, ICTs tend to be destructive of the very same values which are cherished by utopians. Bleak images of life among new information tech-nologies are sustained, of course, by some of the most well known and powerful literature of the twentieth century, including Huxley's *Brave New World* and Orwell's *1984*. However, a host of academic writing has also challenged fundamentally the comfortable assumptions of the utopians, laying emphasis upon issues of control, surveillance, inequality, disinformation and risk.

Control is a keyword in the lexicon of those who counter the utopian view. Three themes predominate, the first of which is that new ICTs are *ipso facto* technologies of control (Beniger 1986). On this reading, it is inevitable that the development of IT-based solutions to organizational problems reflects a search for greater control, because of the rising 'economic demand for control' which follows from the speeding up of industrial and business processes. The best way to interpret the uptake of new ICTs, therefore, is to recognize it as the search for greater degrees of certainty and predictability at all levels of society, whether in the workplace, the home or the state.

A second theme in the social control literature derives from Marxist perspectives on the 'labour process'. Here the core argument is that 'machinery comes into the world not as the servant of "humanity", but as the instrument of those to whom the accumulation of capital gives the ownership of the machines' (Braverman 1974: 192). Here is a direct refutation of the utopian view that technology could possibly be liberating. Rather, technology should be interpreted as a search for social control by the owners and representatives of capitalism. Computers are perceived to be deeply implicated in the requirement for control of individual employees as management secures the 'one best way' of doing things. Counting the key strokes of data input clerks in social security offices, using networks to monitor the workrates of computer-intensive workers such as library counter assistants and applying global positioning systems (GPS) to track the movements of peripatetic workers, such as salespeople or ambulance staff, all provide contemporary examples of ICTs as control technologies. Here in a nutshell is the thesis that ICTs lead to the 'dehumanization', rather than the liberation, of the workforce, signalling the arrival of intensified forms of Taylorist control (Giordano 1993).

Finally, a third theme in the control perspective is that, far from producing more flexible production and distribution arrangements, as the literature on post-Fordism supposes, ICTs are being used to harness small suppliers to large producers in ways that produce enhanced forms of dependency. Thus what appear, *prima facie*, to be more *flexible* arrangements for producing, distributing and consuming services and goods are better seen as instruments of more intensive supervision. Rather than characterizing the present era as a post-Fordist age, therefore, it would more accurate to style it a neo-Fordist age, one in which new technologies are being used to reinforce and widen the scope of, rather than to challenge, the imperialist power of the big corporations (e.g. Elam 1990).

Surveillance and disinformation

Closely linked to this emphasis on control is the dystopian concern with surveillance and threats to personal privacy. As computers and telecommunications systems enter more and more into the daily life of individuals, so these technologies offer enhanced capabilities to the employer, the producer and the government for closer identification, monitoring and scrutiny of employees, consumers and citizens. Suspicion about an employee's work rate or honesty, for example, can now be investigated by means of tracking 'footprints' left on systems, without the knowledge or the consent of the subject (Taylor and Williams 1994; Lyon 1994). Likewise, as camera surveillance of shopping centres, filling stations, motorways, urban housing estates and city centres becomes more commonplace (Lyon 1994), so the social control capabilities of the state are enhanced. As the computer systems of government are able to capture more and more data on individual citizens, and as the same kinds of records are built up by financial services organizations and retailers, so the capability for detailed scrutiny of individuals is enhanced, especially as the growth of interoperable computer systems increases the technical feasibility of automatic data-matching between the records held in these different systems.

At the same time that individuals become more transparent to corporations and government, so big bureaucracies are also acquiring more flexible and effective ways to target information on individuals, and thus control better the information that particular individuals receive. For example, we will see that one of the more ubiquitous applications of ICTs by government in Britain is the packaging of information for consumers of public services. The construction of electronic public information systems (EPIS) represents a one-way flow of information from government to the public, allowing, at best, only highly restricted opportunities for interaction or feedback. At the same time, applications which are claimed to be more interactive are becoming more commonplace in some countries of Europe and in parts of the USA. These initiatives include broadcasting political debates over local cable TV and providing opportunities for recipients to register their preferences on policy choices. While initiatives such as these have been heralded as opportunities for creating more open political debate, they can equally be characterized as 'disinforming' (Laudon 1977).

The information rich and information poor

There is also a dystopian view that, far from being a source of equality, new ICTs are in fact inherently inegalitarian. Again these arguments proceed at a number of levels. In the workplace, for example, there is a reflection of the increasingly genderized division of labour in information-intensive employment, as higher paid ICT-intensive work is colonized by men, and lower paid, part-time, casualized, word processing work is undertaken by women (Webster 1996; Barker and Downing 1985). At the macro level, the uneven distribution of enhanced telecommunications threatens to exacerbate the already uneven development of local and regional economies (Taylor and Webster 1996), a point which translates at a broader level to a concern about the patterns of development within the global economy. Thus, much of the energy being devoted by governments, nationally and locally, to developing information infrastructures is based on the perception that important and irreversible divisions are emerging between 'information rich' countries and localities and those which are 'information poor'.

Threats such as these are further underlined as powerful organizations, including governments themselves, disperse their activities geographically around electronic networks. Thus, some countries, cities and regions will gain from these redistributions and others will lose, although the precise calculation of gainers and losers requires close examination of the kinds of jobs which are being redistributed. For example, the relocation by the Department of Social Security of relatively low-paid back office work from London to Glasgow raises different issues for local economic development from those raised by the large-scale movement by the Inland Revenue of professional and administrative work from London to Nottingham (Taylor 1992).

Technology and risk

Finally, the spectre of technical failures is also commonly raised through dystopian perspectives on the information age. While ICTs might, by this view, promise advantages of many kinds, the risks to which they give rise outweigh those advantages. Financial trading disasters, air crashes and spectacular administrative failures all provide grist to the perception that it is the *technology* which lies at the root of the problem, by offering the possibility of development beyond the range of human control. Here, then, is a popular, neo-Luddite view of ICTs, one which builds from the assumption that development ineluctably gives rise to failures which threaten lives as well as balance sheets. One such example in British government is the London Ambulance Service's Computer Aided Despatch System (LASCAD), which failed with tragic consequences in October 1992. Reports in the press estimated that twenty or thirty people may have died unnecessarily as a direct consequence. More considered analysis of the system has shown that it was introduced over-hastily into the operational environment of the service, and was, in consequence, unable to cope with an unusual flood of 999 calls (SW Thames Regional Health Authority 1993). However, while this detailed investigation points to the 'political, economic and social nature of information systems failure' (Beynon-Davis 1995: 1168; Lyytinen and Hirscheim 1987; Peltu et al. 1996), there remains a popular belief that fault lies in technological hubris. In the same vein, there is a view among some social scientists that certain kinds of technologies, especially those which are inherently large scale and therefore require long-term planning to bring to fruition, are particularly liable to failure because their very inflexibility renders them unmanageable (e.g. Collingridge and Margetts 1994).

The power of ICTs

These, then, are the main dimensions of what are essentially technologically determinist debates about social *impacts* of ICTs. As we have said above, our view, in contrast, is that, while information and communication technologies are undoubtedly powerful, they are not so autonomously (Scarbrough and Corbett 1992). On the contrary, the deployment of computers, telecommunications and information systems is the consequence of human choices which are themselves constrained and shaped by social context. Nor do we subscribe to the view that the information age is only to be analysed, or, indeed, is best understood as a *technological* revolution. Rather, what is significant about *these* technologies is that they are *information and communication* technologies. That is, their specific importance derives from the potential for supporting new informational capabilities, as well as for introducing changes in the way that information is communicated. By the same token, much of the resistance to ICT-induced innovation lies in the political and cultural significance of information and communications processes.

Thus, it should be clear that we endorse the observation that the information revolution is not about *atoms* – that is, physical objects – but about *bits* (Negroponte 1995). It follows that it is the digitalization of information, the bits, and their communication, which should be the core focus of social scientific enquiry of the information age. While the physical machinery has become the common-sense focus of attention, this process has meant that we have become purblind to the distinctive properties of these technologies. What, indeed, are the specific properties of information and communication technologies which have lent themselves to such a dichotomized view of the information age? What is it about these technologies that leads commentators to adopt such definite, but contradictory, convictions about their social implications? To address these questions we will refocus our discussion on the informational and communications capabilities associated with ICTs.

Characterizing new ICTs

It is our view that there are, at bottom, two interrelated qualities of ICTs which help us to answer these questions. Each of these qualities is concerned with information. The first highlights the significance of 'informatization'. The second relates specifically to new capabilities for communicating information.

Informatization

The use of the term 'informatization' can be confusing, because it is used in the literature on ICTs in two different ways. It is often used generically to refer to the increasingly intensive exploitation of the capabilities associated with ICTs (Frissen 1992a). However, the term 'informatization' is being used in this book more precisely, to refer to the distinctive properties of ICTs which were first identified by Zuboff when she coined the notion of ICTs as 'informating' technologies (Zuboff 1988). Zuboff developed the insight that information technology provides a distinctive foundation for innovation, because it adds 'an additional element of reflexivity: it makes its contribution to the product (or service) but it also reflects back on its activities and on the system of activities to which it is related' (Zuboff 1988: 9). Unlike other technologies, ICTs inevitably produce *information* which enables reflection upon the organization into which it has been introduced, and thereby changes, in intended or unintended ways, human perceptions of the context in which that technology is employed. ICTs cannot, therefore, be interpreted simply as *production* technologies, designed simply to speed up and otherwise improve production and administrative processes. While they might well bring greater efficiencies to transaction processing, the distinctive importance of ICTs lies in their reflexivity. As Zuboff shows in her own, richly detailed, empirical study, the 'informated' worker can be emancipated and empowered by a computerized machine because the information which it generates necessarily illuminates the activity within which that worker is embedded. Equally, however, the same worker could be more effectively controlled by management as a result of the information liberated through the informating properties of this technology.

This analysis applies as well to service industries, including government, as it does to manufacturing industry. Thus, as public service providers come to use these technologies extensively, so they could learn more about the relationships involved in their activities, particularly those between themselves and their employees, customers and citizens. For example, professional librarians can learn about their customers' preferences from their computerized circulation and control systems. In other words, the data which are generated by the processes of issuing, returning and reserving books can be exploited to permit the reshaping of book handling activities, so that libraries become more efficient in the use of stock. At the same time, the 'informatization' of library management in this way can raise the quality of customer services, while providing employees with more rewarding work. This example shows how computer systems that use data to accomplish an operational task can capture those data and convert them to management information. Here is innovation in the use of information at its most beneficial and benign (Taylor and Williams 1989).

Communicating and networking information

The second important characteristic of ICTs is identified by the 'C' of ICTs. It is one which, when taken in conjunction with the first, establishes a *prima facie* case for understanding why it is that exploiting ICTs has more ambiguous effects. As we have seen, information systems open up possibilities in contemporary organizations for enhanced forms of self-control by employees and customers alike. However, the networking of information inevitably permits control by others as well. Here looms the potential for the Big Brother State and the control revolution adumbrated by dystopian writers. A hypothetical example will illustrate the point. Many immigration authorities in Western Europe are now equipping themselves with computerized systems which allow officials to cross-check passports against an index of unwelcome individuals. This facility will enable improvements in cross-border procedures by speeding up the necessary checks. It will thereby offer better quality service to people entering a country, as well as, almost certainly, reducing costs, thus bringing an additional advantage for taxpayers. Equally, however, a combination of the informating property of IT, together with the networked character of ICTs, could produce results much less benign than those in the libraries example referred to above. While cross-referencing data from scanned-in passports against an index of suspects stands as the explicit objective, such systems could feasibly begin to open up opportunities for data matches with other government systems. In turn, this possibility would allow officials to identify particular groups of citizens (for example, the unemployed, social security claimants or convicted criminals), and to monitor their movements around the world.

Similarly, the workrate of customs officials, for example, can be automatically recorded on computer and stored in management information systems. While officials might want to use their computers to manage their own case-loads, a networked machine is also capable of providing work-rate information to supervisory management, possibly without the knowledge of the employee. Thus computerized machinery is performing the specific and self-evident functions for which it was designed: speeding the flow of activity and reducing the labour content of transaction processing. What it may also be doing in more or less covert ways is reflexively supplying productivity data to management.

Information, communication and innovation in government

Even from these brief illustrations it can be seen that, especially when exploited in combination, the informating and communications dimensions of ICTs can be the source of powerful step changes in information and communications capabilities. The examples we have given here of information age innovations illustrate four main types of capabilities associated with ICTs, which underpin the radical nature of the social changes with which ICTs are so commonly associated. First, electronic networks can permit the integration of data which are held in different computer files, in different information systems, in different places and, even, in different organizations or jurisdictions. They enable a vast expansion in the volume of information resources which can be put at the disposal of specific organizations or actors. Second, electronic networks allow for the cross-matching of data, enabling new kinds of information to emerge, information which can significantly extend the 'intelligence' possessed by those who have access to such processes. Third, networking can bestow much more flexibility and precision in the targeting, tailoring and differentiation of information flowing to and from specific groups of businesses, customers or citizens. Fourth, the flexibility and connectivity associated with electronic networks can permit organizations and individuals, alike, to acquire much more autonomy and selectivity in the ways in which they retrieve, disseminate and communicate information.

It is these capabilities which underpin contemporary opportunities for innovation in government. A wide range of contemporary innovations are set out in Table 1.3, where they are arranged by ICT function. The significance of this table for our discussion here is that it illustrates three categories of innovations which depend on the information and communications capabilities associated with ICTs. The first of these categories concerns innovations in the ways in which information resources are valued and exploited in the business of government, a process which may be referred to as the 'commodification' of information; the second concerns innovations in the delivery of public services

Table 1.3   Types of public electronic service delivery arrangements

ICT task	Sample applications	Systems that could be used
Narrowcasting	Public meetings; education	Cable and satellite networks
	Up-to-date information (including multilingual)	The Internet; multimedia kiosks; CD-ROMs; bulletin boards; videotext
Transactions	Welfare benefits advice; electronic benefits transfer; payments for services, licences, transport, etc.	Multimedia kiosks; expert systems; smartcards; automatic tellers; electronic funds transfer
	Voting; referenda; public opinion polling	Interactive TV; voice mail; screen phones; the Internet
	Criminal parole checking	Fingerprint-check kiosks
	Electronic tax returns	Phone + voice check; PCs
	Road charging systems	Automatic vehicle monitors
Information retrieval	Access to government information	The Internet; on-line databases
	Answering routine public queries	Voice response; electronic mail
	Supporting public officials and professionals to deliver services	Executive information services; expert systems; electronic mail
Remote communication	Forums on public issues; help for voluntary and professional groups	The Internet; computer conferencing; bulletin boards
	Citizens' complaints, requests; emergency support	Low-cost access to ICT networks; the Internet; kiosks; voice mail
	Intercommunity meetings; consultation with voters	Video and audio conferencing; videophones; local cable networks
	Parent–teacher interaction	Voice mail

Source: Dutton (1996a).

to consumers; and the third concerns innovations in the processes associated with the practice of democracy and citizenship.

The commodification of information

First, governmental organizations are innovating in the ways in which they provide information to the public. Information is being directed primarily at addressing the needs of their service customers, but it can also be aimed at enhancing levels of civic and political awareness. Government organizations are, therefore, increasingly concerned with the *commodification* of information, in the sense that they are acquiring a heightened awareness of the packaging of information, of the processes and costs which are involved in its production and of the choices that must be made between providing it as a free good or as a commercially valuable commodity. Governments are now paying more attention to recouping the costs of meeting the growing expectations for information, expectations which we can expect to place an increasing strain on their financial and administrative resources. As far back as 1983, the UK government produced a paper which encouraged the commercial exploitation of information (Information Technology Advisory Panel 1983). In the 1990s, governments are facing even more urgent questions about their own exploitation of government information, and these questions are being raised more and more loudly as greater volumes of information are offered on-line (Office of Public Service 1996b). Debates about electronic access to *Hansard* provide a good example of the dilemmas involved in this issue (House of Commons 1995–6). *Hansard* has, historically, been sold through HMSO. Making *Hansard* available over the Internet would, arguably, enhance democracy by increasing resources for public debate, but it may simultaneously reduce the income currently generated by sales. Nevertheless, the decision has been made that *Hansard* will be available on-line at the House of Commons Web site. What the debate about it has illustrated, however, is that one of the more important issues raised by the commodification of information is how pricing policies can and should be used, deliberately or otherwise, to structure access to public information resources.

Electronic public services

Second, Table 1.3 illustrates a number of ways in which ICTs are being exploited in the delivery of public services, as governments search for greater efficiency and enhanced quality. Whereas, in our first category of innovation, the production and consumption of information is the subject of innovation, in this second category new information and communications capabilities are being harnessed to secure enhancements of other kinds of services (Bellamy *et al.* 1995a; Taylor *et al.* 1996). Many of these innovations are currently emerging in the welfare benefits field. For example, the American state of Wyoming uses a commercially available smart card, which is being heralded as a major inhibitor of welfare fraud (*The Independent on Sunday*, Business 24 November 1996: 1). The card can be encoded with data about the amount of money to which a claimant is entitled. The claimant is allowed to 'spend' the allowance on a range of permitted goods by conducting electronic transactions with shopkeepers. Likewise, in the UK, the Department of Social Security is interested in enhancing the use of smart cards, to permit money to be drawn through automatic telling machines, and, in the north of Scotland, the DSS is cooperating in an EU-funded project which enables clients and officials to use video-conferencing equipment in order to process claims.

However, while all these examples appear to be benign, we will be interested in exploring how such innovations also create new opportunities for discriminating actively between groups of consumers, and why electronic transactions also increase the transparency of citizens' behaviour for government.

Electronic citizenship and democracy

Finally, a third set of innovations is occurring in the area of 'electronic democracy'. Here we are seeing the introduction into the polity of ICT applications which are designed to strengthen democratic processes, applications such as electronic public meetings and policy forums, e-mailing elected representatives and officials, and virtual community groups. In such ways, ICTs are involved in innovations designed to recast the relationships between citizens, citizens' groups, politicians and government (Donk and Tops 1992; Donk *et al.* 1995; Raab *et al.* 1996). Again, we will wish to emphasize that this recasting is not without its problems. The new information and communication capabilities associated with ICTs are also the source of enhanced capabilities to manage democratic processes, by permitting the deployment of refined market research techniques. Similarly, while new on-line communities may extend opportunities for human connectivity and the development of new forms of civic consciousness, the seductive resources of cyberspace may also isolate human beings, focusing their attention on interactions which are socially detached.

ICTs as ambiguous technologies

We can see, then, that the conjunction of new capabilities and innovations in the workplace is permitting these technologies to become, at one and the same time, agents of employee empowerment and agents for control and oppression. By the same token, if we translate these scenarios to the wider society, we have the basis for more and less subtle forms of monitoring and control of citizens, on the one hand, and for their liberation and enrichment, on the other. It is for this reason that ICTs have been characterized as being, inherently, 'ambiguous technologies' (Frissen 1992b). They offer fundamental choices to the institutions which control the strategic direction of a society. That is, reflexive electronic technologies *simultaneously* hold within them tendencies towards Orwellian control of individuals and tendencies towards enriching the experience of employment and the meaning of citizenship. Neither tendency can be entirely suppressed, but nor does either represent an overwhelming imperative.

This is why taking polarized positions on the *impact* of ICTs is misguided. The intensity of antonymous debate offers a restricted form of debate from which to develop our understanding of government in the information age. Polarized views have high value in raising profile, or for bringing forward specific issues for celebration, investigation, vigilance and condemnation: they have low value if their effect is to create twin Procrustean beds. The specific danger is that the force of these opposing ways of understanding new ICTs may lock successive generations into ideological legacies which will in turn crowd out the development of new ways of thinking about information and communication. It follows that, as we move to a new era for governments, we need to undergo a process of intellectual divestment. The intellectual fashions of the utopians and dystopians should now be deemed *démodé*.

In particular, we should be less willing to ascribe a deterministic role to technologies. In particular, we need a more complex analysis of the opportunities and problems associated with specific technologies. Information and communication are important sources of innovation for government organizations, but the academic emphasis must be on understanding the interaction between the particular institutional and organizational settings which shape innovations and the effects on governance of new information resources and information flows. It is such an understanding that we seek to develop in this book. We will proceed by examining a series of topics which we see as relating in the manner of Russian dolls. As we open each doll, so more fundamental issues become apparent, going more and more to the core of government. Thus, from the broad gauge introduction to the intellectual and technological contexts of the so-called information society in the present chapter, we will proceed in Chapter 2 to an exploration of approaches to ICT-mediated organizational and managerial change in British government. This is followed in Chapter 3 by a focus on the normative issues raised by the consumerist agendas which have come to the fore in contemporary proposals for 'reinventing' government, and in Chapter 4 we will go further into issues posed by the ways in which new information and communications capabilities are mediating relations between the individual and the state, by locating the consumerist agenda within debates about electronic democracy and citizenship. In Chapter 5 we will explore the implications for citizenship arising from the tensions between public service and market approaches to the development of telematics infrastructures, otherwise known as the information superhighway. Lastly, in Chapter 6 we will draw on institutionalist analysis to offer our own interpretation of the role of information and communication in underscoring tensions between continuity and change, tensions which are shaping both the practice of government and the experience of being governed in the information age.

2

Re-engineering the government machine: new technologies and organizational change

Improvements in the machine are needed to assist elected politicians think their way through the complications of 21st century social and economic circumstance. The need is to design cogs and wheels to fit the policy rather than have the policy spatchcocked into old, traditional or unsuitable machinery.

(Kemp and Walker 1996: 1)

Unfolding visions of information age government

In 1966, the Fulton Committee, a major committee of inquiry into the UK Civil Service, asked the Treasury for a note on the implications of computers for public administration. Specifically, the Committee wanted to know whether computers would provide the means for halting, or even reversing, the expansion of the civil service. The Treasury replied with two memoranda (Fulton Committee Report 1968, Vol. 4: memoranda nos. 5 and 54). The first described the use of what was then called 'automatic data processing' in government departments, making the point that almost all expenditure on computers had been justified by projected cuts in staffing. The second memorandum went on to argue that 'although such savings will continue to be made, the trend will in future be downwards rather than upwards. This is because new computers . . . will be used increasingly to do things which it was not previously possible to do without them' (Fulton Committee Report 1968, Vol. 4: 281).

This exchange is interesting because it captures two sides of a continuing debate about the significance of 'computerization' for organizational change. On the one hand, there is the view that its main purpose is to save money by shedding labour. This view has been firmly embedded in the attitudes of the

Treasury and the Public Accounts Committee and, inevitably, has also influenced trades unions' reaction to the introduction of new technology. On the other hand, however, the second memo betrays an inkling that the impact of computers on organizations could be more complex because it opens up the possibility that ICTs could permit new kinds of processes and services to be developed. Indeed, the central question which has come to be posed by business computing in the present era is no longer 'How can we apply computers to our business?' but 'How should we do business now that we have computers?' The significance of computers and associated technologies is that they might enable governance itself to change, ultimately in quite radical ways.

The central assumption underpinning this second, much more heroic, question is the one that we discussed in some length in Chapter 1. The assumption is that ICTs will be the prime instrument for overcoming practical constraints on conducting business, which traditional forms of organization impose. More specifically, the main significance of new technologies, it is assumed, lies in their capacity to challenge the bureaucratic form of organization, as well as the geographical and occupational divisions of labour, associated with business organization in the industrial age. For example, it has long been argued that new ways of communicating information will encourage the de-layering of hierarchies and the emergence of new techniques of organizational control. This argument stems from an analysis of formal organization which identifies hierarchy as an instrument of communication and control specifically associated with the large, monolithic corporations of the Fordist era, an era characterized, as far as information and communication were concerned, by paper-based records and pre-digital telephony (Yates 1989). In this analysis, the primary role of middle management is to sift, process and transmit information passing up and down the hierarchy, between street level workers and top management. This type of information worker would become increasingly redundant in the information age. Not only would electronic networks be capable of supporting instantaneous, interactive communications that are quite independent of the lines drawn on formal organization charts, but the informatizing qualities of ICTs would replace old-style reporting, monitoring and supervisory functions. It follows that organizations would be flatter and trimmer in the information age (Taylor 1992).

ICTs are, therefore, deeply implicated in proposals for innovation in business organization, because of the flexibility which they create for reconfiguring transactions. One consequence is that many commentators believe that the transaction cost structures of organizations will be substantially reconstructed (e.g. Child 1987). They assume that the centrally managed, integrated, monolithic organization will be replaced by decentralized, loosely articulated networks which are the 'emerging organizational form of our world' (Castells 1989: 32). So, for example, the hierarchically articulated unity of command could be dissolved in favour of 'loose–tight' networks of semi-autonomous workgroups, enveloped in a mesh of quasi-contracts. Similarly, 'teamnets', networks of groups working across traditional bureaucratic jurisdictions, could be formed and dissolved according to changing business requirements, to secure greater economies of scope and scale (Lipnack and Stamps 1993). Or longer-standing, value-adding partnerships could emerge between free-standing businesses, in order to secure the benefits associated with vertical integration without the disbenefits associated with long hierarchies. All these kinds of arrangements appear to offer managements much more flexibility to 'make or buy'. Indeed, as a study in 1980 concluded, they could have far-reaching implications for the machinery of government:

> The outcome of all these forces, apart from stressing the old administrative style to breaking point, will be to evolve a nucleated pattern of organization of agencies, staff groups, centres, and project teams in place of the rigid, scalar hierarchy. There will be nuclei of operational units, some permanent, some assembled for specific projects, with far greater delegation of authority over the resources of manpower and money allocated to them . . . Within all of them, we can expect a lessening of bureaucratic rigidity, with more highly trained and specialized staff tending to define their own jobs in the course of their work. Such nucleated organizations will demand a very high quality of management at all levels and highly developed information and planning systems.
>
> (Garrett 1980: 80)

In the same sorts of ways, it is claimed that ICTs will permit much more flexibility in the geography of production and consumption (Castells 1989: Ernste and Jaeger 1989; Hepworth 1989). For example, networked information flows could release public services from the constraints imposed by the informational logic of paper-based records, in particular the need to locate operational staff where customer records are kept. They would therefore permit public services to be redesigned to take more account of the cost structures associated with other factors of production, including variations between local labour markets. Or they could permit them to be reconfigured in ways that are more sensitive to the needs and convenience of customers; for example, by decentralizing customer-facing services to neighbourhood offices or high street caller offices. In all these kinds of ways, new informational flexibilities point to the construction of a radically different distribution network for public administration.

A report prepared in 1990 for the Department of Social Security (DSS) put forward the notion of the 'logical office' (Department of Social Security 1990). A 'logical office' is conceived as a set of interdependent functions which are conducted and managed in ways that are independent of physical distance. In the case of the DSS, it was argued that advanced telecommunications would permit the concentration of back office claims processing into large computer processing centres located in geographical areas where suitably qualified labour was plentiful and cheap, while customer-facing services would be decentralized from local offices to neighbourhoods. The back office and front office functions relating to the same locality would be managed as a single command, despite being located hundreds of miles apart. By extrapolation, the 'logical office' may be seen as a first step towards a 'virtual corporation', an organization conceived as a set of interdependent information–mediated processes conducted over the wires across a network of suppliers, distributors and customers. A virtual organization would offer ultimate flexibility to business strategists, being constrained neither by geography nor by formal organizational structures. Thus:

> to the outside observer it will appear edgeless, with permeable and continuously changing interfaces . . . from inside, the view will be no less amorphous, with traditional offices, departments and operating divisions continually reforming according to need. Job responsibilities will constantly shift, as will lines of authority . . . Thus it is better to talk of the virtual corporation in terms of patterns of information and relationships.
>
> (Davidow and Malone 1992: 5–6)

Such arrangements also offer flexibility to workers and customers, because of the apparent ease with which they can support remote transactions; for example, through teleworking or telesales. In this sense, the virtual corporation will produce a new kind of product, a 'virtual product', that 'can be made available at any time, in any place, and in any variety' (Davidow and Malone 1992: 3).

In Chapter 3 we will explore in more detail some of the important issues which these scenarios present for the delivery of public services. In the present chapter we propose to focus on the relationship between ICTs and change in the organization of government, by considering how ICTs are implicated in processes of institutional change. As a prelude to this discussion we need to observe three points about this kind of organizational analysis. The first point is that it is capable of, and has frequently been subjected to, both utopian and dystopian interpretations as far as its social and human implications are concerned. As we saw in Chapter 1, these intepretations stem in large part from assumptions about the nature of organizational power associated with what appear as new 'hands-off' control techniques. Thus, utopian visions cast ICTs as the instrument by which, for example, much more freedom could be delegated to street level staff, releasing their creativity and commitment. On this reading, the information age organization has the potential to be much more flatly structured, to be much more egalitarian. On the other hand, there is a counter interpretation that hierarchical relationships will be not only reinvented but made much more effective because of new capabilities which new ICTs introduce for top-down control (e.g. Blackburn et al. 1985). On this counter interpretation, ICTs will vastly increase opportunities for surveillance and regulation of staff, as well as of customers and citizens.

The second point is that all these visions of information age organizations are rooted in a technological determinism, having been arrived at by extrapolating from the properties of ICTs to features of organizational design. Furthermore, these visions beg an important question about the dynamic of change. Why should organizations be remoulded to respond to changes in technology? One answer comes from a literature on business computing which adopts a position associating ICTs with the logic of their 'technological implications'

(Child and Loveridge 1990). From this position, technology is perceived to be a major factor 'impacting' on business strategy. This impact is deduced from two highly questionable assumptions. The first assumption is that organizations of all kinds face the same kinds of problems, and that applications of new technologies will therefore tend to cluster around the same kinds of solutions. The second assumption is that business strategists must exploit those solutions or face the loss of competitive advantage. In these ways, technology is elevated from a resource which is at the disposal of management to an imperative which should drive management. For this reason, we see this literature as exemplifying a technicist position, a position which is captured in the tone of this all too typical homily:

> All businesses face the unrelenting pressures of a business environment characterized by intense global competition . . . Moreover, this increasingly competitive world has developed against a backdrop of difficult economic conditions . . . The interaction of these two variables – information technology economics and a challenging business environment – has generated what might be called the economic imperative of information technology. Organizations that do not take advantage of the growing opportunities provided by IT are likely to slip behind in the competitive business world.
>
> (Benjamin *et al.* 1984: 4)

ICTs in government: driving the new public management?

This analysis leads directly to our third point, a point which concerns the implications of this technicist position for interpretations of the derivation and nature of the new public management (NPM). The patterns of organizational change which are so commonly associated with the information age are remarkably consistent with the patterns associated with current forms of managerialism in public administration. So, for example, Hood identified the 'shift to disaggregation of units in the public sector' and the 'unbundling of U-form management systems' as important doctrines of NPM (Hood 1991: 5), while Pollitt (1993: 180) referred to the 'intensified organizational and spatial decentralization of the management and production of services' as one of its four key themes. More recently, Walsh has argued that the pronounced shift to the use of contracting and markets involves a reconceptualization of public services 'as a nexus of contracts'. 'Even if contracting is internal, the organization itself becomes a network. Different organizations within the network concentrate on specific activities in which they may have a comparative advantage. The management of contracts is then a management of networks' (Walsh 1995: 117).

The conjunction of the literature on information age organization with this kind of analysis of NPM prompts obvious questions. Should NPM be understood specifically as a form of public management for the information age? Are new informational and communications capabilities driving, or at least facilitating, NPM, and how powerful are these capabilities in shaping the outcomes of the managerialist agenda? We propose to address these questions by considering the interrelationship of changes in information systems and the developing managerial agenda in British government. To organize this discussion, we will utilize an intellectual framework for conceptualizing the relationship between IT and organizational development which emerged from a major study of the corporation of the 1990s conducted at the Massachusetts Institute of Technology. This study concluded that organizations pass through three stages in exploiting ICTs: from 'automating' to 'informating' (or informatizing), and thence to 'transforming', their business (Scott Morton 1991). We are utilizing this schema in a spirit of profound scepticism that technological change does, in practice, constitute the strategic imperative which is driving organizations inexorably through these stages, and our conclusions endorse this scepticism. Nevertheless, we believe that these three categories, *automating*, *informating* and *transforming*, are useful in delineating contrasting managerial approaches to the role of new technology in relation to organizational change.

Automation

The essence of an 'automation' approach lies in its emphasis on the importance of technological innovation. Moreover, this approach is founded on a conception of computers as a production technology rather than as an information technology. While automated processes often generate information as a by-product, little or no attempt is made to exploit that information as an organizational resource and nor, therefore, is the enhancement of information resources the primary motivation for computerization. Rather, automation is undertaken 'to take the cost out of production' (Scott Morton 1991: 14). Automation also carries with it the notion that ICTs are being used solely to make existing data processing activities more efficient, rather than to challenge, replace or connect them. Indeed, students of business computing have often referred to the presence of 'islands of automation', a term which reflects the selective concentration of IT development in discrete projects focused on data-heavy processing functions. Automation is, therefore, typically associated with the continuing use of paper for capturing and disseminating computerized information because these processes in the information-handling chain typically remain uncomputerized. Thus, the timeliness, scope and usefulness of computerized information are seriously compromised. Not only do data handling costs remain high, but the information yielded is only as reliable as the weakest link in this chain. Here, then, we can begin to detect some of the reasons why computerization-as-automation appears frequently to underperform compared to the resources which are devoted to it. We will see that such problems have been rife in British government.

Automating British government

Computerization in British government has been much more frequently associated with the reinforcement of traditional bureaucratic structures and processes than it has with challenging them, an association clearly in line with the automation perspective. As recently as the late 1980s, most investment in government computing was undertaken to secure greater efficiency in high-volume data processing rather than to develop new ways of conducting the business of government. Hence, the use of computers for operational purposes has been concentrated in those public services which depend most heavily upon large-scale processing of standardized data.

The first computer to be used for administrative work in government was installed in January 1958 to process the payrolls of the Ministry of Aviation and the National Assistance Board (Fulton Committee Report 1968, Vol. 4: 634). By 1967, there were 73 computers in use for administrative purposes, supporting central functions such as accounting, payroll, statistics, storekeeping, tax collection and pensions processing (Fulton Committee Report 1968, Vol. 4: 279). From the 1970s onwards, the use of mainframes to 'batch process' data spread from central, internal housekeeping functions to vertical service producing departments. The enormous computing installations which were created to reap efficiencies of scale in central government services – for example, the Department of Social Security's central offices at Newcastle and North Fylde, DVLC (now DVLA) at Swansea, the central Passport Office at Peterborough and the Inland Revenue's PAYE processing installation at Reading – all date from that period. This use of large-scale, semi-automatic data processing marks an important stage in the geographical dispersal of government employment away from London, but it had little impact on organizational design. Its major significance for public administration was that it became much more possible to cope with the growing scale, scope and complexity of public services. A case in point is the extensive elaboration of the social security system which took place in the 1970s. This process not only saw the introduction of Child Benefit and the State Earnings Related Pension Scheme (SERPS) but, by 1980, had led to the creation of over thirty different benefits (Department of Health and Social Security 1985). It can plausibly be argued that – throughout government – computerization was masking growing problems to which NPM was a later reaction. In particular, new technology permitted successive governments to bolt functions on to government departments, increasing volumes and complexity, while failing to recognize and address the dysfunctions endemic in big, producer-dominated bureaucracies.

The automation of large-scale data processing was also important in the construction of stereotypical attitudes to new technology. The typical government computer installation of the 1970s was a clerical factory, in which Fordist work processes came to be most fully realized in public administration. It concentrated large numbers of clerical workers into highly repetitive, machine-paced labour processes redolent of assembly line production. Similarly, it forced the users of public services to accept rigidly structured interactions with remote government offices, conducted largely by means of standardized forms and letters. In this way, it encouraged the dystopian belief that new technology would lead to public services that were more, not less, unresponsive, inflexible and bureaucratic.

As we saw in Chapter 1, the increasing synergy of computing and tele-communications created the possibility for distributing computing power and computerized information to front-line staff, and, therefore, for decentralized or flexible administrative arrangements. In practice, however, most computing projects in the 1980s did not represent a sharp disjuncture in the trajectory of government computing, but rather a process of slow and uneven evolution. Computing was clearly ceasing to be the special preserve of central computing installations and was spreading to the desks and counters of mainline administrative and professional staff. Direct, unsupervised access to computers was becoming a routine, everyday occurrence. For example, by the late 1980s there had been a 'progressive diffusion' of computer usage within local authorities, extending even to public service customers through such innovations as on-line catalogues in public libraries (Taylor and Williams 1989). Accordingly, both the Audit Commission and the National Audit Office were forecasting major increases in the number of devices which would be needed to link 'user areas' to computers (Audit Commission 1986; National Audit Office 1991). However, as this formulation reveals, it was assumed that diffusion would occur primarily by widening the networks that were being constructed around centralized mainframe computers.

The exploitation of distributed computing has therefore been somewhat restricted, for reasons that are as much cultural as technical. In particular, government computing continues to be shaped by two major constraints, the first of which is the powerful legacy left by earlier systems. Given the enormous costs of the large-scale, centralized computing systems developed in the 1970s and 1980s, there has been an understandable reluctance not to use these systems as the platform for further development. Moreover, systems leave less tangible but equally important legacies, especially the skills base of the organization, the experience of its technical and managerial staffs and the orientation of technology suppliers and business partners. It is these factors, particularly, which continue strongly to influence choices about technological investment. A second, even more influential shaper, however, has been the prevailing attitude to modernization and management reform in British government.

Automation and impoverished management: reinforcing perspectives?

For many commentators, 'managerialism' represents a distinctive break from earlier ways of thinking about public service: 'the injection of an ideological "foreign body" into a sector previously characterized by quite different traditions of thought' (Pollitt 1993: 11). A major reason for this perception is a widespread belief that, especially in the 1980s, the managerialist agenda was constructed largely through the language of business strategy and economics, at the expense of the public service ethos. According to this view, the prevailing emphasis on cost cutting as the main criterion of success reinforced an 'impoverished concept of management' (Metcalfe and Richards 1987). Management was understood, too narrowly, as the strengthening of hierarchical control over executive functions of government, rather than as the taking of responsibility for the quality and performance of the system of governance as a whole (Metcalfe and Richards 1987: 216). In a similar vein, managerialism in British public services has been characterized as 'neo-Taylorism': a relentless exercise in screwing more productivity from labour, so that most public service workers experienced 'better management as tighter control far more than as any other form of enhancement' (Pollitt 1993: 86).

Given this context, it is unsurprising that the exploitation of ICTs should be heavily influenced by an automation perspective. In the UK, the Conservative governments' concern with efficiency during the 1980s was manifested primarily as a preoccupation with reducing the numbers of public officials, and new technology was harnessed to this end. For example, the White Paper on Efficiency, which announced the first plans for driving down administrative costs in Whitehall, discussed the contribution of computers solely in terms of monitoring workloads and introducing economies in staff, declaring that 'an intensified search for cost saving applications of new information technology is an integral part of the drive for efficiency' (Civil Service Department 1981: 9). This attitude to ICTs in Whitehall was shared by MPs at Westminster. In 1982, the Treasury and Civil Service Select Committee investigated efficiency and effectiveness in the Civil Service, and asked departments about the contribution of 'office machines, including computers and other electrical and electronic devices', to the promotion of efficiency. The Committee did not inquire about the contribution of new technology to enhancing effectiveness in the provision of public services (House of Commons 1981–2).

The most important consequence of this attitude is that the application of telematics to government operations has most frequently taken the form of 'distributed automation'. A common stratagem was to use telecommunications to link deconcentrated workplaces, particularly the regional and local offices of government, to central mainframe computers, in order to extend the economies of scale associated with ADP. In so far as these projects reflected a concern with quality of service, improvements were usually of a kind that stem from increased control over the labour process; for example, faster throughput, greater consistency and lower error rates. At least in the short-term, they were not usually designed to provide a platform for new forms of service delivery, including those intended to empower front-line staff and their customers.

Distributed automation: the Operational Strategy of the DHSS
The Operational Strategy of the Department of Health and Social Security (DHSS) the largest computerization project in British government in the

1980s, provides a well documented case in point (Margetts 1991; Fallon 1993; Bellamy 1996). The strategy was a huge programme of some fourteen projects, which was formally announced in 1982. It established a common technical platform for computerizing the processing of a number of high-volume social security benefits, including locally administered benefits such as Income Support, Social Fund and Employment Benefit (which was subsequently replaced by the Jobseekers' Allowance) and short-term incapacity benefits. According to the department's top management, the motive of the DHSS was to cope with the vast increase in caseloads and the growing complexity of social security administration (House of Commons 1983–4: 8). It also anticipated that computerization would reduce errors, delays and fraud. But the rules imposed by the Treasury and the Public Accounts Committee obliged DHSS to promise, too, that the Operational Strategy would deliver substantial savings in staffing costs and, in the event, project managers were forced to reduce the range of functions offered by the systems in order to keep to the timetable for reducing staff numbers. In particular, the DHSS jettisoned a project which would have permitted it to monitor local offices' performance and to define the department's client base more accurately. That is, the potential benefits of informatizing the DHSS were traded in against maximizing the benefits from automation.

The Operational Strategy was much constrained by legacies from the DHSS's earlier mainframe systems. The DHSS's computing staff resisted the technical leap to networked, on-line computing, because their experience, competence and professional contacts were oriented to mainframe computing and ADP (Fallon 1993). For this reason the department also eschewed the introduction of PCs into local offices, although hindsight teaches us that the availability of intelligent computing in local offices could have supported a more flexible, customer-oriented approach to the delivery of street level services (Collingridge and Margetts, 1994). For example, the DHSS already knew that PCs could be used to run knowledge-based, or 'expert', systems which would have permitted front office staff to offer individual claimants tailorized welfare advice by running 'what if' scenarios through the mass of the DHSS's complex administrative codes (Dawson et al. 1990).

The Operational Strategy relied instead on mainframe computing systems, each capable of processing only a single benefit, which were linked electronically by digital telecommunications to 'dumb' terminals on the desks of DHSS local office staff. This decision was to have two major effects. First, the introduction of mainframe computer routines into local offices substantially increased management control over the throughput of cases, while reducing the discretion allowed to street level officials. The replacement of Supplementary Benefit by Income Support in 1988 – a change to a less discretionary benefit – was recognized to be a precondition of computerization (Department of Health and Social Security 1985). Thus, the Operational Strategy shows clearly that connecting mainframe computers to remote terminals can just as easily hook front-line staff into centralized administrative routines and neo-

Fordist working practices as increase local discretion and responsiveness to the individual public service user. Second, the systems which were developed in the 1980s were laid over existing social security benefits codes, replicating and reinforcing their complexity. The Operational Strategy therefore did little to simplify the DHSS's relationship with 'customers'. Indeed, it was to prove a handicap rather than a help in developing a more consumer-sensitive approach to benefits delivery in the 1990s (Bellamy 1996).

The automation of management information systems: reinforcing top-down control

Just as operational systems tended to reinforce existing bureaucratic structures and processes, so too did many of the information systems which were developed to support the emerging managerialist agenda. This statement is, perhaps, somewhat surprising because, as we have seen, managerialism in UK government has long been associated with doctrines which run closely in parallel with prescriptions for organizational change in the information age. For example, the Fulton Committee Report of 1968 provided the seminal discussion of the implications of an apparently simple principle: that managers at all levels should be held personally responsible for results. In particular, the report identified a number of ways in which the traditional, monolithic, bureaucratically organized civil service might need to be quite radically reformed, including:

- the need to free managers from top-down control techniques based on long, hierarchical reporting structures, by moving to flatter organizational configurations;
- the incompatibility of extensive delegation of responsibility with the conventions of ministerial responsibility;
- the challenge to standardized resourcing control regimes and the unity of civil service management arising from the diversity of departmental activities and their management requirements.

The report also recognized that implementing the managerialist agenda would require new kinds of informational resources. In particular, information systems should be developed in two directions. First, traditional financial accounting systems would have to be reconfigured. The problem was that the structure of financial information reflected the demands of parliamentary accountability, which required departmental accounting officers to show that expenditure matched parliamentary votes. In consequence, financial systems were entirely focused on inputs, or finance, rather than outputs, or performance. Moreover, inputs were expressed as aggregate departmental expenditures and were useless for supporting the devolution of financial responsibility to divisions within departments. Second, Fulton understood the need to develop both the methodologies and the information systems for measuring performance.

In the event, the development of management information systems (MIS) in the wake of the Fulton Committee was slow and uneven. There was substantial progress in establishing measures of performance in labour-intensive clerical operations in the DHSS (Matthews 1979), the Inland Revenue and Customs and Excise (Garrett 1980: 124). But in other parts of government most of the interest in MIS petered out by the end of 1972 (Garrett 1980: 123). The Expenditure Committee's review of progress in implementing Fulton found that management accounting systems remained 'haphazard and limited' (House of Commons 1976–7: xviii). Indeed, it was not until the early 1980s, when the Financial Management Initiative (FMI) was launched, that a strong, government-wide drive was undertaken to develop information systems throughout Whitehall. The White Paper which followed the initiative was clear about the informational implications of the managerialist agenda, and, in contrast to Fulton, it showed more understanding that the growing scale and complexity of government's management information needs implied the wide-spread computerization of MIS (Cabinet Office 1982). The White Paper was also emphatic that the purpose of MIS was not simply to monitor efficiency and drive down costs, but also to shed light on service delivery. In turn, better information would also enable the effectiveness of policy decisions to be as-sessed. However, this would not occur without harvesting data from oper-ational as well as from administrative systems. In other words, government was to be 'informatized'. New information flows would be established, including new horizontal flows across boundaries between management commands as well as stronger vertical flows between different levels in departmental hier-archies. The White Paper therefore recommended that departments should develop integrated information systems strategies, which would encourage interoperability between the systems set up for management and the systems set up to undertake departmental operations.

In practice, the development of MIS in government was very restricted, and, a decade and a half later, the aims of the 1982 White Paper had still to be fully realized (Office of Public Service and Science 1994b). Some of the problems can undoubtedly be laid at the door of shortcomings in the manage-ment of IT and information systems (IS) in British government. As with operational systems, administrative computing projects have been subject to investment appraisal techniques which assume that each and every project must pay for itself by cutting cost, regardless of its contribution to a wider strategy. This approach has, unsurprisingly, encouraged a continuing focus on large-scale data processing at the expense of other aspects of information manage-ment. Moreover, the persistent emphasis on mainframe computing meant that most MIS were first developed as centralized mainframe systems. In conse-quence many MIS were designed to be fed with data on paper or magnetic tape generated by existing departmental accounting and statistical routines. The upshot was that many FMI systems were laid over existing datasets and infor-mation flows, rather than providing new kinds of informational capabilities (HM Treasury 1986; Metcalfe and Richards 1987).

A second set of problems has arisen because the construction of MIS laid bare unresolved political tensions in implementing the managerialist agenda. Computerization is intolerant of confusion, and, in practice, managerialism in government has been confused. One problem is that departments have been asked to deliver a variety of not entirely compatible management information, reflecting the plurality of stakeholding in MIS. Departments were required to develop: top management systems, to provide high-level information for top officials and ministers; budgetary control systems, to support devolved management arrangements; performance indicators for providing information about performance; alongside financial management systems, for recording expenditure and reconciling it to Public Expenditure Survey (PES) allocations and parliamentary votes (Cabinet Office and HM Treasury 1983). However, the piecemeal approach to computerizing information systems meant that there were perennial complaints about failures to integrate or share data between the systems that were developed for these rather different purposes, leading to inflexibility and fragmentation in the information which they could be made to yield (National Audit Office 1986: 4). This failure was owing not only to problems in achieving *technical* interoperability, but also to unresolved differences in accounting conventions and data definitions. The problems went far beyond questions of technical accounting conventions, to the politics of information systems in government, and reflected conflicts about the intentions and nature of management reforms. For example, the Treasury was reluctant to disaggregate responsibility for parliamentary votes, fearing that such a process would weaken the visibility of, and therefore its control over, expenditure totals. A change would therefore undermine Treasury control of public expenditure and challenge established interpretations of constitutional propriety. As a contemporary study concluded:

> Changes in IS are not neutral in the sense that they leave organizational structures and the distribution of power as it was. The impact of new IS is not limited to their manifest functions of improving the quality, reliability and timeliness of information available to decision-makers. In addition, IS have significant implications for accountable management and public accountability which call into question established constitutional conventions.
>
> (Metcalfe and Richards 1987: 61)

The outcome of these difficulties was that new information systems were frequently laid into existing vertical information channels, reinforcing top-down control in ways that were entirely compatible with the impoverished concept of management which gave rise to the FMI. Moreover, this approach to MIS has bestowed long-lasting legacies on Whitehall. Thus, over a decade later, a scrutiny of resource management systems in government rehearsed a familiar litany of shortcomings in the quality, accessibility and reliability of management information, including: the reliance on *ad hoc* gathering of information for senior management and ministers; a widespread failure to develop strategies for integrating management systems; and a continuing and restrictive emphasis on *vertical* flows of information, including the flows of detailed data from 'Next Steps' agencies to be processed in core departments (Efficiency Unit 1995). This litany signals the persistence of 'inward and upward' hierarchical control paradigms in government. But what may also be significant for the longer run is that when scrutineers examined Next Steps agencies' *internal* information management regimes, they found more cases where information systems were being substantially redesigned to support new ways of doing business and delivering services, a finding which points up the existence of political forces which may now be challenging longstanding barriers to informatization in government.

Informatization

The discussion above suggests that the terms of the debate about computerization in government have been changing, however slowly. There is now a stronger awareness than hitherto of the information resources and information flows which are required to underpin the developing managerialist agenda, and of the changing contributions which new ICTs might make to the business of government. In other words, there has been some shift from a focus on automation technologies to an emphasis on the information which can be liberated by ICTs. According to some analysts, this second approach can bestow specific advantages on organizations which adopt it (Scott Morton 1991). First, ICTs bestow competitive advantages most strongly on organizations which develop procedures and skills for capturing and analysing the information which is an inevitable but often wasted by-product of operational computer systems. In the public sector, this might involve, for example, the capturing and identification of significant trends from data generated by telephone help-lines or complaints services. Second, electronically generated information can be used to support new kinds of 'information tools', based upon new information-handling techniques. An example of a public sector application might be a front office clerk who is enabled to access multiple databases in different local authority departments, in order to provide a one-stop service to a local neighbourhood. Third, new kinds of information, analysis and skills can open up new business opportunities, by identifying new markets or permitting the development of product or service innovations.

These examples demonstrate how informatizing organizations can create new information *resources*. However, the history of MIS in British government shows that the greatest advantages may be reaped by establishing new ways in which information *flows* around organizations. In other words, the significance of networking information is that it becomes, in principle, a more dynamic, flexible resource, as it becomes possible to integrate or share data and to establish new organizational networks of information-based relationships. In short, the significance of electronic networks for managing data is that they:

- permit the integration of data from a number of sources, thus enabling the memory of organizations to be vastly magnified;
- permit the significant enhancement of organizational intelligence, by enabling new ways of integrating or matching data that will yield much more information about its external environment (including information about markets and customers) and internal processes (including the movement of stock or the performance of employees);
- permit greater flexibility in arranging who may access and exploit information resources, and how information-dependent processes are undertaken;
- permit new kinds of interactive communications within and between organizations (including between organizations and their suppliers or customers).

Moreover, it is these kinds of facilities which appear to be demanded by NPM.

The new public management: informatizing public administration?

In 1991, Hood identified new technology (he used the word *automation*) as one of four 'megatrends' linked with the emergence of NPM. Hood used NPM as a 'loose term' to capture 'the set of broadly similar administrative doctrines which dominated the reform agenda in many of the OECD group of countries from the late 1970s' (Hood 1991: 3–4). In line with this eclectic approach, he used NPM both to embrace doctrines which had long been associated with the managerialist agenda – for example, the drive towards more explicit standards of performance – and to identify other doctrines which became much more prominent in the late 1980s and 1990s, including the drive towards greater competition and the extensive use of contracts in public administration. Subsequently, Pollitt has used NPM more precisely, to refer to a 'second wave of reforms' through which, in the 1990s, governments have emphasized quality management, consumerism, competition and contractorization, alongside, and frequently in tension with, the more strongly established, efficiency-oriented managerialist agenda (Pollitt 1993). What distinguishes the *new* public management from earlier forms of managerialism is a new emphasis on the management and delivery of public services, and how those services are accessed and used. Increasingly, this emphasis implies the divorce, in Osborne and Gaebler's terms, of *steering* from *rowing:* the separation of operational responsibility from the political responsibility for defining priorities, specifying service levels and allocating resources (Osborne and Gaebler 1992). This divorce is typically achieved by establishing contract-based performance measures and the question of whether these contracts are with external contractors or with quasi-autonomous internal units is increasingly irrel   C   ᵗ-based relationships in public administration are manife⸱
vertical relationships – for example, tho⸲
tives of Next Steps agencies – and new
new horizontal relationships have

providers in the NHS internal market, between internal customers and suppliers in service level agreements, and with external contractors. Indeed, management by contract is now deemed to be 'a dominant element in the emerging pattern of public management' (Stewart 1993: 7).

It is this extension of contractorization, whether accompanied by competition or not, which may be breaking down the use of hierarchy as the prevailing means of organizational control. Thus, Walsh has argued that, in contrast to the Taylorist approach of the 1980s which is best seen as 'not a rejection of bureaucracy but its fulfilment' (Walsh 1995: xiv), NPM involves 'market-based coordination': 'The new public service is characterized by networks of organizations rather than integrated bureaucratic hierarchies, with independent organizations or quasi-autonomous internal units, operating with devolved control, providing services on a contractual basis. The pattern is one of increasing differentiation, either between or within organizations' (Walsh 1995: 196). What is clear, however, is that the coordination of public administration through a nexus of contracts creates huge new demands for information resources. Contracting parties need information both before and after a contract is made. *Ex ante*, purchasers require information about the needs of their customers or stakeholders, about the activities to be specified, about budgetary constraints and about potential suppliers. Contractors need financial information to estimate costs, information about the market in order to propose a price and detailed information about activities in order to programme and control implementation. *Post hoc*, purchasers need information to track flows of finance, as well as to monitor contractors' performance. Contractors need information to manage activities, control costs and assess performance against the contracted specifications.

Less obviously, contractual relationships also require the reconfiguration of information flows. Information needed for the hands-on management of contracts must be both timely and robust, placing new emphasis on speedy dissemination and widespread, on-line access. Contractual relationships require information held in financial, budgetary and operational systems to be capable of integration, and also demand that data can be aggregated and disaggregated so that they can be utilized in a range of organizational units. And, above all, if front-line staff are not to be swamped by demands to supply and verify the raw data needed for performance measurement and contract monitoring, many more data than ever before must be captured automatically from street level transactions with customers. In other words, public services must not only be computerized, they must be informatized.

Given this formidable list, it is hardly surprising that much academic discussion of the merits of shifting from 'management by hierarchy' to 'management by contract' h~ focused on information issues. Much of this discussion ha~   v institutional economics, particularly that
                                           sing the transaction costs associated with
                                           lysis has generated considerable scepti-
                                           be gained from contractorization can

outweigh the administrative costs involved in specifying, negotiating and en-forcing contracts (Bartlett 1991; Keen 1994a). It has also pointed up the risks attached to managing contracts with imperfect information (the bounded ra-tionality problem), including the risk of being exploited by contractors who possess better information (the problem of asymmetrical relationships).

Informatization promises to help both to control costs and to reduce risks by permitting the flow of more flexible, robust, timely and accessible informa-tion. As Hepworth has argued in relation to local government: 'In essence, the so-called "Thatcher revolution" has cast local authorities in the role of "quasi-firms", whose survival depends on mobilizing information resources . . . [This revolution has] raised the transaction costs of public services provision, and thereby the information requirements of local councils throughout the UK' (Hepworth 1992: 149–50). However, even this formulation may understate the nature of the changes which are taking place. The shift from integrated bureaucratic hierarchies to market-based coordination, articulated through a nexus of contracts, points paradoxically towards more holistic conceptions of information management. As we saw above, the FMI identified a need for the integration of management systems *within* government departments in order to support the management of devolved units. By extension, the disaggregation of public services into devolved management units creates an equally pressing need for systems capable of exchanging information *between* agencies. In short, contractorization focuses attention on the interfaces between organizations, and it therefore prompts questions about the conditions under which informa-tion could be made to flow across organizational boundaries. We will illustrate this important point by a second case study: the Information Management and Technology Strategy of the NHS Management Executive.

Informatizing public service: the NHS Information Management and
Technology Strategy
The introduction of the quasi-market in the NHS stimulated the development by the NHS Management Executive in 1992 of a centrally determined, national Information Management and Technology (IM&T) Strategy (NHS Management Executive 1992). This strategy was based on five principles:

- information will be person-based;
- systems may be integrated;
- information will be derived from operational systems;
- information will be secure and confidential;
- information will be shared across the NHS.

These principles mean that a single NHS number should be created for each patient, to be used wherever his or her records are held. The introduction of a single patient identifier is the essential condition for exchanging patient infor-mation electronically between different NHS units and implies the eventual creation of an integrated, comprehensive 'virtual' record for each NHS patient, the main points of which could be accessed throughout the NHS.

Clinical data to be used for keeping patient records, for conducting epidemiological studies and for preparing contracts would all be captured using 'common clinical terms' capable of being coded for entry into computers. Electronic administrative registers would be created to hold details of treatments and costs. All this information would eventually pass around the NHS by means of a dedicated network capable of conveying data, voice and radio communications.

This strategy is based on a simple point: that a significant proportion of the existing difficulties and costs in managing the internal market derive not only from the vast range of incompatible IT systems which are currently used within the NHS, but, more important still, from the considerable diversity in the specifications of the same kinds of data within those systems. However, as we began to see in our discussion of MIS in central government, it is the problems which stem from the multiplicity of ownership and control of data which often prove most intractable, for there are many difficulties in the way of resolving them. In the NHS, these difficulties include:

- the costs to individual NHS units of respecifying datasets which are the legacy of existing systems;
- professional jealousies between medics and management over such matters as the coding of common clinical terms and access to patient records;
- data privacy issues (Keen 1994b).

Increasingly, too, the very introduction of the internal market has commodified information, by bestowing commercial significance and value on the data held separately by health purchasers and providers. Indeed, a general problem in reconstructing IS in contemporary government is that contractorization has introduced strong commercial disincentives for sharing data (Muid 1994). For all these reasons, the NHS IM&T strategy has been highly contentious, and has generated strong opposition from within the NHS, perhaps most importantly from the British Medical Association. Meanwhile, it is difficult not to conclude that the problems of securing speedy exchange of information around the NHS have severely exacerbated the information asymmetries and administrative costs laid bare by the internal market (Walsh 1995).

What this brief history shows is that developing new IS would substantially facilitate the implementation of NPM in government, at both operational and management levels. In particular, the shift away from hierarchical organization and management by command towards more devolved, loosely coupled, organizational forms does seem to imply innovations in the exploitation of ICTs, innovations which go beyond the simple automation of existing information flows. However, recognizing this dependency is not the same as asserting that technological change constitutes an independent, strategic imperative. Nor does it imply that new organizational forms and processes will inexorably emerge as business strategists seek to maximize the advantages to be derived from technological innovation. On the contrary, this discussion illustrates the equally strong effect on organizational development and technological investment of socially constructed attitudes to technology and management. It shows how, in practice, information systems are shaped by, and reflect, these attitudes, which IT and IS then embed even further into the routines of organizational life. Moreover, as Coombs has argued, these routines acquire important significance for organizational cultures, by making tangible many of the qualities, the 'way we do things here', which give meaning to organizational life:

> IT systems . . . often elicit a greater degree of political behaviour; partly because of their proximity to the core strategic issues . . . but also for another reason. Organizations are in some senses defined for their members by the way they are portrayed and captured in the information systems. Therefore whenever you define a new information system you are putting 'into play', in the political sense, some very central features of the organization itself.
>
> (Coombs 1992: 14)

It is their role in embedding organizational routines which explains why new IS so frequently constitute the arena where those routines are most visibly challenged by intended reforms, and why, in consequence, they also provide the means by which those reforms are effectively resisted and undermined. These are points to which we shall return at length in Chapter 6. In the meantime, however, we will simply note that the defensive strategies which IS innovations provoke become more salient as business strategists seek to move from automation, through to an informatization perspective, and thence to one within which organizational transformation is the clear imperative.

Organizational transformation and business process re-engineering

Scott Morton states boldly that he deliberately chose the term *transformation* to express his sense of the 'fundamental difference in character exhibited by organizations that have been through the first two stages [automation and informatization] and have begun on the third' (Scott Morton 1991: 15). His view is that organizations which fail to transform themselves by means of ICT will fail to be competitive because they waste many of the resources which they devote to technological investment. Scott Morton is therefore endorsing a fashionable explanation of the 'IT productivity paradox': the uncomfortable fact that it is often difficult to prove that investment in IT impacts significantly on business productivity. Indeed, a high proportion of projects in both private and public sectors fail to deliver measurable benefits (Willcocks 1994). This state of affairs is often put down to the way ICTs are used to prop up failing methods of doing business rather than to transform radically the way that business is done. The following is a typical diagnosis: 'heavy investments in information technology have delivered disappointing results largely because companies tend to use technology to mechanize old ways of doing business.

They leave existing processes intact and use computers simply to speed them up' (Hammer 1990: 104).

The fashionable solution to the inertia and to the internal politics that are blamed for frustrating radical change is 'business process re-engineering' (BPR), or 'business process innovation', propounded by gurus such as Michael Hammer and Tom Davenport (Hammer and Champy 1993; Davenport 1993). The reforming zeal which they threatened to unleash at the beginning of the 1990s was matched only by the extravagance of their claims that they were, at last, unlocking the potential power of ICTs to secure dramatic improvements in business performance. Thus, BPR might be taken as standing for 'business paradise regained' (Grint and Willcocks 1995). The evangelical fervour with which the 'gospel according to St Michael' has been proselytized (Jones 1994) masks, however, a hard-headed purpose, for BPR offers considerable succour to the IT professionals, management consultants and high-tech industries who need to maintain business confidence in the value of IT investment (Taylor 1995). Thus, there are strong interests supporting its claims, a factor which goes a long way to explaining the visibility and influence of what has become a powerful movement.

The fundamentalist fervour of the BPR movement is revealed when its founders write of the 'fanaticism' necessary for its success (Hammer 1990: 112). Thus BPR involves harnessing the energy and determination of its converts both to confront the incrementalism and to subdue the politics which are endemic in organizational life. This process is intended to create a blank canvas on which new, ICT-enabled, business processes might be drawn. Hence, the secret of exploiting ICTs is to 'stop paving over the cowpaths'. 'Instead of embedding outdated processes in silicon and software, we should obliterate them and start over' (Hammer 1990: 104). Thus, BPR is 'inherently distinct from business as usual' (Davenport 1993: 23). BPR demands this radical, even revolutionary, approach to managing change, because its supporters seek to recast organizations on the basis of a fundamentally different principle from that used in most large-scale bureaucracies. That is, they seek to replace the time-honoured functional principle of organization by one which places emphasis on orienting processes towards the outputs for customers. The logic is that the organization of bureaucracies around a vertically controlled, functionally based division of labour represented an effective solution to the problem of managing large-scale, complex enterprises in the industrial era. It was a solution obtained at a price, however; the price being the segmentation of both understanding and control of organizational processes. The advent of new ICTs means that this price need no longer be paid. In the post-industrial age, business processes can be integrated by a continual flow of information, connecting and unifying the activities needed to effect outcomes of value to customers. These new information flows are said to be especially important in integrating activities across organizational boundaries, including the boundaries between suppliers, producers and customers. Thus, BPR is intended to reverse the division of labour, no less: 'it is to the next revolution what specialization was to the last' (Hammer and Champy 1993: 5).

There is, however, a major contradiction in this revolution. On the one hand, its advocates believe that BPR will at last release businesses from the organizational constraints associated with the industrial age and liberate the power of the technologies which define the information age. However, as the use of the discourse of *engineering* implies, the BPR movement is suffused with a rational technicism of a kind which is seen, more appropriately, as the apogee of industrial age thinking. It is tied into hierarchical, even authoritarian, conceptions of organizational dynamics, and it assumes the dominance of a technologically driven rationality over other aspects of business strategy. Moreover, although it is said to involve procedures which are 'organization free', in the sense that they are supposed to be untrammelled by social or political considerations, BPR is suffused with assumptions about organization and power (Taylor and Williams 1994; Taylor 1995). In particular, its advocates assume that the hierarchical power of managers will be left intact to drive forward BPR. And, in an approach which is the very epitome of the Taylorist approach to work process design, it assumes that the way humans are used and managed is also to be subjected to the technicist imperative. As Grint and Willcocks have argued, one of the most marked features of BPR is that the aggression of this approach 'derives from an essentially mechanistic . . . view of how organizations function and can be changed . . . In this respect the use of the word "re-engineering" is not accidental but symptomatic of a world view seeking to treat politics as aberrant and dysfunctional' (Grint and Willcocks 1995: 107). The problem is, of course, that organizational life is messier, less easy to order and more political than the advocates of BPR pretend.

Re-engineering the business of government: bridging the islands?

BPR was officially adopted as a favoured management technique in British central government in the two White Papers on the Civil Service published in 1994 and 1995 (Office of Public Service and Science 1994b: 28; 1995: 14). 'Process re-engineering' was to be adopted 'by considering what final service, or output, is required and how it can best be delivered, *ignoring current functional and organizational boundaries*' (emphasis added). This brief prescription is, of course, silent as to the size, scope and significance of the projects that are envisaged. The guidelines and case studies subsequently published by CCTA envisage that many BPR projects would simply consist of what may be called 'business process re-design' (CCTA 1994b). That is, they would be fairly self-contained projects, undertaken mainly to reduce costs by eliminating unnecessary tasks, automating workflows to minimize delays between functions and reducing the amount of paper handling by using electronic communications. In these ways, for example, a departmental payroll service was able to increase its efficiency in order to compete successfully in a market test (CCTA 1994b: 30). However, there are other projects already established in Whitehall, some of which predate this interest in BPR, which can be seen as a response to many of the same, fundamentally important, problems which BPR is an attempt to confront. We will discuss below two case studies of what Venkatraman (1991) has labelled 'business network redesign'. We utilize this term to signal a shift towards the establishment of a collaborative, information-exchanging, network between organizations which are divided by formal jurisdictional boundaries. However, we will see that, far from being 'organization-free' or politically neutral, such a shift raises highly sensitive issues for the organizational and institutional framework of government.

It has been said that ICTs are 'greedy technologies', and one sense in which this may be interpreted is that the high costs associated with a never-ending process of investment in, and refreshment of, technological systems generate a continual search for increasing returns. As we have seen, the notion of business transformation follows from the assumption that this search can ultimately be sustained only by securing radical changes in the cost structures of organizations. In this light, the NHS IM&T Strategy can be seen as a response to a conjunction of two problems. One is the problem that the transaction costs associated with NPM have become an important issue: the other is that the NHS has reached the limits of efficiency gains to be won from automating processes which are bounded by discrete management domains.

We argued above that computerization was an important factor permitting the growth in bureaucracy and the increasing complexity of public services. However, the paradox is that this technologically supported elaboration of governmental structures has become a source of enormous expense and inconvenience. Organizational complexity keeps internal administrative costs unacceptably high and restricts the financial returns from new technology investment, as vast amounts of paper continue to flow between information systems which are fragmented by the functional segmentation of government. Moreover, as our discussion of MIS illustrated well, most information systems have been designed to fit into organizational jurisdictions, because the design and funding of projects inevitably reflects the structure of budget heads and existing budgetary and managerial responsibilities. That is, bureaucracy has imprisoned data within functional jurisdictions, preventing technology from liberating information as a freely flowing resource.

Building electronic bridges between 'islands of automation' – integrating business processes between discrete information systems, both within and, even more importantly, across organizational domains – is, therefore, widely believed to hold the key to releasing the benefits of ICTs. For example, establishing automatic data exchange between operational and top management systems could liberate valuable data about patterns of service usage, as well as much more accurate data about customers. These data could be made to yield much more reliable statistics for policy-making purposes and much more timely information for management. Electronic links between agencies would also enable bureaucracy to be streamlined, by permitting more sharing of data between public services. For example, by reducing the occasions when data are captured from external agencies, agencies could reduce the compliance costs falling on customers and suppliers, and begin to remove bureaucratic burdens from the backs of individual citizens and businesses. Finally, increasing the flow of data across organizational boundaries would increase the effectiveness of public services, by permitting operations to be based upon more complete and appropriately structured information. Thus, there are many reasons why governments organizations might be interested in business network redesign, and why this is a major theme in the reinvention of government, both in the UK and abroad.

Cross-boundary information flows figure prominently in the US National Performance Review, most prominently in a major report commissioned by Vice President Gore on re-engineering government through IT (Office of the Vice President 1993b). The report identified seven demonstration projects, all designed to secure more efficient and effective use of information by sharing it more widely in government. In addition to proposing the introduction of government-wide electronic mail, and the establishment of electronic public information services, the report recommended five projects. Each of those projects requires substantial cooperation in exchanging information: across agencies; between federal, state and local governments; and between government, business and individuals. The five projects are:

- *Integrated electronic benefit transfer:* to exploit IT currently in use in financial services to consolidate the delivery of welfare benefits across federal, state and local tiers of government.
- *A public safety network:* to coordinate communications among and between federal, state and local enforcement and public safety agencies, by setting technical and information standards to exchange information.
- *Intergovernmental tax filing and payments processing:* to permit individuals and businesses to file a single tax return, by networking information flows between federal and state revenue agencies.
- *International trade data system:* to create an inclusive database for international trade data for use by government agencies and businesses.
- *National environment data index:* to coordinate the development and use of data gathered by government, academics, businesses and individuals.

In similar fashion, the development of electronic facilities for sharing and exchanging information between different parts of government, and, indeed, between governments and individuals, and governments and businesses, has been identified as a major element in the G-7 Government On-line (GOL) project. Thus, it is an explicit, if optimistic, target of GOL that 'most' government information transactions should be on-line by the turn of the century (Kerry and Harrop n.d.).

However, such changes in the conduct of the business of government raise significant issues for governance. For example, the proposals for welfare administration, tax collection and law enforcement put forward in the US *Re-engineering Government through IT* report assume not only a major re-engineering of the internal business processes of a raft of local, state and federal agencies, but a high degree of sustained collaboration between them. Moreover, this collaboration must take place across organizational boundaries which, in the US system, are held in immense constitutional significance. In similar fashion, several other US *re-engineering* projects assume the routinization of information-exchanging partnerships between governments and external organizations which will create important mutual power dependencies and which would therefore have significance for power structures in and around government.

Re-engineering business networks also have important symbolic meaning in relation to the evolution of institutions. If we are right to believe that the sources, flows and content of data held in information systems are of significance in the management of meaning within organizations, then they will also be significant in reflecting and shaping perceptions about political institutions. In particular, the patterns of, and especially the breaks in, information flows across jurisdictions will embed politically significant assumptions about the nature of the governmental system. For example, what is being proposed for the administration of US taxation and welfare benefits is the unification of important, routine transactions conducted by the public with tiers of government whose separation has been seen as constitutionally significant. Thus, the routine receipt of consolidated tax assessments and welfare cheques may eventually undermine consciousness of the formal separation of powers within the US federal system.

We propose to explore the political implications of the transformational properties accorded to ICTs by considering two case studies from a sensitive arena within the British system of government, namely the criminal justice system (CJS). We will begin the discussion by analysing the National Strategy for Police Information Systems (NSPIS) before going on to look at wider changes in the institutional relationships within the CJS.

Transforming public services? The NSPIS

The National Strategy for Police Information Systems was developed in 1992–3 as a collaborative venture between the Home Office Police Department and the Association of Chief Police Officers (ACPO). It is formally 'owned' by ACPO on behalf of the police service, not by the Home Office, a point of some political significance. Policing in England and Wales, for example, is in the hands of forty-three police authorities, each directed by a chief constable. The chief constable is operationally autonomous, but is accountable for the use of resources to the local police authority, which in 1995 become a local quango. Although all police forces perform very similar functions, they have developed a wide variety of computer systems to support them. The development of an IT department within each force, together with the formation of long-term relationships with its own IT suppliers, has created powerful professional and commercial pressures to maintain this diversity. However, the downside is that it has produced severe practical difficulties in sharing information electronically between forces, for the purposes of criminal intelligence, crime statistics or operational control and command. Indeed, diversity has been the reality of police IS, even where the case for a national strategic application has been widely recognized. For example, in the 1980s, ACPO and the Home Office Police Department responded to the operational problems exposed by the notorious Yorkshire Ripper (serial killer) case by developing HOLMES, the Home Office Large Major Enquiry System. HOLMES involved the specification of national standards for a system which was to be installed by every police force and which was designed to facilitate the accumulation, management and interrogation of large-scale datasets which are thrown up by such inquiries. The Ripper case had highlighted the problems associated with conducting major investigations by means of paper records. The facility for data-matching, including between forces, which extensive computerization would have introduced, would have enabled investigating officers to identify the numerous links to the murderer at an earlier stage than they subsequently did. However, the fact that HOLMES was implemented by forty-three different police IT departments, and was contracted to four different suppliers, meant that, in practice, systems are much less compatible than was originally hoped. In other words, the usefulness of HOLMES has been seriously compromised by diversity of provision and local customization (Taylor and Williams 1992).

It is problems such as these which have led to the development of NSPIS (Home Office Science and Technology Group 1994). NSPIS is intended to inject greater urgency into the development of centrally managed, national systems: for example, the successor to HOLMES and the national automatic fingerprint identification service, NAFIS. More radically, NSPIS also proposes the development of standard applications for local police forces, covering the most important functions such as administrative support, custody procedures, command and control, crime reporting and recording and MIS. It is intended that these standard applications will gradually replace the diverse applications currently being run by local police forces, and they will almost certainly reduce the number of commercial companies involved in the supply of police IS. In return, the standardization of data flowing around the police service will enable significant enhancements of:

- the quality of, and access to, operational information, especially for the purposes of criminal investigation;
- the flexibility of response across police authority boundaries (for example, in reaction to major disasters);
- the ease of transferring data required for the administration of criminal justice;
- the quality and timeliness of national crime statistics and performance indicators.

In addition, by nationalizing the technical development and procurement of systems, NSPIS will generate major efficiency savings in police procurement taken as a whole.

The migration to NSPIS is perceived, too, to be crucial for the successful local implementation of the White Paper on Police Reform, by helping to reduce the diseconomies resulting from the decentralized structure of policing (Home Office 1993). For example, it is intended that systems will be made more compatible within, as well as across, police forces, allowing for improved flows of management information to chief constables, police authorities and the Home Office. New information systems will permit the police to generate more reliable and, particularly, more comparable data about levels of performance, particularly in relation to the key objectives established by a former Home Secretary (Home Office 1995a). In addition, they will support the streamlining of processes and the rationalization of bureaucracy within individual police forces. It can be seen, therefore, that NSPIS fits well with the view that policing could become much more business-like. However, it also implies a more centralized approach to police IS, because it severely reduces local autonomy in systems design and in the choice of contractors and suppliers. As the White Paper recognizes, 'over the next few years, the national element in police information technology will be substantially enhanced' (Home Office 1993: 39). In fulfilling this aspiration, NSPIS may therefore be a manifestation, as well as a driver, of the nationalization of policing, which, it is believed, is taking place in the interests of greater efficiency and effectiveness (Oliver 1996).

The Council of ACPO, which represents all forty-three chief constables, has agreed to the strategy. However, central government has also taken powers to drive it forward. NSPIS is being enforced by means of the annual inspections of forces. These inspections are now linked directly to the Home Secretary's increased powers under the 1994 Police and Magistrates Courts Act to intervene in the management of local police forces where they are deemed to be inefficient or ineffective. At the same time, however, the Home Secretary took active steps to distance the implementation of NSPIS from the Home Office, by setting up a new quango, the Police IT Organization (PITO), to implement the strategy and manage national systems (Home Office 1996). PITO reflects the existing tripartite management of the police service and in this way legitimates the process of nationalizing police IS.

It can be seen that NSPIS illustrates well many key issues arising from the electronic networking of information. On the one hand, electronic networks support the current managerialist agenda by offering opportunities to secure more effective operational IS and to capture better management and policy information. Moreover, the sheer costs of developing these IS, together with the additional economies of scale and scope which stem from interforce cooperation, mean that there is bound to be pressure from ACPO and PITO for near universal adoption and exploitation of these systems, just as there is pressure from the NHS Management Executive for implementation of the NHS IM&T Strategy. However, in the cases of the police service and the NHS, for example, these opportunities and calculations raise obvious questions about the continuing justification of traditional patterns of decentralization.

This is not to say that new informational capabilities will lead direct emergence of new institutional arrangements. It is, however, to argue capabilities and economies they offer are beginning to impact significantly on the nature and distribution of cost–efficiency ratios within public services. In consequence, they are bound to become a factor in discussions which attempt to balance efficiency and effectiveness in the use of public resources with less tangible considerations. These intangibles include such value-laden issues as the trade-off between (what may be, in practice if not in name) a national police force and local accountabilities. In other words, the opening up of new choices and new opportunities may well change the terms of debates about institutional change, by undermining the rationale for existing arrangements.

In the cases of both health and policing, contemporary plans for net-working information also expose important issues about the relationships between public services which share the same client group. Once information flows are critically analysed, the mutual dependence of public services on exchanging information resources become more explicit. For example, health authorities exchange considerable quantities of information about their patients with local authorities. Police forces are the first points of contact for most criminals with the CJS, and consequently the police are major suppliers of data for other criminal justice agencies, including courts, the Crown Prosecution Service (CPS), the probation service and prisons. In BPR terms, information strategies which do not acknowledge external flows and informational interdependencies will not maximize efficiency and effectiveness in the performance of information-dependent processes. In practice, therefore, this kind of analysis is exposing serious frustrations with the existing institutional order. In order to explore this point further, we will examine a fourth case study, which sets changes in the police within wider issues being raised in the CJS.

Transforming government? The Coordination of Computerization in the Criminal Justice System

The initiative which is known verbally as 'Triple C JS' (and is usually written as CCCJS) stems from two sets of longstanding concerns which converged in the mid-1980s. At that time, all the major organizations within the CJS were developing, or thinking of developing, strategic, nationwide information systems. The main impetus behind these systems was automation, to secure economies of scale and operational efficiency. But officials within the Home Office began to realize that significant improvements in the quality, reliability and timeliness of criminal justice statistics could also be achieved by securing interoperability between these systems. It was strongly suspected, too, that cross-service flows could yield important, long-term improvements in operational efficiency and effectiveness, by rationalizing the data collected, used and reported within the CJS, and this suspicion was subsequently confirmed by detailed analysis (Goldman 1986).

The strategic systems which were being developed in the CJS are set out in Table 2.1. As with other initiatives we which have considered in this

Table 2.1 The major strategic systems being developed in the criminal justice system

Services	Central agency/ department	System	Description
Computer Bureau	Home Office		Home Office police and crime statistics
Magistrates' Courts	Lord Chancellor's Department	MASS (Magistrates' Courts Standard System)	Case management support basic administration functions including: bail admin., results, courts lists, fine collection, licensing records, warrant tracking, legal aid admin. and stats
Crown Courts	Lord Chancellor's Department	CREST (Crown Court Electronic Support)	Case management, court lists and statistics
Crown Prosecution Service	CPS	SCOPE (Standard Case Operations)	Case tracking and file management, some statistics
Prisons	Prisons Service (Home Office)	LIDS (Local Inmates Database System)	Data about inmates, including their activities, antecedents, movements and records
Probation Service	Home Office	CRAMS (Case Records and Administrative System)	Case management system and MIS
Police	Police IT Organisation	Phoenix: the Criminal Justice Records System	National criminal records and criminal intelligence
		Police National Computer	Operational data, messaging, fingerprints, crime patterns

Source: Bellamy and Taylor (1996).

chapter, the experience of CCCJS shows that there are major problems, as well as significant benefits, involved in building electronic bridges across organizations (Bellamy and Taylor 1996). Some of these difficulties are technical. In the case of CCCJS, the problems of securing inter-operability are severely exacerbated by the fact that systems are in very different stages of development. For example, LIDS was successfully rolled out in all 136 prisons in the early 1990s, whereas it was gradually realized that the systems being developed for the magistrates' courts would not be fully operational until well past the millennium. It has been said that the magistrates courts are the information crossroads of the CCCJS, but, at least in some areas, information may not pass that way freely for several years.

These kinds of technical difficulties underscore resourcing problems. While it is easy to make a rational case which stresses the 'common good' benefits which will accrue to the CJS as a whole, individual organizations must come to terms with the fact that there is a very uneven distribution of costs–benefits ratios arising from CCCJS. For example, the Prisons Service is at the end of the CJS when it is conceived as an information-handling chain: it receives considerable volumes of data from other agencies, but sends very little to them. It therefore has problems in identifying major administrative savings from CCCJS. Moreover, it will be obliged to incur the costs of converting LIDS, which has been operational for several years, to CCCJS standards. In contrast, the magistrates' courts stand to secure major efficiency gains because they distribute large volumes of information to other CJS agencies. For these reasons, the magistrates' courts would, in principle, secure major savings from CCCJS.

CCCJS illustrates the problems we identified above, in securing inter-agency cooperation under the new public management. There is increasing pressure on each stakeholding agency to provide a robust business case to justify its involvement in CCCJS. The Prisons Service became a Next Steps agency in 1993, and the administration of the courts was devolved from the Lord Chancellor's Department to the Courts Services Agency in 1995. At the time of writing (1996), the CPS was also a candidate for agency status. The significance of these changes is that each of these organizations is, or will be, more autonomous in operational terms, and, moreover, will be subject to rigorous financial targets and performance measures. In other words, the CCCJS illustrates well how NPM provides every incentive for agencies to act individually and every disincentive to provide resources for the 'common good', whether this be in the circulation of information or in the support of capital investment.

At a more fundamental level, CCCJS is exposing issues which go to the heart of the institutional order within the CJS. In the UK, the CJS has been highly compartmentalized and decentralized, and this serves two important purposes, both dear to liberal values. First, the decentralization of the police force into forty-three police forces, the separation of functions between the police and the independent CPS, and the separation of the administration of justice, which is the responsibility of the Lord Chancellor's Department, and responsibility for law and order, which lies with the Home Office, are all thought to provide safeguards against the concentration of power. Similarly, the compartmentalization of the organizations of the CJS is seen to be important for protecting individuals' rights and interests. In other words, the organizational boundaries and the breaks in information flows within the CJS are, rightly, bestowed with constitutional significance. It is, therefore, inevitable that there will be profound reservations on the part of stakeholders about exchanging data. Most data exchanges will therefore be of administrative, rather than case-sensitive, data and they will be made under conditions which are strictly controlled by the originating organization. One important consequence is that CCCJS is making CJS agencies more conscious of information stewardship as a key operating value.

CCCJS is also generating issues of high symbolic value which go well beyond practical issues raised by inter-operable computing. One such issue was the development of the Criminal Justice Network (CJN), which will form the communications network of CCCJS. The lowest cost solution was to make use of the newly upgraded and externally sourced Police National Network (PNN). Technically speaking, the PNN is simply a broad highway which accommodates a 'virtual' private network for CCCJS. Nevertheless, there was deep concern among CJS agencies about the symbolic implications of using the police network. Despite this concern, the proposal went ahead, although the CJS network was given its own name to establish its distinctiveness from the PNN.

This analysis shows that, like the pressures which led to NSPIS and the NHS IM&T Strategy, the pressure for CCCJS is symptomatic of widespread perceptions of inefficiency and ineffectiveness within major public services, perceptions which, in many other countries, have stimulated the development of *reinventing government* programmes. The promise held out by ICTs for securing major improvements in efficiency and performance identify CJS, the NHS and the police service as obvious targets for institutional rationalization, which, in a period of unprecedented financial retrenchment, they are finding hard to resist. All these services, too, are rising up the political agenda, and governments are under increasing pressure to deliver better results.

Re-engineering government: towards cross-national data flows

The logic which leads from the search for both efficiency and effectiveness to attempts to secure much more sharing and integration of information across organizational boundaries within national governments does not cease to apply at the point where data flows hit national boundaries. Indeed, in a world where capital, goods and people are increasingly mobile, there are significant efficiencies to be gained, and many operational advantages for public services to be reaped, from international cooperation in the interchange of information. Moreover, this kind of international cooperation is seen as possessing high political value for the cause of European integration, as well as carrying obvious practical utility for European governments. Thus, the European Union has longstanding interests in the principle of exchanging data between national administrations in respect of functions such as company taxation, social security administration, customs and excise, health care and the control of the movement of goods and agricultural products. Much of the groundwork has already been put in place through the Third and Fourth Framework Programmes (Ridge 1994). The Bangemann Report therefore placed considerable emphasis on building on this work to develop a Trans-European Public Administration Network, a network which the European Action Plan proposed to put in place by means of a three-year programme of long-term infrastructure investment. The thirty or so projects in the IDA (Interchange of Data between Administrations) programme will connect national governments and European institutions in an electronic network which is seen as providing crucial operational and symbolic underpinning to the post-Maastricht European Union (European Commission 1994a, b).

Conclusion

The cases which we have brought forward in this chapter raise a fundamental question. This question is whether the enhancements in efficiency and effectiveness to be gained by greater cooperation in the management and sharing of information are capable of creating a political momentum sufficient to overcome constitutional objections and political resistance to changing longstanding governmental arrangements. In addressing this issue, it is important to understand that the political strength of these agendas does not lie solely in a technicist logic, or with the powerful interests which are undoubtedly arraigned behind it. This chapter suggests, too, that they draw some strength from the renewal of the economic promise long associated with new technology, a renewal which has found expression in the widespread conviction that government can at last be 'reinvented'. The significance of the digital revolution is that new informational and communications capabilities are becoming increasingly powerful factors in the managerialist debate, specifically and profoundly because they are changing its terms and expanding its significance. That is, the power of ICTs lies in their proleptical vision: one that promises new opportunities for conducting business, for reconfiguring organizations, for securing new forms of inter-organizational, and international, cooperation. In all these ways, the information and communications capabilities associated with ICTs are profoundly challenging the institutional order of governance.

We will see in the chapters that follow that these capabilities are also challenging traditional ways of conceiving of relations between governments and citizens. Specifically, the notion that government can be 'reinvented' derives from the belief that governments can be relegitimated in the eyes of taxpayers and public service users. Re-engineering business processes with ICTs promises to secure major efficiency gains which will help to remove government from taxpayers' backs, while, bringing about significant improvements in the quality of public services. To begin to test the force of this claim, we turn in Chapter 3 to a more detailed examination of the ways in which new ICTs in general, and the doctrines of BPR in particular, are implicated in plans for re-engineering the delivery of public services to 'customers'. In this way, we will begin both to open out our analysis of the role that ICTs are perceived to play in renewing relations between governments and citizens and identify some of the factors which may shape it in practice.

3

Forging high-tech public services

This Green Paper marks the beginning of a new phase of . . . radical and wide ranging reform . . . It will change fundamentally and for the better the way that government provides services to citizens and businesses. Services will be more accessible, more convenient, easier to use, quicker in response and less costly to the taxpayer. And they will be delivered electronically.

> (Roger Freeman, Minister for Public Service, introducing the Green Paper, *government.direct* 1996)

At the heart of visions of government in the information age lies the simple but hugely potent claim that liberating the power of new technology will drive down the costs of public services and, at the same time, help to rebuild relationships between governments and their citizens. To borrow from the slogan of the American National Performance Review, it will create 'government that works better and costs less' (Office of the Vice-President 1993a). It is this belief that the circle can be squared, that there need to be no inherent contradiction between relieving the burdens on taxpayers and at the same time improving the quality of government services, which runs as a leitmotif through 1990s prospectuses for reinventing government.

As the quotation from the UK government's Green Paper on electronic services (1996) makes clear, new technology appears to offer a means of escaping from the dilemma presented by what have hitherto appeared to be opposing forces: the efficiency objectives which came to the fore under the Conservative government in the 1980s and the consumerist objective of improving services which became more prominent in the early 1990s. It is a promise which its proponents are exploiting to the full. For example, the Canadian *Blueprint for Renewing Government using Information Technology* sets out an 'integrated approach to improving the delivery of government services whilst significantly reducing associated costs' (Treasury Board of Canada 1995: Executive Summary), while the Australian government's *Clients First* programme promises 'more and better client service . . . without escalating costs' (Information Technology Review Group 1995: para. 3.0), a promise based on the belief in IT as 'a major catalyst for change and a major enabler of its implementation'

(Information Technology Review Group 1995: para. 2.1). It is, therefore, entirely consistent with these widely voiced aspirations that the UK government has now determined that 'in addition to providing better services to businesses and the citizen', its proposals for electronic services 'should also benefit all taxpayers by reducing the cost of government administration' (Office of Public Service 1996b: 34).

The Green Paper illustrates how the developing rhetoric of 'reinvention' has come, more and more, to connect a technology-led agenda for information age government to the aspirations of reformers who perceived that the rise of the 'postindustrial, knowledge-based, global economy' was exposing the outdatedness of arrangements fashioned for the industrial age (Osborne and Gaebler 1992: xvi). Despite acknowledging this broad thesis, Osborne and Gaebler's own proposals were a-technological, saying nothing about how governments might exploit the power of information age technology for their own reinvention. It was Al Gore, Vice President of the USA in the Clinton administration, who most explicitly began to shift the terms of the reinvention debate, bringing to bear a technology-intensive perspective on the ways that governments might 're-engineer' themselves. Gore's long-held conviction that new technology would be critical to securing the USA's role as a leading nation in the global economy has been consistently augmented by the belief that ICTs also provide the means for enhancing democratic and civic life.

In this chapter and the next, we propose to pay critical attention to the proposition which lies at the centre of this thinking: that new informational capabilities could support significantly improved relationships between government and individuals, whether those individuals are seen as customers or as citizens. It is a proposition which demands hard analysis, for its claims are fulsome. They reflect the belief that these new capabilities will permit wider, more inclusive access, greater choice and more flexible, responsive public services capable of being tailored to the increasingly disparate needs of consumers. In particular, new ICTs hold the promise that the producer-oriented segmentation of government bureaucracy can be overcome so as to support services which are simultaneously more holistic and less standardized. Public bureaucracy could thus be significantly rationalized, yet rationalization could go hand-in-hand with higher quality services. By this reading, the progressive adoption of ICTs becomes a dominant imperative for contemporary government, enabling transformation to occur in all its aspects. Moreover, by changing the terms of trade-off between efficiency, effectiveness, quality and democracy, ICTs offer, in turn, a further, particularly alluring promise: that of shifting the so-called 'trust deficit' between governments and citizens from red to black (Gore 1993: x).

In contrast, our own analysis will show that the promise of ICTs is not as unambiguously benign as the advocates of reinvention suppose. As we began to show in Chapter 2, technologies *can*, undoubtedly, be used to alter the trade-offs between competing values in government, but whether, how and where those trade-offs are made is, in practice, influenced by many factors, including the political and bureaucratic motivations which underlie contemporary re-forms. Consumerism in public services thus serves as a particularly important illustration of the central thesis of this book: that it is institutional factors which shape the interplay of technological change and governmental reform, and which thereby determine the actual balance struck between the ambiguous effects deriving from ICTs.

Electronic service delivery for the information age

Seen, as it is, as underpinning information age scenarios for reinventing gov-ernment, electronic service delivery (ESD) is becoming closely associated with the consumerist movement which has swept into governments since the late 1980s. The significance of ESD for both government and the governed is underscored by the typology of innovations which we set out at the end of Chapter 1. This typology demonstrated why ESD is at the core of innovation in public services, including the packaging or commodifying of information and enhancing services through informatization, as well as playing a broader role in mediating democracy and citizenship. Our discussion also began to reveal the contradictory tendencies within ICTs, which have led them to be perceived as 'ambiguous' technologies. Accordingly, it is a major purpose of this present chapter to explore further the nature and implications of the contradictions within ESD.

In many areas of public service provision, the growing use of ESD promises significant changes in public perceptions of government services, both for better and for worse. On the one hand, it renders the experience of public service consumption more like that of using private-sector high street services. Thus, technologies not only offer increases in flexibility and consumer choice but may also help to reduce an age-old problem, by mitigating the stigma associated with the uptake of public services. On the other hand, ESD may disadvantage those service users who are uncomfortable with its remote and dehumanized nature, or who are otherwise ill-equipped to exploit information age technology. More positively, the generation of whole-person, 'virtual' records could enable officials to make more appropriate decisions about their clients, just as they could help to tailor services to the needs of specific neigh-bourhoods or client groups. Again, there is a reverse side to these capabilities, however, for they also carry the consequence of making clients more trans-parent, thus enlarging the scope for selectivity, discrimination and surveillance by the state.

Similarly, the commodification of information reflects a fundamental, underlying dilemma about the way in which ESD is being applied. New systems offer opportunities for the sale of a progressively wider range of infor-mation, as well as increasing opportunities to supply information as a public good. Thus, the flexibilities associated with ESD allow consumers to be offered basic information resources on public service terms, with more sophisticated services offered on a pay-per-use basis (Bellamy et al. 1993). However, ESD not only implies enhanced capabilities for the sale of information to members of the public, it also facilitates the sale of data about members of the public. Sophisticated, large-scale computer systems can permit public service providers to assemble a greater volume of commercially valuable data and can, in consequence, create pressures for its exploitation. Moreover, as the control of more and more government datasets is contracted out, increasingly to the same few private electronic services companies, so the commercial uses to which those data are put become ever less visible to public service managers and their clients (Margetts 1995).

Furthermore, ESD holds within it the potential for changing the nature of democracy, citizenship, control and power in the state. In principle, new informational and communications capabilities will widen access to public services, enhancing consumer knowledge and enriching consumption. Greater equity of provision, the empowering of customers and the strengthening of the political competence of citizens are all potential consequences of the application of ICTs. However, what is also enriched by those applications is the capacity of government for monitoring and surveillance, and with it the potential for large-scale abuses of liberal democratic norms.

For all these reasons, information and communication, together with the new possibilities which ICTs convey, are at the heart of the consumerist movement as it applies to British public administration. Such is the influence of this movement that its rhetoric is being adopted on most points of the political spectrum. Consumerism has given rise to ostensibly different policy proposals in these various political contexts, but what is common across this movement is its growing, though often implicit, dependence on the information age capabilities of ICTs, with all the important normative issues that this implies.

Focusing on public service customers

British government presents no exception to the interest in the 'client orientation' which has been growing ineluctably during the present and past decades. Moreover, even in the UK, consumerism has reached well beyond the ambit of the governments headed by Margaret Thatcher and John Major, drawing its energy and succour from both right and left, as well as from ideas in general currency in public and business management.

Initially at least, consumerism could be interpreted as the application to the public sector of prescriptions promulgated by the highly influential 'culture management' school, which exhorted managers to build value-driven organizations that 'smell of the customer' (e.g. Peters and Waterman 1982). Here, emerging from a distillation of current best practice among some of the best-run American corporations, was an apparent revolution in management thinking. Big, bureaucratic companies should no longer preoccupy themselves with inward-looking strategies for achieving efficiency and effectiveness: rather, they should understand the chain of activities in which they formed a link. In so doing, they should apply themselves to enhancing their relationships with other links in the value-adding chain, especially their customers. In that way, corporate renewal programmes would focus organizations where they should be focused, on the improvement and reorientation of critical relationships. Broadly speaking, this kind of managerialist thinking has been around in public sector management since the early 1980s, though the elevation of consumerism to the pinnacle of corporate rhetoric and restructuring has been more recently achieved. The conversion in the early 1990s of the Conservative government to a particularly emphatic version of consumerism was, however, stimulated by more immediate political calculations. John Major was at this time seeking a 'big idea' that would distinguish his administration from that of his predecessor, Margaret Thatcher. What emerged was an attempt to bathe the managerialism of the 1980s in a more positive light, superseding its negative associations with cost cutting and public sector job losses. As it was made manifest in the Citizen's Charter movement, consumerism was to provide managerialism with a human face (Pollitt 1993: 180).

The Conservative government and consumerism in the 1990s

A key dimension of the public management strategy adopted by the Conservative government of John Major was to attach a soft, consumerist rationale to the growing emphasis on contractorization and competition which we explored in Chapter 2. Thus, the argument, captured by the very title of the White Paper *Competing for Quality* (HM Treasury 1991), was that quality would be enhanced by expanding and regulating competition in ways that would create more transparency about performance and costs. Consumers (or their surrogates, such as general practitioner fund-holders) would be empowered to demand higher quality services by means of the establishment of markets or quasi-markets. Hence, the watchwords of the Conservative government's position on public services came to be consumer empowerment and choice: 'the market has been thought to be the paradigmatic institution for extending these values, particularly in areas . . . where it was thought producer interests and professional culture had become far too powerful in shaping the nature and delivery of services and goods' (Plant 1990: 4). Information and communication sit at the heart of this new approach. Quite apart from the information resources and information flows needed to support contractorization, the new consumerism is also creating ever growing demands for new information resources, from purchasing authorities, local authorities, ministers and public auditing bodies, all of which are required to publish Citizen's Charter targets and performance indicators (PIs), from which public service league tables are compiled.

Given the tenor of our discussion in Chapter 2, it is hardly surprising that the implementation of the new consumerism has been limited, rather than facilitated, by the existing state of information systems in public services. This is a point which clearly demonstrates the centrality of information and communication to the provision of services. Older information systems, regardless of whether or not they are computerized, have been established within a particular perspective, a 'paradigm of provision'. As that paradigm shifts, so the limitations of existing information systems are exposed, and demands for their replacement come to the fore. In the information age, however, the emphasis has been not only upon the renewal of existing information systems, but also upon the application of computing, and particularly of networking, to those systems.

The first problem to be identified by the new consumer paradigm was the underdevelopment of management information systems in government, a state of affairs which was restricting the range of PIs which could be applied to public services. For example, in fulfilment of its obligations under the 1992 Local Government Act, the Audit Commission initially established 152 performance indicators across the whole gamut of local government services. While this might appear, at first sight, to be a large number, it represented the bare minimum of some four or six indicators for each local authority service (Audit Commission 1992: 6). Nevertheless, there is no doubt that, for some authorities at least, gathering, recording and reporting even this limited run of data has constituted a considerable extra burden, one which has, belatedly, stimulated more interest in the reconstruction of information systems.

The second problem for government information systems has been the familiar point that performance indicators are shaped, in practice, by the limitations of existing datasets and information systems (e.g. Carter 1989). Performance measurement is inevitably 'data driven', so that the 'performance' being measured is inevitably defined by the data which are available. For example, in an earlier study of Department of Social Security, it became clear that there were important shortcomings in the range, reliability and value of the indicators used in social security benefits administration, but also that the *methodology* of performance measurement was being limited by the restricted development of the department's information systems (Bellamy 1994). These findings explained, for example, the emphasis on a few, rather simple throughput indicators, such as the time taken to clear social security claims, and the general absence of measures of service quality and consumer satisfaction, a state of affairs that was cruelly exposed by the establishment of a Customer's Charter (Greer 1994).

A third and profoundly important difficulty in the implementation of the new consumerism has been the legacies bequeathed by the efficiency-driven emphasis on back-office automated data processing, at the expense of technological support for customer-facing processes. Computer systems were supporting internal administrative routines rather than consumer choice and flexibility. The upshot is that much of the burden of capturing performance data, particularly the throughput data which continue to dominate PIs, has fallen on front-line staff (Bellamy 1994). In consequence it has become clear that there is a more or less direct trade-off between the energy devoted to the *production* of front-line services and to the objective and subjective *measurement* of consumer satisfaction with those services. The recognition of this point has, doubtless, been an important factor in the relatively stronger, but still patchy, investment which began to be devoted to management information systems in government in the 1990s (Efficiency Unit 1995).

In addition to putting more pressure on the internal information capabilities of public services, the new consumerism of the political right has also stimulated greater awareness of information as a *public* resource. For example, the Open Government initiative of 1993–4 was introduced primarily as a follow-through of Citizen's Charter principles, to be taken forward by the Citizen's Charter Unit. The White Paper on Open Government made abundantly clear the direct connection between the new consumerism and the Open Government initiative:

> The Government believes that people should have the freedom to make their own choices on the important matters which affect their lives. Information is a condition of choice and provides a measure of quality. Even where there is little effective alternative to a public service, information enables citizens to demand the quality of service they are entitled to expect and puts pressure on those running services to deliver high standards.
>
> (Office of Public Service and Science 1993: 7)

This belief shaped the Open Government *Code of Practice* which came into force in April 1994 (Office of Public Service and Science 1994a). Equivalent codes of practice were subsequently published for the NHS (Department of Health 1995), and in June 1995 the local authority associations recommended the adoption of a good practice guide for local government. Similar initiatives were also developed by individual government departments (Office of Public Service 1996a). This pressure accounts, in large part, for the growing interest in electronic 'public information systems' (EPIS) or 'community information systems', especially in local government. Many EPIS take the form of videotext systems run on community access terminals, situated in libraries or council offices. However, by the beginning of 1997, over two hundred local authorities had World Wide Web sites, some as a complement to, some in place of, videotext terminals. By means such as these, local authorities are making available a range of electronic information about services, councillors and contact points. Around two-thirds of systems also offer more general 'community information', including information about other local authorities, health authorities, government departments and voluntary bodies (SOCITM 1996: 31). Several central government departments, too, are developing information packages specifically for use in these kinds of systems.

The development of EPIS on a significant scale is being restricted, however, by two kinds of resourcing issues. The first of these is cost. Despite the Open Government initiative, public authorities are still under few statutory obligations to make information publicly available. EPIS are inevitably regarded as a luxury, with benefits accruing mainly in relatively intangible, public relations terms. In production-led cultures, such benefits are inevitably seen as of secondary importance (Audit Commission 1995), and in consequence, a chronic problem in justifying the development of EPIS has clearly emerged (Bellamy *et al.* 1995b). Second, these difficulties are unquestionably compounded by problems in the sourcing of information. Managers of EPIS are highly dependent on the data and information held in the back offices of government agencies, or those of external bodies such as health, community and voluntary organizations. Supplying adequate information to EPIS becomes a burden on such bodies, one made more onerous by the paucity of facilities for automatic, electronic data exchange that would permit information to be cheaply updated. In practice, therefore, most EPIS offer a relatively inflexible and restricted information service, often amounting to little more than the computerization of pre-existing information leaflets. Nevertheless, the growing pressure to publish consumer and performance information means that there will be progressively stronger incentives to develop applications such as EPIS. Furthermore, there are important economies of scope to be secured by inter-agency collaboration in disseminating information by such means. As we saw in Chapter 2, however, the increasing emphasis on 'bottom-line' calculations of the cost and value of information provides a powerful inhibitor of information flows around government, including those which are demanded by the new consumerism. At the same time, the pay-backs from the financial costs involved in collecting, storing and disseminating public information remain difficult to measure, especially by the business case methodologies to which capital investment in government is subjected.

Consumerism from the political left

In contrast to the emergent consumerism on the right of British politics, the wellspring of consumerism on the left can be traced less to a politically driven wish to sensitize public service managers to costs and quality of provision, and more to an equally political desire to defend public services from privatization and contractorization. While this undoubtedly represents a sharply contrasting approach, it nevertheless remains the case that the consumerism which has emerged on the left is as characteristic of information age government as is the consumerism of the right.

As it was originally developed in the early 1980s, the strategy of the political left involved the mobilization of public sector workers and users around a renewed vision of public service. For local government this strategy can perhaps most readily be traced to papers published by the (then) Local Government Training Board, which advocated the development of a 'public service orientation' (PSO), an orientation which would encourage stronger ownership and control of local services by local people (Clarke and Stewart 1985, 1986a; see also Stewart and Clarke 1987). The PSO was based on the simple, though profoundly important, recognition that 'the activities of a local authority are not carried out for their own sake, but to provide service for the public' (Clarke and Stewart 1986b: 1). It offered a vision that would inspire the development of 'excellent' authorities by injecting new life and meaning into 'words so familiar that their meaning has been lost: public service' (Clarke and Stewart 1986b: 2).

One of the aims of the PSO was to put a managerialist gloss on a political strategy adopted by several Labour-controlled city councils in the early 1980s. Local authorities such as Sheffield City Council, the Greater London Council and the London Boroughs of Lambeth and Brent were dominated by the 'urban left', a coalition of mainly younger and intensely active Labour councillors, community activists and radical public service professionals (Gyford 1985). The new managerialism of the urban left had a two-pronged purpose, for it not only offered a readily comprehensible alternative to the Conservative government, but it also challenged the paternalist approach of the 'old' left to running local councils. As David Blunkett, Leader of Sheffield City Council in this period, argued, it was impossible to defend socialism 'if it is encapsulated in a service (like council housing repairs) which is paternalistic, authoritarian or plain inefficient' (quoted in Stoker 1988: 194). Hence, the new urban left aimed to promote more active, responsive, democratic local government, as a way of rebuilding popular support for socialism. Among its the most prominent ideas was the decentralization of local authority service delivery, by means of neighbourhood offices, one-stop services or area-based management (Hoggett and Hambleton 1988). The urban left also looked to the widening of participation in local government, through community forums and local committees. In these ways, local government would be brought nearer to its users, and both front-line staff and local people would be given a stronger voice (Hambleton et al. 1989).

Localizing and informatizing public services

Although its origins lie in the political left, the shift towards area-based service delivery is now one of the most prominent and pervasive elements of consumerism in UK local government. Moreover, it is one which has secured an important place across the political spectrum. Its attraction derives, in part, from the belief that it offers a highly visible way for local authorities to 'get closer to citizens' and to renew their relations with local communities (Burns et al. 1994). For this reason, decentralization offered a particularly attractive strategy to county councils, particularly those which were threatened with abolition by the Reviews of Local Government in Great Britain between 1992 and 1995. Many county authorities in England and Wales, as well as the regional authorities in Scotland, committed themselves to establishing new kinds of front office arrangements, to demonstrate that large local authorities need not be remote from the communities they serve (Bellamy et al. 1996). In some cases, such as that of Highland Council in Scotland or Oxfordshire County Council in England, it was a strategy for survival which worked. The promise of ICT-supported area decentralization was, in both cases, a major factor in securing their survival and, in the case of the former Highland Regional Council, its augmentation.

While decentralization was initially promoted by the left as a means of defending and relegitimizing the principles and scope of collective production and consumption, it has since been embraced, too, as a broad-based response to contractorization and marketization. Its evolution into an alternative community-focused approach to public service delivery is one which, when compared to the 'old' public administration, more explicitly seeks to be sensitive to a greater range of social needs, to promote wider access to public services and to incorporate a more diverse set of political interests. For these reasons it is being interpreted as an agenda for the post-industrial information age, reflecting a paradigmatic shift in public services from 'mass production without Ford' to 'a new form of collectivism, one founded upon the celebration of diversity' (Hoggett and Hambleton 1988: 224). For example, in place of centrally managed, functionally compartmentalized local services, many local authorities are developing decentralized neighbourhood offices, to provide immediate local access to a more inclusive range of services.

One-stop neighbourhood services therefore form part of a general response, for users and managers alike, to the complexity, remoteness and costs endemic in large-scale, mass-produced, public service. One-stop services have also come into favour, however, as a specific response in British public administration to the problems of managing local services in the era of NPM. For example, a study for the Association of County Councils advocated their development as a way of managing the new vertical division of labour between the 'enabling' local authority and its contractors, arguing that 'the potential for one stop shops to act as monitoring agents for the client side, and, indeed, marketing outlets for the contractor side, is ripe for development' (Holman 1994: 10). More recently still, locally based one-stop outlets reflect aspirations to establish 'community governance', by providing horizontally integrated responses to local communities' needs across the increasingly complex and fragmented pattern of contracted out services and privatized utilities (Leach et al. 1994).

The shift from functional, production-dominated services to area, consumer-oriented services depends on developing new information capabilities in ways that are not always explicitly recognized. In the first place, the kinds of decentralized arrangements described above assume just those kinds of information-supported flexibilities in configuring organizations that we discussed in Chapter 2. The delivery of horizontally integrated, one-stop services depends, too, upon many of the informational capabilities which we have discussed in the present chapter. For example, holistic, customer-facing services assume the presence of a capability for collecting, accessing, integrating and utilizing consumer information, as well as for deploying other kinds of organizational intelligence to the front line of government. Conversely, the absence, by-and-large, of these kinds of capabilities in UK local government has constrained innovation. For example, our own empirical research has shown that, for the most part, one-stop services and neighbourhood offices are being crudely 'bolted on' to local authorities in ways that assume only minor adjustments to internal information flows and organizational arrangements, with the result that those initiatives are, in practice, severely restricted (Bellamy *et al.* 1995b). In other words, the practical experience of decentralization almost exactly mirrors that of developing EPIS, where we saw that public service innovations were insufficiently matched by new information flows and only weakly embedded in new informational relationships.

Consumerism and business process re-engineering

The significance of these kinds of empirical findings is that they appear to support the case for re-engineering the business processes which lie behind public services. Indeed, it is the weakness of much that has passed for organizational innovations around information-intensive service provision which has given succour to the radical approaches to delivering change that we began to discuss in Chapter 2. These approaches stress that systems innovations must be accompanied by the fundamental re-engineering of business processes if ICTs are to become more than an expensive and inadequate 'technical fix' for problems which are the legacies of industrial age bureaucracy. For example, Al Gore believes that the 'root problem' which is being confronted by the US reinventing government programme is that government is modelled on the private sector 'as it was in the age of US Steel, not the age of Microsoft, Apple, Wal-Mart and Federal Express' (Gore 1993: xiii). Public services, and the organizational arrangements through which they are developed and delivered, must not only be supported by information age technology, they must also be *transformed* by it.

Business process re-engineering is nothing if it is not customer-oriented. Indeed, the most common conceptualization of a 'business process' identifies the customer as its *raison d'être*. Thus a business process has been defined variously as 'a set of activities that, taken together, produce a result of value to the customer' (Hammer and Champy 1993: 3), and as 'a structured, measured set of activities designed to produce a specified output for a customer or market' (Davenport 1993: 5). Moreover, its proponents claim that BPR can produce leaner, as well as more effective, organizations because BPR provides the means of overcoming the 'Humpty Dumpty syndrome', which describes how functionally segmented organizations fragment problems, with the consequence that huge costs, 'all the king's horses and all the king's men', are incurred to put them back together again (Davenport 1993: 29). BPR offers an opportunity, therefore, to rationalize government both because it is based on a comprehensive approach to business process design and because it supports a holistic conception of consumers and their needs.

Two characteristics, in particular, mark out a process approach to organizational redesign, the first of which is an emphasis on the *horizontal* integration of existing organization. BPR prescribes cross-functional responses to customers' needs, even where those responses challenge the integrity of existing formal organizational jurisdictions (e.g. Davenport 1994: 4). Second, especially in its highest order variants such as 'business network redesign' (Venkatramen 1991), BPR encourages *vertical* integration between procurement, production, distribution and consumption processes. For this reason, BPR can be interpreted as challenging the very distinction between what is internal and what is external to government, by placing emphasis on the nexus of relationships in which public services provision is embedded. For example, the recognition that customers are an important source of operational data – that processing a welfare claim depends upon information lodged by the claimant – leads to a growing awareness of the customer as a significant contributor to the production process. The appreciation that 'the modern business process is a workflow which can extend beyond the boundaries of the organization back into its suppliers or forward into its customers or clients' (Taylor 1995: 84) draws attention to the point that the supplier and the customer may often be the same. Hence, production and consumption in the information age will be characterized by a pronounced shift to what Toffler calls 'prosumption' (Toffler 1980), the drawing in of the consumers of goods and services more actively into their production, reducing costs, streamlining processes involved in sourcing information and enabling the tailoring of services more precisely to consumers' needs. It is this emphasis on vertical integration, based as it is on a reconceptualization of relationships between the producers and consumers, which places BPR at the centre of the new consumerism.

In sum, therefore, BPR promotes the view that sustaining a customer focused approach implies:

- a client- or consumer-centred approach to both *production* and *delivery* of public services: a breakdown of functionally segmented bureaucracy and a shift to holistic service delivery based on greater horizontal integration;
- vertical integration between producer and consumer, including a greater emphasis on '*prosumption*';
- a client-centred approach to the *consumption* of public services: a shift towards the 'whole person' principle.

Three important points are exposed by this alignment of consumerism with BPR. First, it underlines the view that a customer-orientation does not simply imply the introduction into the supplier organization of enhanced technological support. Rather, BPR exposes the extensive ramifications of the new consumerism for work processes and relationships throughout both front and back offices of government. Second, this alignment underlines the case for significant 'business network redesign', because it implies a radical review of the way government relates to, and conducts business with, external actors and bodies. Third, it suggests the need for a thoroughgoing rethinking of government's relationships with the public. This rethinking would include, especially, how the nature of this relationship could be redefined in an era characterized by enhanced opportunities for improving flows of information between government, as provider, and the public, both as suppliers and as consumers, of public services.

Re-engineering public services with ICTs

The rhetoric of BPR is strongly in evidence throughout all the blueprints for renewing public services and recasting organizations published in the 1990s. While few of these documents offer rigorous cost–benefit analysis, they are suffused with the conviction that ICTs must be introduced so as to drive radical, institutional change. For example, the Danish Dybkjær–Christensen Report on *Info-Soc 2000* calls for extensive business network redesign involving: 'a renewal in the functioning and interplay between . . . institutions at central, county and local level. The performance of tasks and the division of labour will be reviewed with the aim to create more efficient interplay with maximum exploitation of those possibilities of rationalisation that are offered by information technology (BPR)' (Dybkjær and Christensen 1994: 43). Echoing these ideas, CCTA's guide to BPR asserts that:

> IT of particular value is that which can support 'network' relationships – that is, communicating across organisational boundaries with customers, suppliers and business partners. It can also support new patterns of work . . . IT that can support the creation, communication and sharing of information is more relevant . . . than traditional data processing. IT can be the driver of business change where technology change allows a highly desirable opportunity to be grasped.
>
> (CCTA 1994b: 16)

In other words, the rhetoric surrounding the radical use of ICTs to bring about customer responsiveness and organizational change is clearly in place. We propose, now to turn from the rhetoric, and to develop a critical analysis of the prescriptions associated with BPR, paying attention to both their practical and their normative implications. To do this we will first return to the three key elements associated with BPR, to which we referred in the section above. That is, we will focus on the contribution which it is believed that BPR could make: first, to establishing more holistic services; second, to the re-engineering of prosumptive processes; and third, to implementing the 'whole person' principle.

Holistic approaches to the delivery of public services

We have seen that one of the most pervasive beliefs in the new consumerism is that horizontal integration can reduce the costs imposed by organizational complexity while, at the same time, offering services which are both more comprehensive and more tailored to clients' needs. Thus, to take one overseas example, the Australian Ministry of Finance's Review Group has identified one-stop services as a central plank of its *Clients First* strategy, arguing that: 'An agreed vision statement common to the major client service agencies in the Commonwealth needs to be established and adopted. The statement should set out the objectives of client service delivery in government, including the widespread use of single points of access by clients to multiple sources of agency services' (Information and Technology Review Group 1995: para. 3.5). This is the approach which the British government brought forward in its own thinking about *government.direct* (Office of Public Service 1996b: 13).

In general, one-stop arrangements, such as those being called for here, are seen as crucial to reinventing government because they are believed to offer:

- economies of scale and scope, by allowing a wider volume and variety of business to be conducted in the front offices of government agencies;
- efficiencies in bureaucratic administrative costs, both by reducing the volume of information exchanges between the back offices of different government departments and by speeding up those exchanges;
- efficiencies for consumers, by offering more convenient and economical ways to transact business with government, less constrained by the departmental divisions of government bureaucracies;
- more holistic, responsive and flexible service, based on a more comprehensive record of the customers' circumstances.

In practice, however, the 'one-stop' badge is being pinned on to differing organizational models, each of which assumes varying kinds of innovation in information systems. An analysis of three of the most developed models will serve to reveal the extensive ramifications for government institutions that are implied by BPR. However, as this analysis will also show, the profound nature of these implications has led to alternative approaches to exploiting new technologies, approaches which are designed to create the appearance, rather than actuality, of streamlining bureaucracy and creating holistic public services.

Information points and first-stop shops
These two terms are associated with a one-stop model which seeks to simplify and enrich first-level contacts with government, by improving the information and support which is available to public service users. This support may be delivered, for example, through a unified reception point, a caller office, an information kiosk, a community access terminal or free-phone, or a telephone hotline.

Information points provide information as a public resource, usually to a generic, but sometimes to a specific, set of clients. For example, recent studies in the UK found examples within sub-central government of business information shops, medical self-help information services and an information service aimed at council tenants, as well as examples of generic 'community' information systems (Doulton 1993, 1994). *First-stop shops* are designed to offer convenient gateways to public services, by helping customers to identify and access the services they need. Sometimes, first-stop shops provide staff who can deal with preliminary queries, issue relevant forms, establish contact with the appropriate part of the bureaucracy or register complaints. Indeed, some of the more advanced of these arrangements in Britain – for example, Bedfordshire County Council's *Action Points* – provide help in initiating or chasing business through the back offices of the authority (Holman 1994). As a cross-national study of one-stop arrangements for the Dutch government found, the essence of this model is that the first-stop shop 'acts as an *interpreter* between the public's demands and the government's complexity' (Humbert *et al.* 1992: 34).

The advantage of the first-stop model is that it offers a relatively easy and cheap way to innovate, requiring neither massive investment in ICTs nor major disruption of existing organizational arrangements. If providers are content to offer more or less stable sets of information, the burdens placed upon information providers can be limited and the need for new informational capabilities can be modest. For these reasons, information points and first-stop shops are by far the most common form taken by one-stop services in UK local government (Bellamy *et al.* 1995a). They offer a feasible means to meet rising political demands for customer-facing innovations, and a low-cost, low-risk opportunity to establish a unified, corporate presence in local neighbourhoods. They may also offer genuine enhancements of public services. For example, Kent County Council sets considerable store by its first-stop shops, which offer an affordable, flexible way to customize information to the needs of local communities in a county characterized by considerable diversity in public service provision.

Nevertheless, this first-stop model suffers from two inherent problems, the first of which is that customers who visit a first-stop point may be offered information about public services when what they actually need is a solution to a specific problem. In other words, first-stop shops may, by design or otherwise, act as a stalling mechanism, sitting between consumers and public organizations, and may cause managers to overestimate the value of consumer information. The second difficulty is the one we identified above in relation to public information systems: the problem of managing the dependencies involved in sourcing information. The obvious solution to overcoming this problem is to automate the flow of information between back offices and front offices, by developing electronic facilities for on-line information transfer. However, the tangible business pay-off required to justify capital investment may be hard to demonstrate. Where it may be most amenable to demonstration is where one-stop arrangements are so designed as to permit the exploitation of new front-office systems to capture operational data directly from consumers, thus significantly reducing internal information handling costs. Alternatively, costs may be saved by transferring back-office functions to front-office counters or telephone lines. That is, costs could be reduced by moving to the second model.

Customer account management

A full one-stop service may be defined as one which allows members of the public to complete all their business through a single point, without direct contact with any of the back offices of public service. The essence of this model is that it *protects* both the consumer and front-line staff from the need to cope with the complexity of government bureaucracy. Its advantage is that it suggests that, given adequate ICT support, integrated account management can be introduced into front offices without substantial reorganization or re-engineering of back-office bureaucracy. This is an important caveat. For example, the Dutch study to which we referred above particularly mentions the value of knowledge-based systems (KBS) in supporting front-line staff and assumes, too, that staff will have direct on-line access to back-office customer records. This conclusion mirrors experience elsewhere. For example, the Norwegian National Public Service Unit is developing a system to provide just these kinds of capabilities for local 'public service offices' (Jøsevold 1994).

The argument for the account management model is, then, that the effective deployment of ICTs can permit public services to tolerate organizational complexity, by enabling public service consumers and front-line staff to be shielded from its inspissated opacity and the dysfunctions which accompany it. In consequence, the implementation of this model is heavily dependent on ICTs. For example, the Benefits Agency in the UK has come to the conclusion that 'one-stop' approaches to benefits delivery not only depend on the strengthening of front-line technology, but will also require massive investment in telecommunications and IS, so as to permit the virtual integration of data already held in the Operational Strategy systems. In a period of sustained retrenchment, an obvious question mark hangs over capital investment on this scale and, in this particular case, the Benefits Agency has been careful not to commit itself firmly to a timetable, emphasizing that 'the pace of these developments, particularly the [later] "one person" and "one time" stages, will be dependent on the availability of resources' (Department of Social Security and HM Treasury 1994: 56). Lending further emphasis to this point, the authors of the Dutch study argue that the costs of technological investment implied by one-stop arrangements may need to be offset by more fundamental transformation of the machinery of government. In other words, their study recognizes the logic of BPR; rather than being used to allow consumers and staff to *cope* with bureaucracy, technology should be exploited to *streamline* bureaucracy.

Internal regrouping around the client group principle
However, while the Dutch study acknowledges this logic, it does not regard it as inexorable. Indeed, its hesitancy in wholly endorsing the transformational logic of one-stop services lies in its clear-sighted understanding of the ambiguous consequences of technology-induced change. The simple point is that breaking down the functional, production-oriented principle of bureaucratic organization implies its replacement by an alternative principle, one which is more sensitive to patterns of consumer demand. The study proposes three ways in which services might be clustered, in order to be more responsive to consumers. First, services might be aimed at clients who share certain demographic or socio-economic characteristics; for example, they could be provided for the

elderly or for children. Second, services might be aimed at clients living in a particular geographical area or neighbourhood. Third, they might be aimed at clients who share the same needs or problems – for example, the sick or the unemployed – a principle which relates closely to the contemporary business principle of organizing services by 'product group'. Here, then, in the new 'consumer-orientation' in public administration, we see the conflation of two principles of organization originally identified by the classical school: organization by 'place' and organization by 'client group' (Gulick 1937).

In moving towards the adoption of client- or area-based orientations in the design of work processes, public managers should be aware of some of the inherent dangers of this approach (Self 1977). As the writers of the classical school acknowledged, the client principle is less than wholly satisfactory as a basis for organizing public service. In the first place, the variety of interpretations of what constitutes a 'client group' reflects the complex and seemingly limitless problem of identifying and classifying those groups to which governments should respond. Second, the client group principle, particularly when conflated with the area principle, hides an insidious trap: the danger of believing that all clients who fall within a specific category share problems ascribed to that category. To take one example, this approach might lead to the mistaken view that all families living in disadvantaged areas are themselves disadvantaged, whereas all those living in more advantaged areas are not. Third, the potential for elaborating specific needs can lead to the fragmentation of services, epitomizing the long-recognized tendency of the client group principle towards 'Lilliputian administration' (Ministry of Reconstruction 1918).

There are also important normative issues involved in reorienting public services in this way. By definition, organization by client group pushes aside the functional or purpose principle, a principle which is relatively oblivious of the users of public services, in favour of one which has, as its very *raison d'être*, a sensitivity to the different needs and circumstances of discrete groups. This sensitivity both implies and reflects new information-based capabilities for targeting services. On the one hand, it permits more selectivity and tailoring of services by service providers; on the other, it suggests rather less benign forms of discrimination. Thus, while the client group principle is intended to lead to greater specialization of services and advice – a process which would doubtless benefit many consumers – its flip side is that government inevitably increases its capability for identifying and discriminating between more or less needy, or more or less favoured, groups of clients. Indeed, organization by client group may be seen as the very antithesis of one of the traditional principles of bureaucracy, that of a blanket form of universal provision which proceeds with very little concern for the individuals or groups being served.

A case study: client-oriented benefits delivery

The dilemmas raised by this discussion can be illustrated by reference to the UK social security system. In July 1992, the social security Benefits Agency published proposals for 'one-stop' services (Benefits Agency 1992). These proposals identified a client group option for administering social security, on the grounds that specialist help might thereby be more appropriately provided for its main client groups: namely, the sick and disabled, pensioners and widows, lone parents and the unemployed. Responses from agency staff and welfare lobbies were uniformly hostile, envisaging enormous problems in assigning claimants unambiguously to client groups. Moreover, there was widespread concern that client-centred organization would stigmatize less favoured clients (Benefits Agency 1993a). As a result, the Benefits Agency was officially agnostic as to how far this approach would prevail, although instructions issued to district managers in 1993 required local office advisory services to be concentrated on two specific client groups, namely the long-term unemployed and lone parents (Benefits Agency 1993c). The immediate political context may be important in interpreting the purpose of this advice. The Conservative government of John Major adopted the rhetoric of a 'return to basics', a mission which legitimated the taking of a strong moral stance in relation to client groups deemed morally unfit in this basic sense; for example, unmarried teenage mothers or the long-term unemployed. Indeed, in keeping with this mission, a wider range of benefits have become conditional upon the behaviour and motives of claimants. Thus, in October 1996, local officials of the Benefits Agency acquired a statutory duty to monitor and counsel claimants in receipt of the new Jobseekers Allowance.

This example helps us to pose the question of whether, by adopting a strong version of the client principle, social security administration is moving towards 'lifestyle targeting'. This term refers to practice in Australia, for example, where the utilization of the welfare system to modify non-conforming behaviour became an explicit objective of social security administration in the early 1990s (Henderson 1993). The tools of the information age, particularly the widespread diffusion of 'virtual' databases, which allow massive scope for the detailed analysis and segmentation of service consumers, are deeply implicated in policy reorientation of this kind. These technologies are not themselves the cause of change, but they do present new sets of capabilities which make it possible. Nor are they to be simply characterized as a force for good or for ill. Rather, as this discussion has shown, ICTs point up longstanding public service dilemmas and issues as new information capabilities bring with them opportunities for fundamental shifts in the operating principles of government.

Prosumption: the self-service state

The notion of 'prosumption', the meshing of production and consumption roles involved in the uptake of services, provides the basis for the second of the ways in which BPR is implicated in consumerism. The belief that 'prosumption' can realize significant savings for public services does not imply that there would be no matching benefits for consumers and suppliers. On the contrary, prosumption may substantially reduce compliance costs by offering consumers and contractors more convenient and transparent ways to transact business with government. Thus, *a priori*, prosumption is not simply to be understood as shifting administrative burdens on to external bodies and individuals, but as a rethinking of the relationship between public services, customers and suppliers.

The possibility of prosumption is already stimulating radical rethinking of the way governments interface with the agencies and individuals who are the source of so much of their operational information. For example, in November 1995 the Deputy Prime Minister, Michael Heseltine, announced three special efficiency scrutinies of the impact of government bureaucracy: on the farming community, on local government and on NHS Trusts (*The Independent*, 10 November 1995: 4). This was an initiative which was in keeping with a general, long-term objective of the Conservative government, to remove government from the back of businesses by reducing regulation and red tape. It also reflected wider international concern about the negative effect of government bureaucracy on the competitive advantage of Western economies, a concern which was highlighted, for example, by a series of OECD reports on administrative modernization in government in the late 1980s and the early 1990s (Glover and O'Dwyer 1990; OECD 1992). The OECD took the view that, *inter alia*, technology could help to streamline the demands that governments made on clients and businesses, by:

- introducing single points for information collection and distribution;
- supporting the use of pre-printed forms, requiring minimum input by clients;
- permitting the sharing of information between government departments (thus reducing the number of data-collecting transactions);
- establishing electronic data interchange (EDI) with clients and taxpayers.

Proposals such as these have, in effect, formed the core of the agenda for reinventing government in the 1990s. They figure prominently in the G-7 Government On-line Project, and have been given a central place in programmes for the reinvention of government. For example, the Danish government is proposing the establishment of a national business network for exchanging commercial documents electronically, especially those associated with government procurement and financial procedures. Many other such proposals are being brought forward under the aegis of the EU, as well as by European and American governments. In line with this approach, a 'key component' of the British government's strategy for electronic government 'is to provide the public (both businesses and citizens) with the opportunity to send and receive, over electronic terminals, the information that currently passes between them and government on paper' (Office of Public Service 1996b: 14). Thus, the PC in the home or place of work would eventually provide an electronic one-stop shop for government services, 'available 24 hours a day, seven days a week . . . and offering as near to instant response as practicable' (p. 15). At the same time, larger corporations would establish electronic links into government, that would 'permit routine information to pass automatically without manual intervention' (p. 14).

Innovations such as these are obviously of greatest interest to departments which conduct high-volume data interchange with clients and external organizations, particularly revenue agencies, licensing bodies and welfare administrations. For example, long before *government.direct* was conceived, similar proposals featured in the UK Inland Revenue's Change Programme, leading, for example, to the introduction in 1997 of self-assessment for nine million higher-rate or self-employed taxpayers. Self-assessment depends heavily on the electronic production and distribution of pre-printed forms and involves considerable modification of internal computer systems. The calculation is that its front-end costs will be offset by the resulting improvements in administrative efficiency and revenue collection, estimated to be worth some £200 million over the first ten years, a heady testament to the cost-cutting expectations which surround prosumption (*The Independent*: 7 July 1995: 13).

The Inland Revenue is also introducing an on-line Electronic Lodgement Service (ELS) for filing self-assessment returns (Inland Revenue 1994, 1995). From April 1997, electronic filing can occur over telephone line and modem by means of secure, dedicated software which is supplied to tax agents. In the first instance, ELS promises accurate processing of self-assessment returns within twenty-four hours, but it is hoped to extend the service to offer electronic tax coding and processing of repayment claims for self-assessed taxpayers by the year 2000. In developing ELS, the Inland Revenue is following the lead of countries such as the USA and Canada, which encourage direct filing from personal computers and touch-pad phones. The Canadian EFILE system, for example, guarantees taxpayers a turnaround time for assessments and the return of overpayments of just two weeks, a facility which was used by three million Canadians in its first year, 1993 (Treasury Board of Canada 1995). In common with many other governments, the Canadian government is proposing to extend direct electronic transactions of this kind to other government business: one current example is the renewal of radio licences.

It is important to be clear, however, that relatively transparent exchanges of information, such as these, are by no means the sole source of government data about customers and clients. On the contrary, as we have already begun to discuss in relation to the importance of informatization, governments can acquire data in less direct ways, quite apart from data gathering through active surveillance. For example, customer inquiries made to information helplines, and scenarios entered into knowledge-based systems by patients, welfare claimants or taxpayers, are increasingly being recognized as potential sources of significant amounts of operational data. Moreover, one of the recurrent themes in contemporary reinvention programmes is that enhancing services while cutting costs demands that governments maximize the value reaped from each data item. The Green Paper on *government.direct* recognizes that:

Once systems are linked together for the purpose of service delivery, it becomes possible to achieve additional efficiency improvements through the use of common services . . . This would not only provide economies which would benefit us all as taxpayers, but would also improve the service government provides: it would only be necessary to tell government once when we changed address, for example.

(Office of Public Service 1996b: 17)

In consequence, there is pressure to develop information systems to support electronic transactions not only as an exercise in *automation*, but also for the purposes of *informatizing* government. This process implies, however, that data could be applied to purposes which may be far removed from its original conditions of surrender. Maximizing the efficiency pay-back from customer-facing computer systems is directly related to the proportion and quality of data which can be captured and disseminated by this means. For example, it would be more efficient if a change of name upon marriage were transmitted automatically to all relevant government information systems rather than being lodged solely at the first point of entry. Thus, to illustrate this possibility from a large government department, the DSS plans to streamline benefits administration by enabling claimants to notify life events, such as marriages, as they occur, rather than to restate their personal details at the point of each benefit claim (Bellamy 1996). There are similar aspirations within the NHS. For example, underpinning the IM&T strategy of the NHS is the hope that some of the data which form an individual's medical history could be captured once, rather than taken afresh each time a patient encounters a new health care agency.

Holistic consumption: towards the single citizen account?

It is the possibilities for rationalizing information-handling in these ways which stimulated an imaginative account of UK government in the information age, published in 1994 (Swinden and Heath 1994). *Wired Whitehall 1999* anticipated that every individual will eventually be offered a smart card, to be called a 'citizen card', permitting a wide range of transactions to be credited and debited from a 'single citizen account'. The card would also permit cross-reference between the services used by a citizen. For example, by 2004, we should take for granted that: 'when we drop into a supermarket or public library, we can use the Infopoint terminal to find out how much credit is left in our road toll account. Also, if we're unemployed and drawing benefit, that it will advise us to call the job agency because a likely vacancy has come up' (Swinden and Heath 1994: 9).

Wired Whitehall 1999 is an overtly futuristic account of government in the information age. None the less, its visions are consistent with similar scenarios in emergent national *reinvention* strategies. For example, the Danish Strategy for the Information Society sets out seven 'principles' which should govern the development of an 'Electronic Service Network of the Public Sector', including the principles that: 'information which has already been submitted by citizens and companies to a public institution, and which can be transferred electronically, shall not be requested by another public institution again'; and that 'data shall be requested only once' (Dybkjær and Christensen 1994: 33, 34). In the same way, the two main objectives identified by the Canadian *Blueprint* are to:

• eliminate the need to collect the same or similar information more than once within a department or within government;
• provide government programmes with access to information collected by other programmes, especially where this would improve the efficiency and effectiveness of government service delivery (Treasury Board of Canada 1995: Information View, unpaged).

The recycling of basic personal data will require the establishment of a common numerical identifier for every person or company, so that the data can be identified in a range of different information systems. At present, an important practical barrier to data interchange in government is the large number of identifiers currently in use. In the UK, for example, there are different numbers used for national insurance and tax administration, for health service records, for passports and (various kinds of) licences, as well as for council tax assessments. Sharing data across government is probably dependent, therefore, on securing political agreement to a common identification number. The Canadian *Blueprint* proposes a 'Single Business Registration Number', to support integrated administration of business taxation, including goods and services, taxes and corporate income tax. In the same way, the Danish Strategy recommends that citizens be offered a single plastic smart card, linking to a common identifier, to be known as the Electronic Citizen Card. This card will eventually supersede all other official personal documents, including birth certificates, driving licences and passports. In the first instance, the citizen card will hold only basic personal data and will be used primarily for identification purposes, but the aim is that it will eventually authorize access to an increasing range of electronic self-service facilities which will be developed in the public and private sectors.

In the UK, proposals for a single citizen account would inevitably become entwined with the politics of identification (ID) cards. The British government has traditionally resisted the peace-time use of ID cards, anticipating that their introduction would meet with public resistance. Nevertheless, the sheer scale of efficiencies to be gained, for government and business alike, prompted a previous Home Secretary to bring forward proposals for a *voluntary* ID card which might, among other applications, provide secure access to a range of electronic public services: 'An identity card would enable citizens seeking access to public services to provide the key data quickly, in a format readily acceptable to the service provider, particularly where the main information was repeated in machine readable form compatible with the service provider's data system' (Home Office 1995b: 15). If implemented, such a scheme would, in the first instance, utilize a new kind of 'photocard' driving licence, capable of being inscribed with basic personal details in machine-readable form.

Information age public services: implications and conclusions

We have sought in this chapter to elucidate and explore the claim that government in the information age will 'work better and cost less'. We have seen that there is an increasingly widespread belief that taxpayers, suppliers and customers alike will gain from streamlining government bureaucracy, rationalizing information-mediated business processes and maximizing economies of scope. At the same time, information-age government holds out the promise of more flexible, more holistic, more integrated and more comprehensible public services, which will be more targeted and tailored to customers' needs.

We have seen, too, that there is an important paradox at the centre of this claim. This derives from the widespread perception that the power of ICTs to secure a real and irreversible impact on costs and productivity lies in transcending the view of IT as a *production* technology, a technology of automation. Rather, realizing the promise associated with ICTs will derive from the informatizing and transforming properties which the technologies bring. While BPR appears to offer a value-free prescription for transforming business processes, its doctrines have politically significant implications for relationships in and around government, especially those between public services, their suppliers and their consumers. This point takes us back to the main question addressed in this chapter: what are the implications of contemporary *reinvention* prospectuses for public service users and for public service values?

The first point to note, in seeking to conclude with some answers to this question, is that the claim that ICT-intensive government will work better and cost less is predicated on securing greater integration between business processes, both horizontally across government and vertically between suppliers, producers and consumers. Securing and maintaining the business relationships on which this integration depends is indisputably an agenda for the information age, because it depends critically on the informatization of government. That is, it depends on new capabilities for capturing, for sharing, for integrating and for exploiting information by means of new kinds of information systems capable of supporting new information flows.

Herein lies the rub, for it is these same capabilities which would also be the source of new possibilities for surveillance and control. For example, we have seen that patient-based records in the NHS and 'whole claimant' records in the DSS both depend on data-matching techniques, enabling the 'logical' or virtual construction of more comprehensive, flexible datasets. We have seen, too, that detailed and precisely tailored intelligence can be formed about individuals' behaviour, by analysing the electronic footprints left on government

IS. For example, it would be technically possible for a system designed to provide job-search facilities to monitor its own usage by individuals who are in receipt of Jobseekers Allowance, thus providing evidence about the assiduity with which they are seeking work. This may seem fanciful, but examples of similar monitoring capabilities already exist. In Minnesota, for example, information kiosks are permitting people on parole or probation to report remotely to their supervisor. What is also happening to this client group, without its knowledge, is that the system is automatically and simultaneously breathalysing them (Taylor *et al.* 1996).

The point of concern here is not so much that big brother capabilities are being explicitly created by informatizing government: it is to be assumed that, in a liberal democracy, an Orwellian agenda would not be constructed as a matter of overt policy. Of rather more concern is that the choices that will be made in deploying ICTs will be the outcome of a much less transparent or conscious process, a by-product of bureaucratically agreed trade-offs by managers who have not engaged fully with issues relating to the loss of privacy or the increased capability of the state for surveillance. In particular, as we discussed in Chapter 1, we would counsel against oversimplifying and dramatizing either the customer-supporting or the citizen-threatening propensities of ICTs. Rather, this chapter has been designed to show that the dilemma here lies in the inherent, and inescapable, contradiction between 'soft sister' informational innovations which promise to improve both the quality and efficiency of public services, and the 'big brother' implications of those same innovations for social control. As Lyon (1994: 18) has observed:

> People trust themselves to complex technologies because they seem to promise convenience, efficiency, security and reduced uncertainty. Simultaneously, we worry that in so doing we may be denying something important to a worthwhile human life . . . We end by depending on the very systems about whose efficacy we entertain nagging doubts. We collude with surveillance systems, whether willingly or reluctantly, wittingly or unwittingly.

Despite the use of this emotive term, it cannot be assumed that 'collusion' is an unwise choice for individuals, or, indeed, that it is even a matter of choice. As Lyon has also argued, adopting a fatalistic or paranoic response to 'the surveillance society' is to be blind to the subtleties and complexities of the capabilities on which it depends, not least the point that the surveillance systems in advanced bureaucracies are the same information systems by which citizens' entitlements to public services are met. Thus, there is real sense in which citizens exist, in relation to public services, only in so far as their identity can be recognized by public service computers. It follows that 'To participate in modern society is to be under electronic surveillance' (Lyon 1994: 4).

It is, of course, the case that access to public services has always entailed having much of the detail of one's life recorded in the files of government bureaucracy. What is distinctive about the information age is not only the more intensive permeation of consumption *by* information systems, but the vast expansion of capabilities for integrating and cross-matching data *between* information systems. The consequence is that most capacity for surveillance is created behind the scenes of bureaucratic life, through processes whose opacity is guaranteed partly by a lack of public awareness. Moreover, although a growing number of individuals probably possess an 'in-principle' understanding of the expanding capabilities of the surveillance society, the very flexibility of information age systems means that, in practice, none of us *can* know precisely what others do or could know about us.

What this chapter has also shown, therefore, is that much of the capability of the surveillance society is being created as the incidental by-product of processes which are designed primarily to meet non-surveillance goals, such as reducing fraud, improving efficiency and enhancing quality. For this reason, it is important not only to analyse the surveillance society at an abstract level, but also to understand the factors which are, in practice, shaping the capabilities on which it is founded. For example, how are values such as efficiency and privacy being traded off in the organizations of government in the UK?

Although the government is obviously determined to find new ways of managing public services, the exploitation of new information and communications capabilities continues to be heavily influenced by prevailing capital investment criteria. The push exerted by the hoped for impact of ICT on costs, together with the pull exerted by the new public consumerism, combine to provide a strong incentive for government to move on from an automation perspective. We have brought forward several illustrations to show that consumerism is, indeed, fast becoming a factor leading to the informatization of government. However, it is also clear that there will be continuing financial retrenchment in UK government, probably for the foreseeable future. Thus, we may anticipate that, as the information age unfurls, investments in new technologies will be increasingly shaped by the promise of economies of scope, just as they were governed in the era of automation by the promise of economies of scale. In other words, the danger is that the trade-offs between 'big brother' and 'soft sister' propensities of ICTs will be overly influenced by the business-driven need to extract the greatest possible value from information resources. On this analysis, the integration of information resources is less likely to be driven by the deliberate expansion of capability for control, and more likely to be stimulated by the renewal of the promise that technology can, after all, take much of the cost out of public services.

In practice, the impact of new informational and communications capabilities on public service customers is likely to be extremely uneven, not least because the information age will almost certainly be marked by a retreat from universal service principles. The second general point to be made about information age relations between public services and their customers is that they will be marked by increasing differentiation. We have already seen that for one commentator, at least, the relegitimation of the public service ethos lies in the celebration of diversity. Again, this is clearly an aspiration for the information age. Its fulfilment is predicated on the increasingly flexible capability for identifying, selecting and integrating information, a capability which will permit public services to be more effectively focused on progressively differentiated demands. It is this flexibility which provides the underpinning for the claim that information age public service is moving on from Fordism, from the provision of standardized services which are both indifferent and unresponsive to individual needs. Nevertheless, this shift can be also perceived as a retreat from the traditional values of public bureaucracy, namely a commitment to consistency, predictability and impersonality in the disposition of its powers. Organization by client group epitomizes this retreat, by erecting as a very principle of public service the doctrine that governments can, and should, be sensitive to differences between citizens; that discrimination and selectivity are integral to the new public service ethos. This is especially so when set alongside increasing capabilities to differentiate service levels; for example, by permitting customers to be billed on a pay-per-use basis.

So how will targeting and discrimination be applied, especially in a climate of financial retrenchment? The danger is that enhanced capabilities for sifting and grouping consumers will lend itself to overcrude categorization and stereotyping. Thus, far from being a gateway to expanded social rights, they will serve to pigeon-hole individuals and restrict or channel access to services. For more favoured groups of customers, information age public services will look and feel more like high street services. The utilization of holes in the wall, modern telephony and comfortable neighbourhood offices will render services increasingly convenient to use, distancing them by geography and style from the drab government buildings and council offices which have so often housed public services. The application of these technologies could eventually enable more public services to be co-located with other high street services or delivered through commercial networks. In other words, for some groups of customers, public services will be experienced in ways that will render the public–private cleavage increasingly blurred. On the other hand, for less favoured groups, the same technologies will make possible a more discriminating public service, one that is more capable than ever before of policing their lifestyles and targeting non-conforming behaviour in the interests of social control.

This retreat from universalism is merely one reason why the meaning and practice of citizenship should be reconsidered for the information age, and it is to this question that we will turn in our next two chapters. First, we propose to look critically at the proposition that the expanding information resources at the disposal of citizens are encouraging a counterveiling strengthening of democratic capability for bottom-up control. Second, we will consider the implications for public service values of contemporary telecommunications policies that are shaping the nature and the direction of the superhighways of the information age.

4

The search for renewal: citizenship and democracy in the information age

> The advanced telecommunications networks being built today . . . could support the electronic equivalent of public spaces, where people could come together as informed citizens – or they could provide only electronic malls, where people are targeted as spectators and consumers.
>
> (Benton Foundation, undated, unpaged)

Chapters 2 and 3 have shown why the 1990s have witnessed a strengthening of the conviction that government can be reinvented through the intensive application of ICTs. What we have also begun to see, however, is that consumer-driven reinvention of government is unlikely to be neutral as far as the values of governing are concerned. There are good reasons to suppose that the technology-enabled search for new economies of scope and for enhancements in public service will combine to force new interpretations of the significance of efficiency, equity and stewardship in government, as well as new kinds of trade-offs between these values.

In this chapter we propose to build on our analysis of the normative significance of consumerism by exploring the ways in which it is implicated in changes of even more fundamental importance in contemporary government. That is, we will extend our conception of consumerism as an information age agenda and, in so doing, explore its *political* significance for the nature of democratic practice and citizenship. This significance lies in the fact that consumerism is being asked to deliver much more than straightforward improvements in the efficiency and effectiveness of public services. Beyond this narrow version of the public management agenda lies the more or less explicit conviction that the traditional institutions of representative democracy are failing to inspire widespread confidence in the democratic basis of government. For example, on the New Right of the political spectrum, Madsen Pirie has contended that the Citizen's Charter represents an important democratic gain because it symbolizes a determination to reverse the chronic imperviousness of

modern governments to popular influence (Pirie 1991: 23). Along similar lines,
the Minister first responsible for the Citizen's Charter claimed that the Charter
offers citizens a usable and effective means of holding government truly to
account, in contrast to formal constitutional doctrines which uphold a state of
affairs 'where control, exercisable in theory, was routinely subverted by producer interests' (Waldegrave 1993: 82).

This discrediting by the political right of the practical utility of representative democracy is matched by a growing disillusionment on the centre left
with the political infrastructure of the social democratic, Keynesian welfare
state. We saw in Chapter 3 that the perception that the welfare state fostered a
paternalistic, bureaucratic system of government is by no means confined to its
Thatcherite critics. On the contrary, it is, for example, clearly reflected in one
of the more interesting recent academic analyses of the issues confronting
public managers in the 1990s, an analysis which shares the conviction that the
processes of democratic government have been subverted by the producer-
dominated oligarchies which control the welfare state:

> the post-war social democratic polity emphasised a passive public, taking its
> lead from professional experts and distant elected representatives. While
> much was achieved, excluding the public from participating in the de-
> velopment of society led in time to a withering of identification and
> support. The vacuum in the polity was the absence of public engagement.
>
> (Ranson and Stewart 1994: 61)

Democratizing the consumption nexus

As on the right, the response on the centre left of UK politics has been to attach
an explicit democratic value to consumerist initiatives, by emphasizing the
need to empower users as direct stakeholders in the material outcomes of
public administration. As we saw in Chapter 3, this response accounts, for
example, for the widespread interest in decentralization strategies as a means of
forging new opportunities for user involvement and democratic feedback in
local government. In these kinds of ways, the consumption nexus, that relationship within which government and its consumers meet, is increasingly
being asked to stand as surrogate for the discredited processes of representative
democracy by operationalizing such basic democratic values as accountability,
responsiveness and participation. On this reading, the new consumerism represents one response to the growing cynicism about the democratic efficacy of
those traditional arrangements which exist on the 'input side' of political systems: that is, elections, parliaments and parties. It is a cynicism which has
resulted in the emergence of a wide variety of single-issue groups and new
social movements which, in turn, have also contributed to the 'decentring' of
representative politics (Self 1985). Where once parties, elections and parliaments occupied, in a relatively unequivocal sense, the centre ground of democratic politics, now that ground has become contested and uncertain.

Turning to the output side of political systems, we can see that attempts to democratize the consumption process go back over several decades. The ombudsman movement of the mid-1960s provides one example, and others are the fashion for public participation in policy implementation in the late 1960s, the community development movement in the 1970s and the public service orientation in the 1980s, with their emphasis upon bringing the physical organization and the decision-making procedures of government closer to the public. Most recently, democratization of the output side of politics has found its strongest expression in the conviction which lies at the heart of *reinventing government*: that governments can best rekindle the faltering legitimacy of the contemporary state by repairing their relationships with taxpayers and public service users through thoroughgoing redesign of the consumption nexus, especially through the intensive deployment of ICTs.

This emergent shift in democratic focus has deep potential significance for flows of information in and around contemporary governance. In particular, this shift both explains and validates the reorientation of the application of new ICTs away from the automation of internal housekeeping functions and towards a much greater concern to informate relations between public service managers and public service users. It follows that a key dimension of information age government is that its popular legitimacy, specifically its claim to be responsive to citizens' demands, will increasingly depend on the effectiveness of what we propose to call 'consumer democracy'. By this, we refer to the increasing reliance on channelling the democratic expression of opinion and preferences through bureaucratic processes and service delivery arrangements which are mediated primarily by public service managers.

In principle, consumer democracy rests upon two different types of information flows, one type generated *by* 'citizens' as explicit and intended expressions of popular voice, by participation in public forums or through market research techniques, for example. However, as we saw in Chapter 3, the informatization of public services also liberates increasingly rich information *about* individuals' preferences, information which is capable of being exploited to shape or legitimate public policy. If we take seriously the doctrine of classical economics, that markets are the most effective way of signalling preferences, then data generated by the informatization of marketized relationships will be an increasingly significant source of 'democratic' intelligence. Thus, an increasing range of resources can be legitimately allocated without the need for direct political intervention or explicit processes of accountability (Phillips 1994). The essence of this position is that citizenship in the information age consists of neither more nor less than the registering of consumer preferences in the information systems of government in the course of undertaking service transactions. It is this simple insight that gives the information-rich consumer agenda that we discussed in Chapter 3 a political significance which goes far beyond the narrow-gauge concern to improve the management of public services.

Relegitimating the political nexus

Despite the bipartisan origins of public consumerism, its close connection with the spread of market-type mechanisms, and thus with individualist values, has provoked, by way of reaction, a renewed preoccupation with theories of citizenship and democratic politics which emphasize collectivist values such as social responsibility, mutuality and community. This attempt to reclaim a conception of citizenship that embraces far more than a stakeholding in public services is one which is reconnecting the agenda of academic public administration to some of the traditional concerns of political theory (Hambleton 1988). It is an endeavour which has been most forcefully pursued in the UK in relation to local rather than to central government, for reasons which are not hard to understand (Richardson and Cram 1992). Local government in Britain is widely believed to have suffered a sustained erosion of its autonomy and powers and a disabling fragmentation of its jurisdictions and functions (Cochrane 1994; Stewart and Stoker 1995), and it has certainly sustained a withdrawal of democratic support. For example, a body of research bears witness to the relatively low turnouts at local elections, extensive popular ignorance about the structure and functions of local government and the chronic decline in willingness to serve on local councils (e.g. Lynn 1992; Rawlings *et al.* 1994). It is entirely unsurprising, therefore, that there has been a sustained campaign, on the part of those who still have faith in local government, to reinvent and renew the idea of local democracy, and thus to relegitimate the principle of elected local government.

The proposition which sits at the heart of this campaign is not simply that local democracy must be strengthened, but that this must be conceived as a process which depends, at bottom, on the rediscovery and revitalization of local *politics*. This proposition draws on a specific definition of politics, as an activity permitting the orderly resolution of the conflicts that inevitably arise from differences of opinion and interest among people who nevertheless wish to pursue collective action for their common good (Crick 1964). In other words, politics is conceived as a process which demands that people look beyond their individual interests to see themselves as members of a political community, a process which involves a willingness to tolerate and reach accommodation with other interests and preferences.

This belief in the importance of politics as 'a social activity which takes people beyond the individualism of the market' (Stoker 1994: 9) leads directly to the rejection of any conception of citizenship that is restricted to the consumption nexus. Rather, this definition of politics relates more closely to a conception of the 'active' or 'republican' citizen, one who 'plays an active role in shaping the future direction of his or her society through political debate and decision-making' (Miller 1995: 443). Active citizenship involves moral and ideological engagement in the issues and problems facing a community, including determination of the fundamental principles of social justice by which public services and resources are allocated (Miller 1989; Plant 1990). It follows from this reasoning that there is a fundamental difference between institutions which exist within the public domain, and which therefore have an inescapably political dimension to their purposes, and those which exist in the private domain. 'A concept of organization that encompasses citizens differs from an organization that knows only customers' (Ranson and Stewart 1989: 5).

The specific relevance of this line of argument to the relegitimation of *local* democracy is that the strengthening of citizenship requires not simply a process of institutional reform, but also deep cultural change. The distinctive contribution to be made by local governance is that it is uniquely placed to provide opportunities for the experience of direct, participative democracy that can encourage the revaluing of political discourse which these writers seek (Ranson and Stewart 1994). In this endeavour, the work of the American Benjamin Barber has been particularly influential, for he believes that the tired, 'thin' processes of Western representative democracy can be revitalized by being underpinned at the local level with new opportunities for active citizenship, including those made possible by ICTs (Barber 1984). 'Electronic communities' could encourage the emergence of a stronger civic culture and help to counter the narrow preoccupation of the liberal right with the promotion of individual and sectional interests. New forms of local participative democracy would help to build a stronger democracy that would be equally effective in 'resisting assaults on community, or justice, or citizenship' (Barber 1984: 4).

Reinventing democracy for the information age

Given this line of argument, the question arises: what kind of contribution to the renewal of the political nexus might be made by ICTs? This is an issue which has been diverted by the widespread, almost synonymic, coupling of electronic democracy with direct democracy. This coupling is reinforced by the simplistic proposition that 'the technical difficulties that until now have made it impossible for large numbers of citizens to participate in policy making have now been solved by the revolution in computer–communications technology' (Masuda 1990: 83; see also Naisbitt 1984; Toffler 1980), a highly questionable proposition but one which, nevertheless, is currently being taken at face value within political science (Budge 1996). However, it is also clear that these optimistic, even utopian, visions of electronic direct democracy – or 'teledemocracy' – are far from being universally shared, for teledemocracy is more commonly associated with forms of direct democracy that are far from 'strong' (Donk and Tops 1992).

Barber (1984: 274) believed that technology could be utilized to invent a form of strong democracy, because ICTs could 'strengthen civic education, guarantee equal access to information, and tie individuals and institutions into networks that will make real participatory discussion and debate across great distances'. However, his work also explicitly recognizes and challenges the power of Orwellian images of direct democracy in Western liberal political thought. These images were pre-dated and nurtured by a long tradition of political thinking which has proved remarkably persistent in modern politics. According to this tradition, direct democracy is susceptible, on the one hand, to the tyranny and venality of the masses, and, on the other, to a high degree of manipulation by elites. Consequently, a major problem for contemporary proponents of 'teledemocracy' is that the very notion brings to the surface deep-seated anxieties that it will lead to the disintermediation of politics and thereby to the emergence of a high-tech form of authoritarian populism (Eulau 1977). For example, the conclusion drawn from a seminal empirical study of ICT-intensive direct democracy (Laudon 1977) was that the main political use of interactive technology was to refine political marketing techniques. At best, large-scale computerization would strengthen 'managerial democracy', by increasing the technical competence and information base of public service and party managers. At worst, it would lead to 'telefascism', destroying local communities and grass-roots groups, and creating the conditions by which socially isolated individuals could be mobilized within a new kind of high-tech totalitarianism.

Scoping democratic forms in an information age

This brief review of the literature on democracy and technology emphasizes the classical polarization of view, the juxtaposition of unquestioning enthusiasm and deeply pessimistic dismissal, which characterizes discussion of tele-democracy. However, taking a somewhat more detached view of the debate which this literature has so powerfully dominated, we can begin to identify three main archetypes of information age democracy. Thus we have identified a 'strong democracy' archetype associated, for example, with the work of Barber; a populist 'managed democracy' archetype associated, for example, with the work of Laudon; and a 'consumer democracy' archetype which we have drawn from our own analysis of the political significance of consumerism in government. Each is associated with a specific notion of citizenship. Strong democracy and consumer democracy are associated with notions of 'active' citizenship, albeit in rather different forms, while populist democracy is associated with 'passive' citizenship.

Before elucidating these archetypes in greater detail, we want to be clear about the purposes behind them. Primarily they are intended to be analytic tools, designed to facilitate understanding not only of the nature and implications of changes in contemporary democracy, but also of the connections between those changes. They have been arrived at deductively as a consequence of teasing out the informational and communications content of these changes. Essentially, we use them here to explore a range of outcomes for the nature and quality of democratic politics and government arising from new capabilities for political control and liberation. We identify the main channels of democratic expression which are embedded in these archetypes and, in so doing, begin to explore the nature and quality of popular influence and participation that flows through, and is structured by, those channels. Moreover, we depict our archetypes in the language of political inquiry rather than that of technological innovation, a process which has enabled us to escape from the tele- or techno-centric nature of so much recent debate about information age democracy.

Strong democracy

'Strong democracy' is used primarily to capture the informational and communications content of an 'Athenian'-like democracy and the active mode of citizenship on which it depends. This archetype depicts information-rich citizens who have become so as a consequence of their universal enjoyment of low-cost access to publicly provided information. Equally, it suggests open communication *between* citizens, politicians and public officials, as well as intensive interaction *among* each of those groups, all leading to rich and active participation in a wide range of civic, cultural and political affairs. Strong democracy is, therefore, predicated on the assumption that the increasingly pervasive electronic networks of the information age will be valued as much as for their communications facilities as for their capability to deliver information resources. ICTs would provide high-quality, comprehensive public information, but they would also be universally deployed to realize the communications intensity of this archetype.

Active citizenship requires that citizens possess certain rights, perhaps the most fundamental of which is the right to access the means of participating in democracy itself. In other words, information age democracy requires universal access to information age capabilities. However, the notion that citizens enjoy political rights as an integral element of social justice underlines the importance within this archetype of the construction of an inclusive political community, capable of integrating citizens and groups on the basis of a pervasive sharing of fundamental social values as well as a mutual commitment to toleration and political modes of discourse. Thus, the challenge which strong democracy presents to the information age is not only to make real its promise of social inclusivity and access – for example, by facilitating popular involvement in an ever widening complex of on-line communities – but to engage in a yet more difficult and important task. This task is to nurture a conception of virtual 'public space' wherein political activity occurs.

Populist democracy

Within the populist democratic archetype, information age capabilities are especially exploited from the 'top' of politics, enhancing the capacity of political and bureaucratic elites to manage democracy and to legitimate government through the construction of numerical majorities that stand as proxies for popular consent. That is, the most significant capability offered by ICTs is their capture and processing of ever more detailed and comprehensive feedback from voters, permitting the precise and effective targeting of political communication. Thus, the most pervasive political uses of new technology within populist democracy are to refine and enlarge the political use of the techniques of mass marketing and to exploit opportunities for increasing the use of plebiscites and referendums as devices for managing politics.

The effectiveness of the management of a mass democracy in the information age is, therefore, contingent upon the universal availability of electronic media for the receipt and transmission of political communication. However, widening access through these electronic means is no more than a political expedient, for engagement in politics is not valued in itself. Nor is there a presumption that there should be freedom of access to public information; quite the reverse. We have already shown why public information is likely to become progressively commodified, in two senses of this word. In the first place, the growth of publicly accessible information services will lead to an increasingly strong emphasis on the shaping, customizing and packaging of information for different groups of users. Second, public information is also likely to be perceived, more and more, as a commodity to be bought and sold. The most obvious reason for selling information is to recoup the growing costs of meeting information age expectations for information resources, a pressure which we can expect to place an increasing strain on the resources of parliaments, parties and public bodies alike. However, trading in information also has an important political significance which should not be overlooked. That is, it both permits and implies the creation of a hierarchy of differentiated information resources, some for sale at full cost, some at zero direct cost to the end consumer and some whose price reflects a compromise between conceiving information either as a commercial or as a social entity. In this way, highly differentiated information markets are created and sustained, enhancing the information producers' control of access to information resources and communications facilities.

In sum, populist democracy is built on the assumption that the availability of fast-growing, flexible information resources holds out the promise of managing democracy more effectively, but also that political elites will seek more and more to shape and control the informational and communications capabilities associated with new technologies. Moreover, for a variety of reasons, this exercise of control will be far from neutral in its impact on politics and government. First, this archetype places considerable emphasis on the management of political communication, including the interpretation of democratic feedback, an emphasis which would inevitably intensify the influence on political processes of political bureaucracies, such as party machines. The management of communication would not only reinforce the oligarchical nature of political organization, it would also carry important consequences for the culture of political elites as it bestowed increasing legitimacy on the kind of technocratic rationality that is succoured by data intensity.

Second, however, the high value that is placed on 'teleocratic' control, the top-down control of information age resources and communications media, points to a highly insulated and conservative style of governance, one that is relatively impervious to the kinds of democratic expression resident in strong democracy. The danger is that governing would become highly dependent upon the internally validated conventional wisdoms and orthodoxies of political managers and public officials. Thus, managing democracy in these ways would weaken the authority and, therefore, the effectiveness of alternative channels of political voice, especially those traditionally provided by representative processes. In consequence, we would expect a populist democracy to be associated with high levels of popular detachment and cynicism, while at the same time insulating policy-makers from its own immediate consequences.

The teleocratic search for more intensive forms of political control is, therefore, one way in which political elites could be expected to seek an accommodation with the information age. Such strategies carry a high risk of exacerbating the problems of legitimation in contemporary democracies, however, by alienating information age citizens who might increasingly expect independent, self-directed access to richly resourced information and communications media. Indeed, populist archetypes assume a high degree of capability on the part of political and bureaucratic elites for containing and controlling informational and communications capabilities, an assumption which, as we will see later in this chapter, is strongly countered by other interpretations of the information revolution.

Consumer democracy

Consumer democracy, as we use it here, represents a more subtle and interesting response to problems of political management in the information age than populist democracy. It is an archetype that has topicality, in that it better aligns with the immediate experiences which citizens have of governments (Corrigan 1996), as well as being realistically in tune with information age capabilities. As with populist democracy, this archetype has also been influenced by the notion of 'managed democracy', but, in contrast to populist democracy, which assumes that ICTs will be exploited to refine the top-down control of democratic expression, the consumer democracy archetype assumes that such expression can be contained by being channelled through the consumption nexus. In consequence, the imperative of political control lies at the interface between governments and the consumers of their services.

In contrast to 'strong democracy', the new public consumerism rests on an instrumental, rather than a republican, conception of the individual's relationship with government. Consumerist democracy derives from a utilitarian or 'protective' (Macpherson 1973) conception of democracy, which, in the early nineteenth century, provided the basis of a powerful claim to political equality and universal civic rights. As with utilitarian democracy, consumer democracy assumes that the individual's interests will be protected only if the individual has the means to protect them, an assumption which, as the Citizen's Charter recognizes, establishes a strong claim by all citizens to information about entitlements to public services. It is an archetype, therefore, which casts the individual as active, competent and rational in the making of choices and in the expression of preferences.

While the concept of citizenship here is active, citizenship in a consumer democracy differs from citizenship in a strong democracy in three important senses. In the first place, consumer democracy restricts citizenship to a notion of stakeholding in public services. In consequence, consumer democracy excludes the citizen from influence over those affairs of state which might be referred to as 'high politics', affairs such as national economy, welfare, external security and internal order. Thus, the form of consumerism promoted by consumer democracy is one whose expression is captured and channelled within a relatively narrow set of vertical administrative arrangements concerned with the relatively 'low' politics of public service delivery and operational management. Likewise, it establishes a claim to public information only in relation to the citizen's stake in the delivery of public services. Second, the reliance within consumer democracy on the consumption nexus to interpret and moderate individual consumer preferences neglects the possibility that citizens might engage with others who may have equally powerful and rational preferences to express and that, as a consequence, individual choice might be moderated by political interactions. Just as it elevates markets as the apogee of rational choice, so consumer democracy legitimates the use of market intelligence as a proxy for explicit democratic expression. Here we have exposed an especially crucial aspect of information age government, for it not only places consumer behaviour at the heart of debates about the democratic legitimacy of government, but it does so in a way which conflates it with the search for greater and greater levels of managerial effectiveness. It is within both the quest to understand better the nature of consumer preferences and the consequent search for improved managerial responsiveness that the role of ICTs is to be found.

Third, active citizenship in consumer democracy differs from its practice in strong democracy, in that it implies the ceding to the state of a myriad of personal data. Consumer democracy embeds into the processes of government the force of Lyon's proposition that the inevitable corollary of participation and citizenship in the information society is the surrender of a mass of data about the individual's behaviour and preferences, a process which is at the root of the enhanced capabilities for monitoring and surveillance possessed by the informated state.

These three archetypes of electronic democracy – 'strong', 'populist' and 'consumer' democracy – provide the basis for a broad understanding of the use by governments of information and communications technologies, developments which are claimed to be significant for both democracy and citizenship. Our primary intention in the rest of the chapter, however, is to bear these archetypes in mind while analysing current innovations so as to offer a sense of the changes which are actually occurring in government. In this undertaking, we will focus in the first place on UK experience, though we will also draw on American and continental European practice to open out debate about the possibilities for, as well as the contemporary practice of, emergent forms of democracy in which ICTs may be playing a significant role.

Information, communication and citizenship in contemporary government: consumerism and open government

It is clear that both central and local governments throughout the world have begun, albeit belatedly and unevenly in most instances, to exploit new informational and communications capabilities in ways which promise to influence, and possibly to reshape, the nature of citizenship and democracy. In Britain, this activity has focused mainly on 'open government', a concept which is being operationalized through the changing arrangements by which government offers public access to certain kinds of information resources. Notable, however, is that, as this initiative develops, it is not promoting freedom of information as its proponents had hoped (e.g. Mitchell 1979; Benn 1980; Wilson 1984; Ponting 1989). Open government is scarcely challenging established relationships between government and citizens, for those new capabilities which ICTs introduce are, in large part, themselves being shaped by prevailing strategies for managing those relationships, as well as by longstanding assumptions about the significance and nature of information.

Two features of the open government agenda are particularly discernible. First, government conceives of information in a particularly narrow sense, as an input and output of the business of government, rather than as a fundamental entitlement of citizenship. In consequence, information is treated largely as a commodity, to be managed by applying the same criteria by which other resources and commodities are managed, with cost and cost recovery uppermost. Second, although the Open Government Initiative has meant that more effort than hitherto is undoubtedly being devoted to providing information to the public, far less effort is being devoted to developing interactive communication facilities that would permit citizens to make more effective contributions to political debate. Indeed, we will see that the most common use of the interactive properties of new ICTs is to add value to public services by enhancing customer inquiry and feedback facilities. In other words, 'open government' is interpreted largely from within prevailing norms of production and consumption. Its radical potential for recasting relationships is reduced in this normative environment to 'more of the same', though increasingly in electronic form.

The growing awareness of issues related to the provision of public information by British central government has been focused mainly around the Open Government Initiative. Open government has been one of the most persistent issues in British central government for many years, coming to particular prominence in the late 1980s as a result of a series of cases, especially the prosecutions of civil servants Sarah Tisdall and Clive Ponting, and the Spycatcher Affair. However, the strong interest in open government in the

1990s has also sprung from rather different origins. While leaks of classified information remain an important problem for governments, the Open Government Initiative is better understood as a direct manifestation of the central place which consumerism has come to occupy within the new public management (NPM). Whereas, until the early 1990s, governments were mostly concerned with protecting their abundant stores of information, they are now much more concerned with the liberation from government organizations of consumption-related data, in order to stimulate managerial efficiency and consumer choice. If the key political objective of NPM was to effect an irreversible shift from producer-dominated to consumer-oriented public services, then securing greater symmetry of information between producers and consumers has come to be seen as crucial to its realization. It is entirely in keeping with this analysis that the (then) Office of Public Service and Science (OPSS) and its Citizen's Charter Unit were given the lead in the Open Government Initiative.

The 1993 White Paper on Open Government (Office of Public Service and Science 1993) was silent on the relationship between the openness of information, on the one hand, and new technologies, on the other. It was a remarkable silence which reflected the almost complete lack of interest within government at that time in the application of ICTs as tools for the improvement of information resources and communication, rather than for automating production. However, the CCTA consultation paper on public sector applications of the information superhighway of 1994 (CCTA 1994a) opened the way for the development of electronic open government projects, at the centre of which was the Government Information Service (GIS) (CCTA 1995c). GIS is a service offered over the World Wide Web, carrying information supplied by around two hundred government departments, agencies and other public bodies, including local authorities. By the end of 1996, there were around 3,000 accesses an hour or 55,000 accesses a day, 75 per cent of which were from outside the UK (http://www.open.gov.uk/daily.stat/index.html). The information on the GIS is continually being extended, but typically includes contact points, ministerial speeches, press releases, consultation papers, citizen's charters, performance targets and departmental briefing papers. CCTA and the Citizen's Charter Unit have also been involved in the development of an on-line, government-wide electronic directory of public services, which can be accessed through the GIS, and also have plans for an *A–Z of Government Services*. The *A–Z* will be a database of central government services for each local authority area, and will, in effect, be a modified on-line version of the ill-fated Charterline Project, piloted in the East Midlands in 1993. The Charterline Project offered public service users a manned telephone help line which provided contact points for local public services. The project was discontinued because its development costs were deemed too high when set against anticipated demand.

Alongside the development of the GIS, CCTA is helping a growing number of government bodies to develop their own on-line information services. One of the earliest such services, established in November 1994, was the Treasury's Internet Service (http://www.hm.treasury.gov.uk). This service offers press releases and ministerial speeches, including the Budget speech, as well as the minutes of the Chancellor's monthly meetings with the Governor of the Bank of England and the reports of the Panel of Independent Forecasters. Since 1994, several departments have established on-line inquiry points, or facilities for sending e-mails, and the Department of Trade and Industry is pioneering a video network which will incorporate some of its business links (CCTA 1995b). Departmental Web sites are listed at, and can be accessed through, either the GIS or the *10 Downing Street* Web sites listed in Appendix II.

It can be seen that CCTA is actively encouraging the use of the Internet in the furtherance of the Open Government Initiative. Government policy assumes implicitly, therefore, that most of those individuals who want to use the Government's information services are, or soon will be, wired up. CCTA is, therefore, involved in the development of dedicated community access terminals, partly through the G-7 Government On-line Project and partly through its coordination of a national project aimed at developing a community access terminal (CAT) suitable for use across public services (CCTA 1995a). CATs will provide free public Internet links to the GIS and, through the GIS, to other government information services. However, while CCTA is clearly interested in exploiting the Internet as a medium for government's information services, it does not follow that it has plans for widening access to the Internet as a generic public resource, one that might also provide access to non-governmental electronic services. Indeed, apart from the *Schools On-line* project, which will place an Internet link in every secondary school (Department for Education and Employment 1995), the British Conservative government was largely silent on the question of public access to the information superhighway. Instead, there was a heavy focus on its own initiatives, which were mainly concerned with the packaging and presentation of public service information, supported by the provision by government agencies of an increasing variety of on-line customer services.

There are good reasons to question, from the citizen's perspective, whether the development of electronic public information systems, such as GIS and the local authority EPIS which we discussed in Chapter 3, is the most useful route for public authorities to take. The standard information packages currently offered on Web sites and videotext systems are aimed at the generic public information user, a concept which is increasingly out of step with the promise of the information revolution that information can be customized to fit the wide-ranging and complex needs of different individuals and groups (Dutton 1994). For this reason, electronic public information systems may well amount to a cul-de-sac off the superhighway. However, the limitations of the approach being taken in UK government may derive from deeply embedded cultural factors. That is to say, these highly controlled arrangements for disseminating information to the public can be seen as reflecting the longstanding belief that effective statecraft depends on insulating government from direct popular influence. From Burke onwards, the English constitutional tradition has valued the representative process less as an expression of popular voice, and more as a buffer between the government and people, saving government from direct exposure to popular clamour and scrutiny. Thus, the dictum ascribed to Sir Humphrey Appleby, that 'Open government is a contradiction in terms: you are either open or you have government', reveals a deep-rooted faith in the value of confidentiality over transparency in government, a faith which legitimizes government's control over the dissemination and exploitation of public information. In other words, the reliance on standard information packages to deliver open government reflects the dominant administrative style and the manner in which it has accommodated itself to democratic forms.

Nevertheless, as a strategy for managing popular access to information, this approach is coming under considerable strain. As CCTA has itself recognized, many users of on-line services 'would prefer more substantial information such as policy documents, legislation and government statistics rather than publicity material' (CCTA 1995c: 9). It is entirely unsurprising, therefore, that one of the effects of the Open Government initiative has been to concentrate minds on the commercial value of government information, a process doubtless reinforced by the rapid proliferation of commercial information services. CCTA has warned central government departments that 'the material best suited for Internet use is data which organizations are prepared to see freely produced and from which they do not expect to generate an income stream' (CCTA 1995c: 9), an injunction which extends to command papers and all material under Crown copyright. One emergent line of development, therefore, is for governments to move strongly into electronic publishing. It can thus be anticipated that British government at all levels will adjust to both the growing expectations and progressively differentiated needs of information age citizens by focusing on the supply of a more flexible range of commodified specialist information, while offering only a restricted range of basic, standard information as a freely available resource. This scenario would serve further to embed consumer democracy into British government. Not only does it strengthen the notion that citizens are to be seen primarily as consumers of government services, but, more insidiously, it reinforces the important distinction between 'high politics' and lower-status operational issues of a kind deemed appropriate to be broadcast on public information systems.

Revitalizing the political nexus?

Among the questions raised by this analysis is whether these new flows of information in the consumption nexus, between government and consumers of public services, are matched by changes in the information flowing through the political nexus, the nexus wherein governments and citizens meet. For example, are there commensurate changes in the informational support provided for elected representatives? Are new information systems and other electronic applications being designed in ways that are likely to increase councillors' and MPs' competence and independence in representing their constituents, or are elected representatives becoming even more dependent on bureaucratic sources of information and interpretation? Are the new informational and communications capabilities of the information age opening up new kinds of 'stronger' democratic interaction between representatives and those they represent, or are these capabilities merely serving to reduce elected representatives to the function of gatekeeping the restricted channels offered through the consumption nexus? As yet, at least in Britain, the answers to these questions are far from clear.

Where externally focused innovations are occurring around the use of ICTs in British government, they are largely concerned with *information* provision rather than the development of opportunities for better *communication*. To date there has been comparatively little concern with the development of new kinds of electronic, interactive political communications. For example, at the time of writing, there are no published plans to establish the British equivalent of initiatives such as the 1980s Alaska Teleconferencing Project, which permitted citizens to talk to their representatives in the state legislature 'over the wires' and enabled them to give evidence to legislative committees (Arterton 1987). Nor are many British cities seeking to emulate 'Amsterdam City Talks', with events that exploit cable TV to enable citizens to participate in or vote on local political debates (Edwards 1995). Moreover, not only is there a dearth of communications-intensive and democratically oriented innovation in the UK, but there is also a marked absence of publicly funded facilities for e-mail communication between politicians and public. In local government the use of e-mail in general is patchy (SOCITM 1995) and, where systems are being developed, in most instances they appear not to include local politicians. There are a few examples of local authorities which claim to provide e-mail facilities for councillors – Swansea City Council is a good example – but they are few and far between (Taylor *et al.* 1995a). As for setting up e-mail for MPs, no facilities are currently provided by the House of Commons for constituents to communicate electronically with their Members. Rather, e-mail is used on an *ad hoc* basis by those MPs who happen to be personal enthusiasts or who are provided with facilities under initiatives funded by political parties.

The application of ICTs to the external relations of the House of Commons has been concerned mainly with raising its public profile by making existing, published documents available on-line, rather than by creating new kinds of information resources, such as voting records of MPs or policy position papers. A public access Web site for Parliament was piloted in 1995, although at the time of writing in December 1996, it offered only basic factual information. In March 1996, the Commons Information Committee proposed that the site be gradually extended over the next few years, in order 'to encourage wider public interest in, and knowledge of, the business of the House' (House of Commons 1995–6: v). Moreover, although the committee was understandably concerned with protecting copyright and with establishing a system for licensing the commercial exploitation of parliamentary documents, it has been agreed that all published House of Commons papers should eventually be made available electronically free of charge. That is, the House has successfully defended the principle of open access to parliamentary information resources, bucking the trends of government policy. What remains unclear, however, is how far the provision of on-line information resources and, in some cases at least, improved communications is impacting on the role and power of MPs, or on public understanding, or on the political influence of the House, particularly in its relationships with government.

Towards stronger democracy in the information age?

This drawing out of examples suggests that the provision of facilities for electronic citizenship and democracy in Britain is rudimentary. Analysis of contemporary innovations in the UK, such as they are, appears to validate the work of scholars who have argued that ICTs tend to be shaped by organizations in ways that reinforce existing power structures and patterns of influence (Danziger et al. 1982). The capabilities of new technologies are being harnessed largely to serve the interests of the most powerful actors in bureaucratic and political systems. The 'reinforcement of politics' thesis makes it unsurprising that the use of ICTs tends to support the power of executive over legislature or of local authority officials over councillors, to take two examples. These purportedly 'revolutionary technologies' are employed to uphold the existing order, and do not in themselves challenge it. Second, and more fundamentally, ICTs are being used in ways which embed into democratic practice prevailing assumptions about the nature and use of information in government. Thus information is, in the main, provided, by central and local government alike, according to their own assessment of need and demand, and at a price which they choose to levy. The extent to which the citizen, *qua* citizen or consumer, can express and access his or her information wants remains limited at present and is unlikely to be extended in the future, unless there is a marked change in the prevailing assessment of the democratic value of information.

Our preferred analysis turns away, therefore, both from the seductive images of autonomous, wholly authenticated citizens capable of using the powerful resources of the information age to monitor and control their governments, and from 'big brother' images of the citizen under close political control. Instead, we are opting for a view which locates technologically supported change firmly as an expression of institutional and cultural continuity. None the less, we recognize that the power of these images is such that there continues to be widespread interest in the development of more imaginative roles for ICTs. For example, a recent book, emblazoned by the publishers with lurid images of the World Wide Web, has proffered a closely reasoned argument to show that 'Direct democracy can . . . be seen as the logical way to modernize our existing regimes. Just as with the nineteenth-century enfranchisements, one can indeed see tentative steps being taken in its direction long before it is officially accepted as the way to go' (Budge 1996: 193). In a rather different vein, a recent report has argued that 'ICTs could make a major contribution to improving opportunities for participation within a system of representative democracy and for making the representative system more democratic' (Percy-Smith 1995: 18). This view has had official currency too. For example, the Chair of the Local Government Review in England and Wales from 1993 to 1994, claimed that:

> he kept 32 of the 39 shires much as they were because to impose a new structure would be to slam the door on evolution to a new style of democratic decision-making . . . as technology takes hold and we enter the era of telecommunicating, I can see relatively small communities with citizens able to access their local government directly and to take part in decision-making.
>
> (Sir John Banham quoted in *The Times* 18 January 1995: 9)

This chapter would not, therefore, be complete without further discussion of the feasibility of moving beyond the present democratic paradigm, one which, to refer to our earlier analysis, might be best characterized as consumer democracy. In particular, we propose to address the question: 'How might ICTs contribute to a shift towards "strong democracy", particularly at the local level, and what would be the public policy implications of supporting such an aspiration?' We begin by contextualizing this question by undertaking a brief review of changing thinking about technology and democracy, a review which illustrates how debates have swung between utopian zealotry and dystopian pessimism.

Teledemocracy to the 1980s

Most of what is a vast academic literature on politics and communications technology has concerned itself with the political significance of the *mass* media, in other words with the democratic implications of broadcasting information as text, voice and image to a largely undifferentiated audience. This literature is focused on a form of communication which is, inherently, unidirectional, non-interactive, not susceptible to control by its receivers and relatively untailored to their needs. Its tendency is to broadcast 'monologic' communication: 'The sound bite and image goes forth and creates a chaotic, constantly shifting pseudocommunity momentarily brought together only by that message . . . [It] need not have class position, worksite, age, gender, geographic area, or ideological predisposition' (Fox and Miller 1995: 52). The argument here is that the absence of opportunity for reciprocity between speaker and listener atomizes individuals and affirms their value only as market research statistics. Monologic communication opens up recipients to manipulation and at the same time divorces them from a social basis for common action.

Set against these images of monological, mass broadcasting are new visions, which began to form in the late 1960s and the 1970s around the potential held out by the convergence and anticipated synergies of communications and computing technologies. Individuals could be recast as more active, selective, controlling participants in political communication. 'Listening' would become a more deliberate and discriminating activity, and the roles of speaker and listener socially reconnected. The new communications media would sustain a 'dialogogic' politics (Fox and Miller 1995). Such was the optimism that US social scientists were encouraged to construct a vision of 'mass information utilities', permitting the 'extension of interactive or conversational computer services to the general public in the natural environment of the user' (Sackman and Boehm 1972: v). Basic information resources would be accessed through touchpad phones and domestic TV screens, and more specialist, advanced services would be available in dedicated information centres. In particular, claims were being made that on-line voting and other new kinds of political communication had the potential to 'revolutionize' democracy (Sackman and Nie 1970; Sackman and Boehm 1972). For example, the MINERVA project (Multiple Input Network for Evaluating Reactions, Votes and Attitudes), which was developed in the USA at this time, aimed to provide technology that would not only establish real-time democratic discussion, but would also permit direct feedback between audiences, broadcasters, experts, candidates and political leaders (Etzioni 1972).

Interactive cable TV, supported by new kinds of telephone services, especially telephone conferencing, was assumed to be the driver of these kinds of project. Together with videotext and teletext applications delivered on home TV screens or community access terminals, these technologies, support-ing, as they did, a greater degree of interactive communication, remained the most promising media for conducting electronic politics until the early 1990s. In practice, however, none of them established a widespread, mass market in this period. In particular, the two-way uses of cable TV were never commer-cially exploited on a significant scale (Dutton 1992; Taylor Walsh 1993). Thus, despite the continuing hyperbole of futurologists (e.g. Toffler 1980; Naisbitt 1984) practical experiments remained thin on the ground, and much of the literature tended to revisit the same, few, American, cases. Among those cases were the much publicized attempts at the University of Honolulu to replicate some of the characteristics of direct democracy by creating 'electronic town meetings' (ETMs) (Becker 1981). ETMs exploited telephone polling and tele-phone touchpad voting, and were supported by the increasingly sophisticated uses of local cable TV, in order to encourage popular participation in local political and constitutional decisions. Other projects in the USA used ETMs to conduct electronic hustings or to expose public service managers to political feedback. At around the same time, the Warner-Amex Cable Communications Company, anxious to obtain municipal franchises for cabling American cities, developed the high profile QUBE system, which provided facilities for push-button, computerized televoting as an accompaniment to televised debates (Abramson et al. 1988).

While experiments like these attracted considerable interest, they confirmed many of the problems which had long been associated with teledemocracy. The first of these was that the use of what were primarily commercial entertainment services tended to trivialize political coverage and force it to compete, usually unsuccessfully, for the attention of viewers. A second problem was that the turnouts in televotes remained consistently low, at least when judged in commercial terms, and ETMs struggled to capture and maintain their audiences (Arterton 1987). Thus, the claim that the QUBE system showed that 'millions of people are already willing to "play and pay" for electronic town meetings, just as they are already paying to shoot down space invaders' (Becker 1981: 9), was somewhat undermined when Warner-Amex terminated its programming support for QUBE in 1984 in response to low audience ratings. The third problem was that of putting agenda setting, information shaping and issue resolution into the hands of those who owned and managed the technology, and who thus acquired enhanced powers to shape and manage the expression of democratic opinion. At least one commentator concluded that most of these experiments in electronic democracy using so-called 'interactive' media would be better understood as using 'interpassive' media, 'for they deny the possibility that people might initiate anything themselves' (Winner 1993: 69).

Thus, the rather sparse evidence from initiatives in the 1980s reinforced the belief that teledemocracy would extend the power of political and corporate elites to manage democracy more effectively, rather than providing a new stimulus for more active, participative democratic forms. Indeed, the assumption that ICTs would do little more than attach more sophisticated market research and opinion shaping techniques to government runs implicitly throughout the best known British academic study of new technology, electoral behaviour and political choice published at this time (McLean 1989).

Cyber-society and cyber-politics in the 1990s

Despite these analyses, which tend to reinforce the populist archetype of information age democracy, faith that ICTs could support a process of change towards stronger democratic forms has refused to wither. On the contrary, what has also emerged, once more largely from an American literature, is a vision of a fully interactive media, capable of evolving into 'citizen technology' (e.g. Laudon 1977; Winner 1993; Becker 1993). Rather than disintermediating relationships between leaders and led, as many commentators feared, citizen technology would encourage horizontal political communication among citizens, through its linking of the multiple, overlapping sub-groups that constitute the fabric of American pluralism. Indeed, according to 'conservative futurologists', such as Newt Gingrich, 'citizen technology' could transfer power from government to people, succouring a new communitarianism (Etzioni 1993; Gingrich 1994). These kinds of beliefs that a new kind of democratic practice might emerge are, in the 1990s, not only fuelling a renewed interest in electronic democracy, particularly at the local level, but also spawning a vast number of projects and studies, all designed to demonstrate the practical feasibility and democratic potential of community networks.

The basis for this renaissance of interest in electronic democracy is the so-called 'cyber-revolution'. The extraordinary growth of the Internet, together with changes in the US, UK and European telecommunications regulatory frameworks, have created a rapidly expanding market for commercial information and telecommunications services that will encourage ever widening access to the information superhighway. Not only do a growing number of people now have direct experience of computer-aided telecommunication and on-line information services in their place of work, but wiring up is becoming a feasible and affordable option in an increasing number of homes and community organizations (Taylor Walsh 1993). The potential political significance of these developments derives from cyber-networks being conceived less as media for disseminating *information* and more as media for interactive *communication*. In short, these networks seem to mark the transition from interpassive to interactive media (Winner 1993).

Why are the interactive properties of ICTs held to be so crucial? First, it is argued that they permit individuals to act as the initiators of communication as well as the increasingly selective and autonomous users of information. Thus, Sawhney has typified the Internet as 'more of a "fetch" technology than a "deliver" technology', with all the implications this has for enhancing personal control (Sawhney 1996: 302). Second, it is argued that interactive networks encourage dialogic communication because they support intuition-rich, immediate, personal connectivity (Jones 1995). It is the very matter-of-factness and conversational quality of new kinds of electronic communication that is encouraging talk of 'virtual communities', communities that will bring the *Gemeinschaft* qualities of face-to-face democracy to the post-industrial world (Rheingold 1993). Thus, the cyber-revolution is changing visions of electronic citizenship through its emphasis upon visions of authentic social interaction at the expense of images of the centralized, Orwellian state. Far from reinforcing the trends to more highly managed forms of democracy, cyber-society is seen to be potentially subversive of the power of political and techno-managerial elites, because of the capacity held within it to generate autonomous networks beyond the range of control by politicians, bureaucrats or media tycoons. It is the Internet, in particular, which has come to symbolize this upbeat interpretation of the potential for challenge to existing power structures in the information age (Weston 1994).

The political significance that is being attached to the Internet does not simply derive from the access which it affords to seemingly unlimited, global information resources, nor from the fact that its use is growing at a dramatic and unprecedented rate to the point where, by the mid-1990s, it connected over three million host computers, 44,000 computer networks and 36 million people worldwide (Castells 1996: 345). The Internet stands, too, as a powerful metaphor for 'citizen technology' because of its apparent immunity to control, and thus to political or commercial manipulation. The Internet is a 'network of networks', some of which, such as the British joint academic network (JANET) and the US scientific and academic network (NSFnet), are the result of strategic governmental or corporate action. However, the Internet as a whole is also the largely uncoordinated and unplanned consequence of the creation of myriads of small networks formed by computer buffs and affinity groups (Rheingold 1993). In this sense, the Internet represents a 'counter-cultural' approach to technological development in a world where technology has been largely owned and controlled by corporate interests (Castells 1996). The following is typical of the heroic claims which are circulating on the bulletin boards of cyber-space:

> The act of putting software into the public domain makes the technology self-propagating and prevents anybody from trying to establish exclusive ownership of the tools. It is the active participation of thousands upon thousands of communities in designing and maintaining their own spaces on the Net that will sustain its rich potential for shared experience and its characteristics as the defining institution of an Information Society.
>
> (Graham 1994: unpaged)

As one author has recently claimed, 'the Net is the world's only functioning political anarchy, but it could soon become a major tool for democracy' (Fenchurch 1994: 11).

From cyber-anarchy to strong democracy? Realizing visions of electronic citizenship

This last quotation contains a major, and highly questionable, leap of logic, one which is crucial to assessing the political significance of the cyber-revolution. For those writers who seem convinced that we may be on the verge of cyber-democracy are resting their case on two specific dimensions of cyber-society. First, they emphasize the rich opportunities which they see for new, more inclusive kinds of human connectedness. Second, they emphasize the detachment of communications networks, perhaps even their insulation, from the power structures of the state. However, of themselves, these claims hardly add up to a new kind democracy, certainly not to a new electronically mediated 'strong' democracy.

The core question in this debate is whether the progressive multiplication of on-line communities is, at bottom, compatible with the 'republican' conception of citizenship, one which emphasizes the importance of political discourse in the public domain as a medium for integration. Why should it be the case that the expansion of flexible, diverse, increasingly specialized networks of communications and information services will expand and enrich the functions of the public domain, rather than balkanize politics and deepen social cleavages by encouraging the proliferation of a fragmented complex of introverted individuals and ineffectual groups (Abramson et al. 1988)? On the contrary, it is just as plausible to argue that, far from encouraging the renewal of the public domain, the capabilities of new ICTs serve to underline the warning that the communitarian renewal of civil society could easily produce communities which are 'ghettoized, divided and stagnant, or will spawn their own forms of inequality' (Keane 1988: 15).

Seductive as the claims are for cyber-politics, it can be seen that they raise issues for public policy and constitutional practice which need to be addressed if serious attempts are to be made to revitalize democratic practice on the basis of 'citizen' technologies.

Building the slip roads to the superhighway: the role of community networks

The paradox which lies at the root of the cyber-revolution is that the fulfilment of the opportunities that it presents is directly dependent on the telecommunications infrastructure and the information services which are being laid down mainly by commercial companies. The first danger is, therefore, that access to technology will be restricted to the 'information rich', which will encourage the emergence of the thinnest form of democracy, an 'information teleocracy' rather than an 'information democracy'. There is, therefore, a widespread assumption that public and, perhaps, philanthropic action is necessary to encourage the use of electronic networks. To borrow a metaphor, 'while the "superhighways" are being constructed, there are not enough "slip-roads" being built, there are virtually no cars, let alone public transport, in mass production, and insufficient driving lessons' (Carter n.d.: 2). This view was significantly strengthened by evidence from the first free-to-users, public sponsored, interactive local communication network in the USA, the Public Electronic Network (PEN), which was launched in Santa Monica, California, in 1989 (Dutton et al. 1991; Guthrie and Dutton 1992; Rogers et al. 1994). PEN demonstrated that it was possible to design a public access network in such a way that it would actively involve people who had no access to PCs either at home or at work, and who came from social groups whose take-up of technology is typically low. Indeed, PEN developed quickly into a successful forum for promoting a radical political agenda by providing a medium for activists to mobilize the city's homeless people and other badly disadvantaged minorities.

The result of this line of thinking has been a growing interest in the notion of the 'wired' or 'digital city', a term which is applied to civic projects designed to provide near universal access to the superhighway (Dutton et al. 1987; Graham and Marvin 1996). Such projects usually involve the construction of civic or community networks that can provide a 'public transport' system around the local virtual community, and may also act as public sliproads to the global superhighway (Beamish 1995). Their civic applications often build on the Free-net® principles pioneered by the National Public Telecomputing Network (NPTN) in the late 1980s. Such was the pressure from lobbies interested in promoting civic applications of superhighways that the American federal government established the Telecommunication and Information Agency's Infrastructure Assistance Programme, which made some US$26 million available in its first year alone for the development of public 'telecomputing' applications. Since the early 1990s, the concept of the wired city has also established a following in parts of Europe.

'Wired cities' are attractive to public policy-makers because they can help to fulfil a number of what are somewhat incompatible policy aims (Graham 1991). First, as we saw above, they may help to reduce social inequalities whose information age manifestation lies in the gap between the information rich and information poor. The aim of increasing social inclusion can be fulfilled once such networks come to operate, at least in part, as 'public information utilities'. In other words, these locally provided networks aim to widen entry to the information superhighway by providing free or low-cost access to on-line communication services, including the Internet. Second, and most crucially for this discussion, 'wired cities' reflect the assumption that local electronic networks can be used to re-create and enlarge local 'public spaces' in ways that replicate many of the cultural, social and political features of face-to-face communities. Indeed, many community networks refer to their facilities as providing 'electronic town halls', 'village halls' or 'public squares'. In particular, the two hundred (or so) Free-nets operated under the aegis of the NPTN specifically emphasize civic and teledemocratic applications. For example, the original Cleveland Free-net, which now has some 250,000 subscribers, offers the use of twelve 'buildings', including a 'public square' or public discussion forum (Telnet/freenet-in-a.cwru.edu). The square includes 'the kiosk', which is an unmoderated bulletin board, 'the cafe' for electronic chat, 'the podium' for making speeches and 'the polling place' for electronic voting. The national syndication of local Free-nets under the NPTN means that users enjoy access to a wide range of special interest groups, both national and local, as well as to national news services and national teledemocratic projects, including those which flourish at election times.

It is, however, the Amsterdam Digital City (http://www.dds.nl) which best illustrates the democratic potential of wired cities. Digital City was first developed in 1994 as a collaborative venture between the Amsterdam Cultural Centre and the local computer hackers' network. In contrast to the Free-nets, which were developed by voluntary action, Amsterdam's Digital City was developed by means of a collaboration at whose centre was the municipal authority. Within months it had attracted over 15,000 participants, who accessed the system over 3,000 times a day, either by dialling up from private computers or by making use of public access terminals (Schalken and Tops 1995). Since 1994, digital cities have been established in over twenty-five Dutch cities. The digital city movement places considerable emphasis on the development and use of 'public open space'. For example, as well as providing a connection to the Internet, Amsterdam Digital City provides local community facilities, including direct links to political parties, election candidates, public officials and municipal information systems. It also offers a platform for a number of well supported public discussion groups which have been formed on a wide range of local and general issues; for example, the extension of Schiphol Airport, the relationship between technology and democracy, and racism and the multicultural society. Moreover, in response to a questionnaire mounted on the system in 1994, 41 per cent of respondents claimed that they wished to pursue political interests through Digital City. This emphasis on teledemocratic applications reflects specific contextual factors in the Netherlands, however. In particular, Dutch municipal authorities have recently become much concerned by a decline of interest in local government, exemplified by turnouts in local elections of less than 50 per cent (Depla 1995). Consequently, several municipalities have also sponsored teledemocratic initiatives; for example Amsterdam City Talks and the Delft City Panel, which seeks to develop on-line, computerized analysis of citizens' views. That is, the digital cities have been created in an environment in which public authorities were already receptive to exploring democratic applications of ICTs.

The main attraction of wiring up cities by means of public action, however, is to ensure that the city is well placed in the global information economy. In other words, wired cities are often regarded primarily as instruments of local economic development (Graham and Marvin 1996). While the rather glib assumption is often made that networks which are designed around this goal will also facilitate the political and community development of cities, there are some important practical reasons to doubt that this is so. The most obvious is that, as champions of Free-nets have often found, it does not follow that individuals and businesses who subscribe to community networks in order to gain access to national and global information and communication services are also interested in participating in civic affairs. This problem has been exacerbated by the fact that, in the UK at least, securing funding for the economic development and employment-generating functions of wired cities has proved much easier than securing funding for their social or political applications. For both these reasons, democratic applications are easily marginalized if not entirely excluded. This point may be illustrated by referring to the experience of the Manchester Host, one of the very few community networks to be established in the UK, the history of which provides a sharp contrast to that of the Dutch digital cities.

The Host was established in 1990 and has since spawned replicas in Kirklees and Wakefield, as well as a number of other similar projects, including the Nottingham EMNET. It originated from a concern about economic development in the late 1980s when, faced with the effects of massive deindustrialization, the city attempted to gain influence over the development of new telematics infrastructures that would allow it to emerge as an 'information city', a fully fledged part of the information economy. A key element in Manchester's approach was to ensure that its own engagement with the information economy would not lead to polarization between the information rich and the information poor. In consequence of this thinking, a decision was made to establish a central 'host' computer which would provide access to electronic communications and information services for small and medium-sized enterprises and voluntary bodies. The Host project was complemented by a series of local economic and community development projects, known as electronic village halls (EVHs), which aimed to develop IT skills and business ideas among specific client groups – for example, women and ethnic minorities – by means of drop-in computer centres, training courses and, more recently, cyber-cafes (Gibbs and Leach 1992).

Manchester City Council recognized from the outset that telematics could be an 'important tool for the development of local democracy, and community participation in economic development' (quoted in Gibbs and Leach 1992: 7) and EVHs have undoubtedly fulfilled important community development functions. Nevertheless, the political and democratic potential of these initiatives has remained largely unfulfilled, for reasons that reflect both their genesis and funding (Graham 1991). Host was set up with initial capital grants from central government's Urban Programme, British Telecom and the European Community's regional development fund. It was never to enjoy stable, core revenue income from the city council or elsewhere. It was assumed that the Host would pay its way by selling subscriptions to its services, while the EVHs would rely on voluntary sector funding. In practice, this pattern of funding has meant considerable reliance on European Union funds, which have been largely geared to employment and structural issues. In consequence, Host has never provided a comprehensive electronic public information service, and, although it has provided information about some voluntary services, the costs and burdens involved in sourcing and mounting public information have deterred many groups from putting up information. For similar reasons, Host has never offered the equivalent of the Free-nets' 'public square', although it supports electronic communication with certain local MPs and councillors. Despite these problems, Manchester has continued to promote itself as an 'information city', one which is also at the forefront of promoting 'wired cities' in Europe. For example, it has promoted the European Telecities Initiative, launched in April 1994, which it coordinates in conjunction with Antwerp, Barcelona, Bologna, Nice and The Hague. This initiative has since grown to include more than fifty cities and is now being promoted within the G-7 Information Society programme.

Public policy and community networks: issues for electronic democracy

As information society initiatives gather pace throughout the UK and Europe, in particular, and as the sense of a deep democratic malaise refuses to dissipate, so it might be anticipated that the building, development and exploitation of community networks might achieve more prominence. As we have seen, the UK experience of these networks has, to date, been one of low key initiatives, particularly in their exploitation of their immanent political and democratic potential. It has also been an experience characterized by the presence of many impediments to the full exploitation of these technologies. Three points, especially, emerge from the experience of community networks which should infuse and inform public policy-making in this field.

The first of these three points is that the creation of an 'electronic public domain', such as that afforded by a community network, must be positively designed into the initiative rather than simply being a taken-for-granted outcome. It is not an outcome which can be left to emerge organically, mainly because it requires to be strongly resourced. Indeed, the experience of the Manchester Host shows how easy it is for political, democratic and public service applications to be marginalized by economic development issues, a process inextricably tied in to the problems of resourcing local electronic networks, particularly once the first flush of enthusiasm, including capital funding, subsides. In contrast to the USA, however the British government shows no signs of providing financial support for community applications, particularly the revenue funding necessary to sustain the public service and teledemocratic functions of wired-cities. Moreover, UK local communities cannot draw on the financial underpinning of charitable and corporate foundations which have an interest in long-term civic initiatives to the same extent as can US projects.

Second, public policy-makers must contend with a contradiction which derives from the increasingly fragmented system of UK local governance. Local governance has encouraged the uncoupling of vertically integrated local governments, yet developing community networks at local level may only be possible through sustained collaboration between and within public, voluntary and commercial agencies. Without such collaborations it will also be difficult to mobilize an effective business case for the provision of appropriate communications infrastructure by the privatized telecommunications industry. Strategic partnerships at local level must be stimulated if these community networks are to be exploited in the UK as they are being in the USA and the Netherlands.

Third, even if such problems could be overcome, there remain to be resolved fundamental issues about the nature and conduct of democratic politics. In particular, it is important to be clear that, for all practical purposes, visions of electronically supported 'strong' government must be made compatible with the broad pattern of existing representative institutions, for it seems fanciful to believe that the information age will herald the wholesale abandonment of longstanding constitutional traditions. For this reason, there is much to be said for harnessing the power of new information and communications capabilities to support current proposals for new forms of popular deliberation and direct participation intended to strengthen, rather than supersede, representative democracy. There is, for example, an emergent view that the processes of electronic democracy could be exploited to supply 'strategic guidance' to elected politicians (Percy-Smith 1995), an approach which is consistent with the conduct of City Talks in Amsterdam. Recent proposals for establishing 'deliberative opinion polls' – that is, polling of a sample of the population who meet regularly for informed discussion – or carefully selected 'policy juries' who deliberate on specific issues suggest other methods of implementing this approach (Fishkin 1991, 1992; Adonis and

Mulgan 1994). ICTs could easily support such processes by helping to make information available to citizen panels, and by making it possible for them to 'meet' in the virtual sense.

These formal, highly structured exercises in participative democracy do not, however, offer a wholly satisfactory response to the electronic networks of the information age, whose democratic value is mainly perceived to lie in the opportunities they present for inclusive, unmediated interaction. These kinds of possibilities raise their own questions for government: for example, how an elected local authority should respond to the emergence of public open spaces on a community network, an issue which needs to be addressed if the processes of cyber-democracy are not to become entirely marginal to the public domain. On one level, this question raises strategic issues for the design of the internal business processes of a local authority, for it is difficult to envisage how the new kinds of electronically-mediated relationships which would ensue from a community network – for example, the extensive use of the network to support discussion between councillors and their constituents – could simply be bolted on to existing ways of conducting its work. At another level still, this question poses issues of deep political significance. For example, what criteria should guide elected authorities in assessing the outcomes of teledemocratic processes conducted in the public squares and the cafes of cyber-society? What procedures might be established for using wired cities to seek authoritative expressions of popular opinion and what basic levels and kinds of public information resources ought to be available to support such processes? What rules of order should govern the conduct of electronic politics? Is it appropriate, for example, that on-line public meetings should be subjected to the same regulations that have been developed to regulate the content of electronic broadcasting, and how should the proper limits of free speech be determined on community networks (Dutton 1996b)?

Conclusions

Two overarching themes emerge from this chapter. One theme has been the ebb and flow of polemical rhetoric on the subject of electronic democracy. We have seen how, over the past thirty years, utopians and dystopians have vied for the high ground of public policy on this subject as technological innovations have set out their promises, threats and expectations in front of succeeding generations. The second overarching theme of the chapter, however, has been the confrontation between the rhetoric of the information age and the *realpolitik* of contemporary government. While vivid and beguiling images of radical change have contended for popular attention, we have shown, too, that there is also a deep furrow of continuity in the practices of politics and democracy. Our core conclusions fall into three parts. First, we have seen that electronic assistance to the processes of democracy has so far done little to disturb the politics of the UK. It is far easier to discern the deployment of the new technologies in the shoring up of old practices than it is to see that they offer profound challenges to established political institutions. In the second place, however, we believe that this shoring up of old practices is itself more significant than it might at first seem. For, while we have argued that the 'reinforcement of politics' thesis provides a powerful explanation of current trends, it begs the question of what character of politics is being reinforced. What is the *status quo* into which ICTs are being so inexorably drawn?

We have argued that the prevailing understanding of democracy in British government tends to 'consumer democracy'. The notion of the 'citizen as consumer' provides the predominant contemporary paradigm for technologically supported innovation around democratic practice. In consequence, the most apposite application of ICTs is to provide government officials with additional and powerful tools for managing new forms of information-rich consumerism. As the rhetoric of consumer democracy continues to nurture the empirically driven production and distribution of public services, so the collection and exploitation of consumption data is progressively shifting to the centre of administrative practice and, as government legitimacy comes to reside largely in its responsiveness to consumer preferences, so, inevitably, the role of political intermediaries, including public representatives, will be brought further into question. We have also seen how few of the current innovations in the UK involve elected representatives, especially to the point where they might strengthen their role. One of the most important questions which falls out of this chapter, then, concerns the role of politicians within the political nexus of the information age. In an era when representative politics has become delegitimated and when, at the same time, bureaucratic and managerial capability is being increased through the application of new ICTs, there is a strong possibility that the information and communications capabilities of the information age will simply augment and speed up the decentring of representative democracy, helping to dissolve it into a highly managed form of consumer democracy.

Our third conclusion concerns the nature of information age reactions to this possibility. We have seen that the advent of the cyber-revolution is revitalizing utopian visions of a renewed democratic politics, in ways that speak directly to the reclaiming of citizenship from the consumer nexus. We have seen, too, that while consumer democracy rests primarily on the capacity of governments to exploit new ICTs to disseminate and capture more and higher-quality information about consumer preferences, so the potential exists for the use of ICTs to 'recentre' politics through renewed emphasis upon their communications capabilities. There are important reasons to be sceptical, however, about a largely technicist logic that extrapolates directly from the observation that new forms of human connectivity are now made possible through new technology, to presumptions about their impact on the complex activities of democratic politics. Even if opportunities to be wired up can be spread more or less universally throughout the population *and* existing political institutions prove receptive to the challenge that this implies – both highly questionable assumptions – this, as we began to explore briefly towards the end of this chapter, would not be the end of the story. On the contrary, the prospect of interactive media should prompt wider discussion about the nature, quality and conduct of democracy. The issues raised by the advent of these new media range from large constitutional questions about the relative merits of existing and new forms of democracy to tactical questions about the conduct of electronic participation and interaction.

The discussion in this chapter serves to underline our central thesis that the fulfilment of the heady visions of information age democracy cannot be expected to flow inexorably from the process of technological innovation; nor can electronic democracy best be considered simply as a bolt-on to existing ways of conducting government. The ways in which information age technologies are already being embedded into contemporary government not only reflect the dominant paradigms which shape institutional change and continuity, but are to be understood as tangible manifestations and validations of particular sets of assumptions about the future of a consumer-based democracy. In contrast, the information and communications capabilities of the information age are lending increased credibility to alternative democratic scenarios, of which the concept of 'strong' democracy is probably the most coherent and prominent. Realizing visions of strong democracy would, however, require a significant degree of institutional change. While technology-led policies, such as the development of wired city initiatives, could undoubtedly do much to widen access to information age opportunities, we have argued that for substantial changes in democratic practices to occur, such initiatives would have to be embedded in major constitutional, political and organizational reforms. Thus, the major question for government prompted by electronic democracy is not 'can technology save democracy?', as so many commentators have asked, but 'can existing political institutions exploit the new flows of information and the new forms of communication associated with ICTs, to help to renew their legitimacy and, thereby, to re-establish their place at the centre of democratic politics?'

5

Wiring up for the information age: telecommunications and public services

The nineteenth century's physical infrastructures of railways, canals and roads are now overshadowed by the networks of computers, cables and radio links that govern where things go, how they are paid for, and who has access to what.

(Mulgan 1991: 3)

Themes in telecommunications and electronic public services

In the opening chapter of his book on the new telecommunications, Frederick Williams provides a number of anecdotes emanating from innovations occurring around what he refers to as 'the coming of the intelligent network' (Williams 1991). Williams stresses that as the digital revolution and the distributed intelligence which accompanies it both take firmer hold, so we can expect telecommunications to be at the heart of innovations in products, services and business processes across all industrial sectors. This book has been devoted to exploring how innovation might affect public administration, including innovations which depend on new telecommunications. In this chapter we propose to focus, therefore, on the nature and implications of the dependence of innovation on telecommunications, and to relate it to important aspects of the telecommunications policy debate as it has unfolded in the UK.

Just one of Williams's anecdotes will serve to underline three frequently made assumptions, which we wish to challenge in this chapter: 'Glued to his Apollo workstation, Arun Sharma of Bangalore, India, debugs a glitch in software used for manufacturing VLSI chips. He "hands" his solution over to Tom Burke, the production supervisor, who gives feedback so Arun can finish the job. They work as a team although Arun is separated by 14,900 kilometres from Tom in Dallas, Texas' (Williams 1991: 3).

The first of these three assumptions concerns the spatial characteristics of digital networks. The image of space which is being purveyed in this quotation is one which has achieved classical proportions in the context of the literature on telecommunications. Modern digital infrastructures are usually said to have removed considerations of geography from strategic decisions about the organization of work, signalling what one American commentator has called 'the passing of remoteness' (Palfreman and Swade 1991). In a much trumpeted recent book, this transcendence of space is given further credibility when viewed not from a business strategy perspective but from the perspective of a worker choosing his or her employment location: 'If instead of going to work by driving my atoms [that is, his car] into town, I log into my office and do my work electronically, exactly where is my workplace?' (Negroponte 1995: 165).

Clearly, the 'end of geography' theme has both currency and plausibility. For example, at a recent public lecture, Martin Bangemann, the author of the European Commission's *Information Society* report, argued that 'distance loses its physical and economic significance' in the information society (Bangemann 1995: 5). There is now no technical reason, it appears, why workers in Bangalore or California, or anywhere else on the planet, cannot supply public services to Britain, including health consultancy, educational materials or bibliographic services, to take some of the more obvious examples. This very feasibility looks set to end the era when public services were characterized by geographically specific provision. The search for 'best-in-world' service production need no longer be constrained by national boundaries, or so it would seem (Quinn 1992; Dunleavy 1994). It follows that professional, public sector knowledge workers can enlarge their own choices of geographic location, confirming the emergence of a new global division of labour (Angell 1995). Thus, leading public service professionals will be able to ply their knowledge from points in physical space which are much more of their own choosing than hitherto. The information age is one in which the necessity of co-locating capital and labour has been broken.

The second assumption which has achieved the status of conventional wisdom concerns the availability of the technical capacity to support the globalization of labour processes which is being depicted in Williams's quotation. In other words, the assumption that can be, and often is, derived from such stories is that the technology of the appropriate type and quality to support these kinds of remote teleworking is, or will soon be, widely available. Again, if we translate this assumption into the public services arena, we see how it strengthens the notion of a globalized future. Indeed, if we assume that there will be a ubiquitous, high quality telecommunications infrastructure, then the kinds of strategic and personal decisions which we are discussing become infinitely more possible than if that infrastructure is of variable quality and less than ubiquitous. For example, offering professional medical services to Britain from the United States will be dependent on the availability of an infrastructure which will support the transmission of high-quality video images as well as text and voice. That is, it will be dependent on a telecommunications infrastructure with consistently high bandwidth.

In practice, this higher bandwidth telecommunication is far from universally available (Davies 1994; Taylor and Williams 1995; Negroponte 1995). Moreover, the significance of its uneven provision goes far beyond technological debates, for, in effect, it reverses the logic of the 'end of geography'. If broader bandwidth is necessary for the successful electronic production of a particular public service, but is not universally available, then, in contrast to the commonly held view, spatial factors, the geographical distribution of people and organizations within the global economy of the information age, acquire stronger, rather than weaker, significance. This geographical imperative is being strongly recognized in the urgency with which so many industrial countries are entering the race to become information economies. However, as we develop our arguments below, we wish to go further even than this important point, for the geography imposed by the telecommunications infrastructures of the information age becomes critical not only for the production, but also for the consumption, of public services. Thus, this chapter will also challenge a third assumption that is too often derived from this debate. This is the assumption that it is mainly the economic development implications of telecommunications infrastructures that are important for public authorities, an assumption that derives from a perspective which emphasizes the new geography of production rather than the new geography of consumption.

The consumption of public services has, historically, stood largely free from geographical constraints, in the sense that public services have been provided according to a principle of equity which is, supposedly, blind to spatial considerations, including those deriving from differential costs of service delivery. In the present era, however, an era which, as we have seen, is more and more characterized by electronic service production and delivery, access to public services may well become increasingly constrained by the quality of telecommunications infrastructures. It follows that the normative basis of public service provision will become influenced to a greater extent than hitherto by the normative content of contemporary telecommunications policy. To touch upon an example which we will develop at length below, changing interpretations by telecommunications providers of the policy norm of 'universal service' will inevitably influence the interpretation by public service organizations of their own universalist norms. The closely interrelated assumptions of the information economy, that advanced telecommunications both transcend space and are universally available, underpin the relevance to public administration of the sharply contrasting policy stances which currently shape the public policy of telecommunications in different administrations. We will see that there is a strongly held view, which has emerged in public policy forums in the USA and the European Union, for example, that much of the telecommunications infrastructure necessary for the successful delivery of electronic public services and citizenship should be conceived as a critical public resource, though not necessarily one provided by public authorities. In contrast, UK public policy-makers have been much more relaxed, preferring to rely on commercially based investments by the telecommunications operators in a regulatory regime which, to date, has applied only the most modest pressure in respect of universal service provision. Public authorities are inevitably caught up in this issue because they are large-scale users of telecommunications. Not only are their activities necessarily shaped and constrained by the available infrastructure, but these activities also form a substantial part of the potential market that could stimulate and influence infrastructure investment, thereby providing an important potential point of take-off for the information superhighway.

Public authorities use telecommunications in varied ways and thus require different levels of sophistication in their electronic networks. They lease private networks from the telecommunications operators for much of their internal administrative activity, though once public service providers seek to provide equal access to their consumers throughout their territories then those private circuits will prove insufficient unless they are extended at enormous cost. That is, existing private circuits reflect administrative requirements for moving data and information within particular authorities. These circuits are made up of variable transmission capabilities, so that high bandwidth capability will typically be installed for major traffic routes, whereas low-speed analogue lines will remain in use where data flows have historically been modest. While these private lines might extend widely across a particular territory, it is unlikely that they will be installed into all the local communities that lie within a particular administrative jurisdiction. It follows that if public authorities are to reach all consumers and citizens with electronic information and communications services, then the quality of the public telecommunications infrastructure is of pre-eminent importance.

Telecommunications policy is as central to the future of public services as it is to economic development. Its implications are as important for the polity as they are for the economy, yet this is a simple point to which the relevant literatures scarcely refer. Accordingly, we move on in the next section of this chapter to examine the origins of current telecommunications policy in the UK. We will then proceed to offer a critique of that policy, particularly in the light of the apparent desire in contemporary governance for innovations in both electronic services and electronic citizenship.

Telecommunications: a public utility with a difference

Telecommunications provides the supreme example of a network technology industry (Foreman-Peck and Millward 1994). Many of the public utility companies fall into this general category, but no other in quite such a complete way as telecommunications. In order for public utilities to provide service, their gas, electricity, rail and telecommunications networks must be in place: the pipes, tracks and wires must be laid before services can be provided to customers. In meeting the needs of large industrial customers, some parts of these physical, service-conveying infrastructures can be private, laid down to meet a specific need and not shared with any other customer. In the case of the millions of domestic customers which these industries must reach if they are fully to meet both statutory obligations and commercial imperatives, the physical network is wholly public, save, in the case of those industries which supply services to the home, for the last short connection. While many networked organizations are public utilities, as this term is conventionally understood, many of them are not. Indeed, some private businesses possess many of the characteristics of networked organizations, the most obvious examples coming from the financial services sector, where clearing banks and building societies have developed elaborate branch networks to reach their customers.

There is, then, a supply side logic at work in all networked industries, for the network is essentially one for distributing a product or service. In these industries, the network is the *sine qua non* of service provision. However, telecommunications can be distinguished from other networked industries in that the logic of networking also applies to the demand side of the consumption nexus. It is for this reason that we describe it as the supreme example of a networked industry. Its demand side logic resides in the maximization of the geographical spread of the basic network in the mutual interests of all its consumers. Whereas in other public utility settings the consumer's interest lies almost wholly in his or her own consumption of a service, in telecommunications each consumer has an equally strong interest in consumption by others. The greater the number of people that are connected to a telecommunications network, the better it is, in broad terms, for each user. The more expansive the customer base becomes, the more the value of being connected is enhanced. Thus, to take a striking example, in the early days of fax machines, 'first mover' consumers bought into a technology whose usefulness lay in its support of business relationships which were possible only with parties who had also invested in the technology. The pay-off from investing in a fax machine was relatively slight in those first years, therefore. Now that the fax machine is to be found in over 90 per cent of business organizations, the pay-off is clear.

This distinctive demand side logic of telecommunications has raised, and continues to raise, powerful questions about how best to realize the positive externalities deriving from optimized provision and consumption. It is a logic which is made all the more acute by the technical revolution which has surrounded, if not engulfed, telecommunications from the 1970s onwards. As we saw in Chapter 1, telecommunications has moved on from the era of POTS to PANS. Both the public switched network and private telecommunications networks can now, in principle, convey fax, text, graphics and moving images, in addition to voice services. The same demand side logic applies potentially to these service enhancements, with each customer gaining, as more and more people and businesses are able to use them. The answers to two questions, in particular, are crucial to the realization of these potential gains. First, what is the appropriate organizational form for the optimal provision of telecommunications? Second, what kind of intervention should occur in the relationship between provider and consumer, if any, if optimal uptake is to occur? It is to these questions that we now turn as we seek to unravel the significance of telecommunications for contemporary governance. In so doing, we turn to telecommunications policy in the UK, because the UK provides what is widely acknowledged as the strongest example in the world of a liberalized approach to telecommunications provision. UK telecommunications policy therefore brings out many of the issues and dilemmas which have accompanied this liberalized policy stance. Moreover, it will help us to examine the links between telecommunications policy and the core themes of this book, related as they are to the conduct and reform of government itself.

Organizing for telecommunications provision

To 1981

The issue of what is the best organizational form for providing telecommunications was debated throughout its seventy-year period in public ownership, as indeed it was before then. When in 1911 the Post Office acquired the assets of the National Telephone Company, it did so after a widespread debate about how best to develop the public interest aspects of providing plain old telephony. Further reports and studies in the 1920s and 1930s, most notably the Bridgeman Report on the Post Office in 1932, led to the establishment of a decentralized structure for the Post Office, with a high degree of regional operational freedom. By the 1960s, the movement to remove the Post Office altogether from the departmental structure of government gathered momentum and, in 1969, the Post Office became a public corporation once more, providing a higher degree of operational independence, though this time for the corporation as a whole rather than for its geographical components. In 1977 the Post Office Review Committee (Carter Report 1977) recommended the organizational separation of posts and telecommunications, a separation implemented by the Conservative government in 1981.

Telecommunications had, therefore, remained since 1911 in the hands of a government-owned monopoly provider, albeit one which had been organizationally decentralized since the 1930s. Internally the organization had come to be dominated by its regional structure, with ten topocratic 'barons' running the regions, each protecting and promoting its patch of the UK (Taylor and Williams 1988). Surrounding the monopoly supplier was a series of stakeholder relationships, with the sponsoring government department, with trade unions, with equipment suppliers and with the consumers' organization and other government departments. This was a set of relationships which both sustained its monopoly powers and maintained 'domain consensus', an unchallenged equilibrium of stakeholder interests (Arthur Andersen 1994). The Post Office commanded this stakeholder network with a combination of financial and knowledge resources (Pitt 1980; Cawson et al. 1990; Mansell 1993; Davies 1994), a command which the Conservative government set out to break from 1981 onwards, when it attempted to establish a consumer-driven industry to replace one which had been so completely dominated by a network of producer interests.

From 1981

The belief that telecommunications was a 'natural monopoly', that production by one organization is more efficient than production by several (Vickers and Yarrow 1985), was ebbing away by the early 1980s. Emerging in its place was a new industrial *Zeitgeist*, from which a view came to be articulated that liberalized markets were the key both to efficient production and consumer responsiveness. Although, ultimately, the process of change was complex and muddled (Newman 1986; Taylor and Williams 1988), by 1984 a new Telecommunications Act had replaced the one which in 1981 had established telecommunications as a public corporation. The 1984 Act signalled the advent of an era of regulated duopoly. Mercury Communications Limited (MCL) was to be licensed as British Telecommunications' main network competitor; the Office of Telecommunications (OFTEL) was established as the regulatory body; and shares in the newly privatized company were offered for sale, producing a dramatic oversubscription.

There have been two distinctive periods of organizational change in telecommunications since 1984. Broadly, the first period, to 1991, was one which consolidated the duopoly. The main regulatory device for managing the onset of network competition was the price cap on most of BT's prices, which began at Retail Price Index (RPI) minus 3.5 per cent in 1985 and at the time of writing (in 1996) was RPI minus 7.5 per cent. In addition, a further duopoly, that in mobile telephony, was consolidated in this period through the creation of two companies, *Cellnet* and *Vodaphone*. A further significant regulatory decision during this period was to permit the resale of telecommunications over capacity by other commercial companies, which, in principle, enabled a further, though small, element of competition to occur.

The second period, from 1991, has been one to which the Conservative government attached the watchwords 'competition and choice' (Department of Trade and Industry 1991). In this period, many more players entered the UK market as further liberalization occurred. Nine cable companies are now offering telephony services, each in its own franchise areas, and there are several other nationally oriented licensed operators, including *AT&T*, *Energis* (a subsidiary of the National Grid) and *Ionica* (Monopolies and Mergers Commission 1995).

The upshot of all this change is that a new policy paradigm for telecommunications has emerged in the UK. This paradigm has been forged from ideas which hold markets to be economically superior to hierarchies, and which hold to the desirability of independent regulation of services, rather than of provision or sponsorship by government. It is not surprising that in this period BT undertook a number of deep restructurings of its business, first, as it went through what has been termed its 'identity crisis' and second as it went through its 'refocusing' stage (Arthur Anderson 1994). The most significant outcome of this organizational redesign has been the company's withdrawal from the geographical principle of organization. The regional structure of the company was abandoned in the early 1980s, and initially replaced by one based on smaller autonomous districts. By 1990, however, a radical organizational departure had occurred as BT created a new divisional structure which was focused primarily on customer groups. Thus, an organizational regime which for almost sixty years had been guided by the principle of geography had been supplanted by one designed to serve BT's customer bases, regardless of the latters' location.

Within this period, too, the stakeholder environment for telecommunications has shifted markedly. The old network of producer stakeholders has been broken up. The 'ring' of equipment suppliers has been replaced by a wholly liberalized equipment market. OFTEL has replaced the official User Body as the watchdog of consumers, as well as taking ownership and oversight of the stimulation of competition. The trade unions have lost much of their ability to influence the industry. The primary locus of Whitehall interest has moved emphatically to the Department of Trade and Industry.

Intervening to secure optimal outcomes in telecommunications

We discussed above the unique demand side logic in telecommunications which brings with it a shared interest among consumers in the expansion and enhancement of the telecommunications network. This logic presents us with what might be described as a core theme in debates about the public interest aspects of telecommunications. In so far as the public interest is synonymous with the communications interests of consumers, then, as we have shown, the realization of the public interest in telecommunications requires full access by all consumers to the network. This argument, in turn, leads on to two sets of questions. First, what level of access is in keeping with the realization of the public interest? Now that telecommunications networks have the potential to provide access to a range of services, does the public interest lie in universal access to all, or to only some, of those services? Second is the question of how to meet the costs of providing comprehensive access. This question draws into the discussion the interests of the providers of telecommunications infrastructure and services. What degree of comprehensiveness is implied by the public interest, so far as the provision of telecommunications is concerned? In a rapidly changing technological environment, such as that which characterizes telecommunications, providers of service undoubtedly have difficult investment choices to make. Thus, investment may be predicated on the principle of equal and universal access, or it may be predicated on a business logic which will benefit some groups of consumers more than others. In the telecommunications industry, these questions have been crystallized in the concept of 'universal service', a concept which, as we shall see below, is not susceptible to easy or agreed definitions, either practically or normatively. The two periods which we identified above, first to 1981 and then from 1981 to the present time, are useful for analysing the history of this slippery concept as far as telecommunications provision in the UK is concerned.

Universal service in telecommunications

To 1981

The concept of 'universal service' in telecommunications began to take shape and meaning in the early years of the twentieth century. The first recorded use of the concept is by Theodore Vail, the President of the American giant *AT&T*, in the company's annual report of 1907, where Vail used the term to capture the perceived need at the time to integrate the competing telecommunications infrastructures of the USA. At this time, the pressing need which gave rise to this concept, and through which the concept was interpreted, was that customers should be able to reach each other without having to be concerned with the self-serving behaviour of competing suppliers. In the UK the integration of the telephone system into the Post Office from 1911 made manifest the UK equivalent of this American concern. Thus, in these early days there was no strong presumption embedded in the concept of universal service in favour of ubiquity of telephony. Rather the concern was that telephony should be as simple as possible to use, that it should not be impeded by the presence of competing infrastructures (Mueller 1993).

The clear implication in this reasoning was that telecommunications should be treated as a natural monopoly, to be provided from a single and unified source, a criterion which the Bell System in the United States and the Post Office in the UK were both designed to meet. Common standards, which permitted full inter-operability among and between customers, were to be secured through monopoly provision. The secondary concern, that of gathering the economic and social advantages of an enlarged customer base, was also to be accommodated in the monopoly. However, as the monopoly settled into place, and as the diffusion of telephony gathered pace, so the interpretation of universal service shifted towards a geographical concept, one that embraced the principle of evenness in regional provision and access to basic telephony at a common price. As we have seen, these shifts in emphasis found organizational expression in the UK through the introduction of a strong regional structure in the Post Office from the mid-1930s to the 1980s, a structure dedicated to ensuring that all regions of the country were taken into account in investment decisions.

Essentially, both these interpretations of universal service were 'supply-led' (Taylor and Williams 1988, 1991b). That is to say, they were interpretations of the concept which were, primarily, expressions of the interests of the telecommunications provider, a consequence of perceiving those interests to be identical with the public interest. Although, latterly, there was concern to provide for access by subscribers on equal financial terms, there was no strong argument during this period for the ubiquity of telecommunications within the nation state. To express this position at its strongest, these interpretations of universal service never implied that the core objective of telecommunications provision was to connect everyone to the network as a basic means of participating in society. Rather, they were interpretations which assumed growth in the number of 'subscribers' (as customers were termed in this period), but which assumed that growth should be carefully controlled. Thus, the objective of allowing more subscribers on to the network was balanced against the costs of the capital investments which were necessary to support it. The primary solution to this dilemma was to suppress demand through imposing queuing by means of a waiting list. Indeed, in the latter part of the period, the 1970s, the waiting list for subscription to the telecommunications network was at times well in excess of half a million people.

In 1922, a House of Commons Select Committee had argued that there was an overriding attitude in the Post Office that the public was made for the Post Office, and not the Post Office for the public (House of Commons 1921–2). To achieve the status of 'subscriber' to the telephone network was something of a privilege and certainly far from a right. The consequences of this kind of thinking were manifest for most of the period to 1981, with little apparent zeal within the telecommunications provider for working with the 'demand side logic' of which we wrote above. If the public interest lay in mass consumption of telephony then that public interest was far from realized throughout the first three quarters of the twentieth century. In 1972, the proportion of households in the UK with a telephone was 42 per cent. One decade later, following the gradual rethinking of the telecommunications business, a rethinking which included a stronger customer focus, that figure had climbed dramatically, to 76 per cent (OFTEL 1994a).

From 1981

From the point of the separation of telecommunications from postal services in 1981, and through into the period of liberalization, privatization and competition which followed, British Telecommunications (later BT) continued a process of strategic business development which had begun to take root in the later part of the 1970s. In part, this process was to result in a pulling away from the geographical basis for the provision of telecommunications. In part, too, this process gave rise to a new strategy for managing the pent up demand for subscription. Rather than use demand compression techniques such as the waiting list, BT now gave further impetus to a process of targeted investment, a process which was to demolish the waiting list and give rise to a huge growth in the numbers of residential customers linked to the network. The old administrative principle of 'first come, first served', a principle which produced the waiting list as a manifestation of seemingly equitable provision, was now replaced by a business principle which meant that BT's investment decisions fell under the influence of a new way of thinking, one which stressed the need for traffic and revenue growth and therefore an investment strategy which would maximize opportunities for attaching new business to the network.

This new commitment to business development in BT is revealed by the 20 per cent increase in the number of households with a telephone which occurred during the 1980s alone (OFTEL 1994a). Although, when measured on an international scale, the current rate of 'household penetration' of telephony in the UK is modest, at around 91 per cent – especially when compared to Sweden's 121 per cent, for example (OECD 1995) – it has, none the less, grown appreciably. Of the 21.5 million residential connections in the UK in 1995, BT was responsible for 20.6 million, with the geographical patchwork of cable providers accounting for almost all the rest, a total of around 4 per cent (Monopolies and Mergers Commission 1995). In the residential market for telephony, BT has remained, therefore, the *de facto* monopolist in much of the country, despite twelve years of competition.

Universal service: the current debate

During the period from 1981 the policy norm of universal service has undergone a process of significant modification, and in so doing has, increasingly, become the focus for public debate. As competition and the contestability in telecommunications markets developed throughout the 1980s and 1990s, so BT came to skew its network investment away from the rough geographical equality which appertained until that time, towards clear, spatially differentiated provision around identified centres of demand. Thus, in the City of London, for example, where telecommunications business is highly lucrative and where, as a consequence, competition is fierce, BT has invested strongly in optical fibre networks and enhanced switching capabilities. In other parts of the UK, where BT remains in effect the monopoly provider but where business revenues are modest, investment beyond the trunk network has been comparatively weak. Thus the predominant view within the company has been that, as competition has developed and telecommunications networks have acquired greater degrees of technical and service-carrying sophistication, so a reinterpretation of universal service provision should occur. In effect, plain old telephony, or the provision of a basic telephone service, as the regulator describes it, should continue to be provided on a universal basis as laid down in BT's operating licence, but all other services should be demand-led; that is, they should be provided only on a fully commercial basis. In effect this means that there will be parts of many governmental jurisdictions at subnational level for which telecommunications services, beyond simple telephony, will not be available.

This shift in the interpretation of universal service has taken place under the twin pressures of infrastructure and service competition, on the one hand, and technical change, on the other, and has brought two major debates in its train. First, there has been fierce debate about the appropriate compensation that is due to the historic provider, BT, in return for providing a geographically comprehensive telecommunications network, including a universal service in basic telephony. This debate has three major strands. First, there is a concern over 'access deficit charges'. BT's network provides the basic network into which all other network service providers must connect if they are to supply a geographically full service. While BT charges for interconnection on a call-by-call basis, this does not compensate the company for the costs associated with the maintenance of its network. The principle of access deficit charges has been invoked to provide compensation to BT for these costs (OFTEL 1995a). Second, there is a concern with identifying the real financial costs of universal service. OFTEL has estimated that the gross cost to BT of providing universal service is in the region of £60–£90 million a year, but that the net cost, after appropriate deductions for the benefits which BT gains from this provision, is between zero and £40 million, depending upon how benefits are calculated (OFTEL 1995b). Third, there is concern that these costs of universal service should be met from a fund to which each telecommunications operator, save perhaps for the very smallest, would contribute. Such a fund is likely to be made up from contributions which are in proportion to revenues from basic services, a fund to be administered by a neutral funding body (OFTEL 1995b).

The second major debate provoked by this shifting stance towards universal service has centred on the concept of 'universal service' itself. In its first major discussion paper on the subject in 1994, OFTEL rehearsed both the case for the universal service obligation which was then applied to BT and the question as to the level of service to which the contemporary universal service obligation (USO) should apply (OFTEL 1994a). OFTEL argued that the governing principles of the present USO were that:

- access to basic telephony should be available regardless of location;
- access to basic telephony should be affordable;
- access to basic telephony should be sensitive to those with special needs;
- access to free public emergency call services should be available;
- access to public call boxes should be available.

This report argued, however, that the concept of universal service should be addressed flexibly through time, as technological change, and changes in lifestyles and consumption patterns, create conditions where higher levels of service – that is, those levels requiring higher bandwidth than basic telephony – might well come inside the operational definition of universal service. Furthermore, OFTEL envisaged an intermediate level of operational sophistication emerging in the near future in the definition of universal service. That is, OFTEL envisaged adding to the notion of basic telephony some supplementary services such as itemized billing and call forwarding. Subsequently the regulator has developed the debate on universal service further by giving support to the notion that there should be a higher-order universal service definition applied specifically within the educational sector (OFTEL 1995b). In this respect, OFTEL has recognized the strength of political debate which had emerged around the need to improve educational provision, as well as recognizing the potential strength of multimedia applications in that provision (e.g. Labour Party 1995; DFEE 1995). Thus the view taking hold within the UK regulatory body is that the public service obligation of universal service provision might best be enhanced through provision of telecommunications to a higher technical standard than is the norm, but only to specified users such as educational establishments.

The power of OFTEL's emergent position lies in the way it is giving a new recognition to public services as potential drivers of higher-order universal service in telecommunications. As governments seek to reinvent themselves by exploiting the new capabilities associated with information and communications technologies, so, logic suggests, they may well find themselves in the vanguard of the information age. That is, they may find themselves collectively establishing and pushing forward the case for the enhanced telecommunications infrastructures from which the much vaunted political, social and economic benefits of the information age will flow. It is an unavoidable fact that most public services have a spatial dimension: they must be delivered throughout a specific geographical area. Public services such as education have inescapable obligations to reach their consumers, and eligible individuals are legally obliged to consume the service or to provide themselves with some lawful alternative. The principle of universality of provision has always been an important element, therefore, both in the operational obligations of public service organizations and in consumer expectations.

The problem that will confront public services in the information age is that while the concept of 'universal service' has been and remains the core policy norm in telecommunications provision, its meaning is not agreed. In its earliest form it was associated with Vail's dictum 'one policy, one system and universal service', as we have seen, but there was no sense here that universal service meant equal and widespread access. In the UK, from the 1980s onwards, the consumption side of Vail's dictum has been sustained by means of interconnection agreements between the telecommunications operators, and the promotion by governments of the principle of open network access. The production side aspects of Vail's concept of universal service have been fundamentally challenged, however, through the demolition of natural monopoly arguments and the erection of competition and choice as a policy paradigm designed to bring greatest efficiency and effectiveness in telecommunications provision. Technical change has combined with these profound shifts in the policy paradigm to move the industry from a monopolistic public utility, providing little more than basic telephony, to an immensely powerful and competitive private sector industrial complex whose products and services are central to the emergent information age. Within that new setting, BT remains the dominant player, a player that is, moreover, taking on an increasingly global business strategy, and for which commercial considerations have become central. While the public utility legacy of telecommunications has ensured that universal service obligations remain in place, BT, as the dominant telecommunications operator, has sought compensation for its inherited obligations, whose purported commercial advantages remain opaque at best.

The core regulatory issue is how to clarify, maintain and extend the public interest aspects of telecommunications in this incipiently competitive market. This is a concern which, of course, gathers new importance as the rhetoric of high public policy, such as that emanating from the G-7 Ministerial Conference, recasts proleptic visions of the information society and the information age. For, pushing up against the pragmatic behaviour of regulatory bodies such as OFTEL, as they balance the public service and market dimensions of telecommunications, is a wave of utopian or quasi-utopian thinking which stresses the heady potential for individuals, economies and democracies that full access to the information age might bring. As this wave of utopianism rises higher, it brings forward with it the question of whether practical, operational interpretations of universal service should fall into line with its higher order values. At the same time, however, it challenges the likely social inequalities to which a pragmatically oriented market in telecommunications seems likely to contribute.

As a utopian concept, universal service suggests idealistic visions wherein citizens have access to information age services regardless of geographic location, income, gender, disability or ethnicity. In such a utopia, advanced telecommunications provision becomes a basic right of citizenship, one which is a necessary condition for the realization of social and political rights. It follows, therefore, that a much enhanced definition of universal service is as a *sine qua non* of social inclusion, helping to prevent the emergence of an underclass of 'information poor' (Doctor 1994; Gans 1994; Sawhney 1994). Thus, within this line of thinking, telecommunications policy acquires a strong affinity to social policy. 'Communication policy must be central to any meaningful deliberations about the future of the modern democratic welfare state' (Calabrese and Borchert 1996: 249).

The re-emergence of the information society: in the age of the superhighway

As we saw in Chapter 1, the rhetoric of the information society has never been stronger than it is in the 1990s, but the intoxicating images associated with the beneficial 'impact' of ICTs on society first began to influence politicians in the 1970s. For example, on entering government in 1979, the late Sir Keith Joseph, then Secretary of State for Industry, included James Martin's seminal book *The Wired Society* (1978) on the list of twelve key texts which he instructed his senior civil servants to read, alongside, for example, Adam Smith's *Wealth of Nations* and Hayek's *The Road to Serfdom*. Martin's book offered the incoming government beguiling images of a better society, one to which enhanced telecommunications was central. At about the same time the findings of the French research of Nora and Minc (1980) were being translated into English, giving further sustenance to technology-inspired visions of the coming information age.

Many of these visions remain highly influential in the 1990s, as the powerful industries of computing, telecommunications, broadcast entertainment and publishing converged to form a new industrial complex whose common interest lies in the development, and promotion by governments, both of their infrastructures and of the services which run upon them. In the past, powerful business interests nurtured and sustained a 'public interest' around the building of road, rail and airways infrastructures, and now information age industries are promoting a new public interest around the notion of a step change in communications capabilities which is advanced under the banner of the 'information superhighway'. This book has shown why, for governments too, the superhighway seems to hold immense promise. As governments seek to scale down their activities and budgets while holding out the promise of a consumer-oriented transformation of public services, so the information and communications technologies of the information age seem to offer a plausible and dynamic means to realize both objectives. It follows that the construction of superhighways takes on a direct significance for governments, in that it offers opportunities for innovations in the ways they organize themselves and deliver their services, as well as opportunities for enhancing the means of political communication and democratic expression. For this reason, the changing definitions of 'universal service' are of supreme importance for information age governance, featuring prominently in contemporary high-level policy debates about the superhighway.

The USA: towards a National Information Infrastructure

Undoubtedly, what has magnified these visions of the information society is their championing from the top of the US administration, with the National Information Infrastructure (NII) initiative being strongly promoted from the Clinton/Gore White House. As the concept of the NII took shape in the late 1980s and early 1990s so improvements in public services became central to it. Two quotations from Clinton's future Vice President bring out the intensity of the visions which had formed around US government at this time:

> Most important we need a commitment to build the highspeed data highways. Their absence constitutes the largest single barrier to realising the potential of the information age. Present policy, which is based on copper wire networks, is hindering deployment of the new fiber technology. There is a policy gridlock – some say a 'graphic jam' – because the interests that built and still run our existing infrastructure resist changes that might intensify competition . . .
> Hundreds of schools are linked by low-speed (1.2–2.4 kbps) networks . . . Networks thousands or even millions of times faster would offer greater benefits. Today a child can go to a library and use a computer to get the title of a book. A faster network would bring the book to the child at home, pictures and all.
>
> (Gore 1991: 100, 110)

These quotations provide a sense both of the optimistic thinking that has surrounded the NII and of the infrastructural issues that have been perceived to be the barrier to its realization. For the American government there are essentially two related issues which are to be confronted if progress is to be made. The first of these is that 'for electronic service delivery to occur on a large scale, all geographic areas of the nation must have access to advanced digital telecommunications services' (US Congress Office of Technology Assessment 1993: 14). The second and related issue is that the definition of universal service be revisited 'to reflect advancing telecommunications technologies', at least in so far as telephony is concerned (p. 15). This emphasis in NII thinking upon the implementation of an extended version of universal service is entirely in keeping with our earlier discussion of the concept, and with the quotation above from the US Vice President.

The NII project appears to be moving forward strongly. Recent steps include decisions by the Office of Management and Budget to sell information at the cost of dissemination rather than of acquisition and the development of a computerized index to all government information. Seven key areas have been identified for public policy initiatives in respect of the NII, including: business to business communications; the delivery of health care, educational and life-long learning opportunities; speeding the delivery of government services and sustaining the role of libraries as providers of information and thereby as agents of democracy (Dutton *et al.* 1996).

The European Union: towards the information society

Many similar themes to those which have developed in the USA run through policy documents of the European Union. Thus, as we have seen throughout this book, the EU has also attached enormous significance to the urgent realization of the potential economic and social gains associated with the information society (European Commission 1994a, b, c). It has brought forward a series of proposals for action, which are designed to develop a 'common vision' among member states, business and other stakeholders across Europe of 'the way to the Information Society'. Like the Americans, the EU has assumed that the information superhighway must be constructed primarily through private investment and it, too, has sought to ensure that the telecommunications playing field is as level and open as possible. Accordingly, it has secured agreement to the liberalization of the telecommunications industry throughout Europe (European Commission 1994a); it has devoted considerable effort to the development of common, unambiguous, telecommunications standards; and it has strongly promoted the principle of interoperability of systems.

Like the US government, the EU has also come to see the development of a ubiquitous broadband network as the 'backbone of the Information Society' (Bangemann 1994: 21). Indeed, Bangemann's High Level Group of Experts defined access to e-mail, electronic file transfer and multimedia applications as 'basic services' in the information society. To a large extent, the EU is relying on the assumption that the information society will create its own demand, that 'the market will drive' (Bangemann 1994: 8). The prime task of governments is to encourage competition and to develop an appropriate regulatory framework, one that includes the principle that *all* licensed operators should share in the cost of universal service obligations. However, it also recognizes that broadband applications require 'critical mass', in two senses of the word. First, each application needs a critical mass of users and, second, the information society needs a critical mass of applications which will encourage further investment, thus creating a 'virtuous circle of supply and demand' (Bangemann 1994: 23). The EU has, therefore, also attempted to stimulate the rapid development of critical mass, in three closely related ways. First, it is attempting to build on a significant degree of technical research and development which it has financed through the Third and Fourth Framework Programmes. Second, it is using its own structural funds to promote ten trans-European application projects aimed at stimulating demand, demonstrating benefits and providing test beds for suppliers. These application projects include several with obvious relevance to government – for example the Trans-European Public Administration Network, the electronic public procure-ment project and the Telecities Project we have already mentioned in earlier chapters – as well as a distance learning project, a healthcare network and a universities research network (Bangemann 1994). Third, all these activities are designed to raise awareness of, and therefore demand for, the economic and social benefits of the superhighway. Thus, we can see that, in ways that are very similar to US thinking, the EU is attempting to promote the information society through policies and funding which are designed as much to build business confidence in the information age as they are to put in place the necessary regulatory framework.

The UK: developing superhighways

The UK government's response to the implementation of the information society and the superhighway has been somewhat different in character and tone from those of the USA and the EU. The main government publications on the subject (CCTA 1994a; Department of Trade and Industry 1994) are both couched in optimistic tones about the delivery of the purported advant-ages of the superhighway because of 'the advanced nature of [the UK's] tele-communications infrastructure and the high level of investment being undertaken by multiple operators to improve provision' (CCTA 1994a: 2), and because, 'By the end of the decade, the cable communications companies alone will have invested £10 billion in new networks. BT, Mercury and the other telecommunications operators are likely to have matched that investment' (Department of Trade and Industry 1994: 1).

Both these documents refer not to a single national information in-frastructure or superhighway but to multiple superhighways. UK telecom-munications policy, which since 1991 has fallen under the rubric of 'competition and choice', is a policy which is, according to government, producing multiple high-capacity telecommunications networks from which information age applications can be fully exploited. The view in UK government has been that: 'efficient infrastructure is best developed by competing providers, rather than by promoting a single all-purpose switched two-way infrastructure . . . A competitive environment tends to reduce the gap between the development and deployment of new technologies, products and services, thereby rapidly increasing the products and services available to customers' (Department of Trade and Industry 1994: 4–5).

In contrast to the US government and European Commission, the UK Conservative government did not identify the need to move forward strongly with infrastructure investment. Both the US government and the EU are clear on the need for the development of high capacity broadband networks and for the need to move forward on the concept of universal service in telecommunications. The Conservative government showed less concern on both fronts, preferring instead to let the existing telecommunications policy work its way out and deliver the advantages which it is deemed regulated market competition can assure. The essence of the UK government's approach was that the investment strategies of the growing number of telecommunications providers in the UK, together with regulatory oversight and appropriate measures, were creating the British superhighways. The role which government saw for itself was to encourage public and private sector applications on the superhighways and to improve its own internal coordination between departments with special responsibilities in this field. Thus the DTI, with its responsibility for telecommunications regulation, the Office of Public Service, charged, as it is, with improving the quality of public service and promoting open government, and the Department of National Heritage, with its responsibilities for broadcasting, should be brought together to take on a more coordinated approach to superhighway provision and exploitation (CCTA 1994a: 11).

A stronger UK voice on the development of the superhighway has come from the Trade and Industry Select Committee (House of Commons 1993–4a). The committee's inquiry was begun out of a concern that government policies could be hindering or not sufficiently encouraging the development of the most advanced infrastructure and services, and it concluded with robust recommendations directed at both government and OFTEL, designed to stimulate both broadband infrastructure development and the uptake of applications. In particular, the committee saw a powerful shaping role for well coordinated public services in simultaneously pulling through infrastructure and applications, recommending, for example, that government should seek to ensure that all public institutions such as hospitals and schools are connected to broadband networks as soon as possible. As we have seen above, OFTEL is presently working its way through the issue of broadband universal service, though its own recommendations at this time fall well short of those of the committee.

Superhighways: public services and citizenship

One practical translation of visions of information age governance is the emergence of a core debate about the nature of public policy for telecommunications, on the one hand, and about the exploitation of telecommunications in the business of government, on the other. In the UK, the positive role that public services and public procurement can play in the development of the superhighway has been clearly recognized. At the same time, the superhighway is increasingly being positioned as being crucial to the 'reinvention' of government. Yet what is equally clear is that the import of these linked debates for UK telecommunications policy has not been fully thought through.

We have seen already that governments have historically observed the principle of universalism in their provision of public services. This is not to deny, however, that universalism has been interpreted in different ways in different services arenas. In its strongest form – for example, in education and health – it has led to the provision of services where there is no formal bar to access and consumption, where there is no user cost at the point of consumption and where the costs of travel for consumption purposes are kept low by means of a geographical spread of basic service units. Even in public service arenas where more selective or targeted approaches to service delivery are present, or where user charges are levied, there has been a presumption of geographical universalism at work. Public administration has, therefore, always implicitly recognized the concept of 'reach'. Governments, both at and beyond the centre, have sought to locate their consumption points throughout their territories, establishing a presence in significantly sized centres of population. The geography of public administration has been, in consequence, a complex one, reflecting these varying notions of reach within public services. Yet this geographical spread is also one that is seldom charted, for there is an implicit assumption that it is accommodated in the arrangements for service delivery and democratic activity. Closures of rural schools and post offices and the rationalization of hospitals, to take some examples, often bring in their train localized political activity. This activity emphasizes the pre-eminent normative centrality of the principle of geographical universalism. Consequently, where changes in provision are being introduced, they are accompanied by assurances, and even by new arrangements such as the busing of schoolchildren, designed to allay fears that access to public service is being restricted by geography (Taylor and Webster 1996).

The implicit geographical universalism in public service provision is, we argue, coming under challenge from a powerful combination of factors. The earlier chapters of this book have provided wide-ranging illustrations of the ways in which governments are beginning to innovate in the use of ICTs in their operational activities. For example, governmental organizations are innovating in the provision of electronic opportunities for public information retrieval; in providing for new forms of transactions between providers and their consumers and in other forms of electronic enhancements in public services; and in supporting new forms of democratic communication and community interaction. We have also seen that these innovations are widely viewed as carrying with them a new business logic and communications strategy. Why should the public finances be used to meet the costs of maintaining a service presence in remote rural localities, when 'virtual' services delivered over telematics networks could simultaneously reduce costs and – so it is claimed –

enhance service quality? Why should public service agencies assume that users must continue to come in person to government offices, when information age services could exploit the potential embedded in technologies to bring services closer to the homes of customers and citizens? Why should elected representatives canvass on the doorstep or book 'surgeries' for their constituents into draughty public halls, when they can reach far more of the public by telephone canvassing or exploiting cable TV or the Internet? These are siren voices, voices whose volume seems certain to rise during the coming years. If it is to be pursued, however, this business logic carries another logic, a public service logic, alongside it. As public administration becomes ineluctably dependent upon information and telecommunications technologies to meet its universalistic obligations, so the presence of these technologies must itself be universalized.

We have seen that the working assumption in information age policy forums is that infrastructure must have the capacity to convey voice, data and video communications. However, while the telecommunications capabilities required for conveying voice and text, such as those used for information retrieval activities, are in principle modest, the quality of telecommunications infrastructure becomes more significant as multimedia enhancements are brought forward. Thus, in many instances – for example, where information is being provided by internal monitoring and control systems – line speed and bandwidth requirements are low, whereas in instances where multimedia terminals or kiosks are to be used for public information systems capable of both providing and receiving information – such as those envisaged by the G-7 Government On-line Project – high-speed high-bandwidth telecommunications is undoubtedly required. Likewise, the development of interactive capability increases bandwidth requirements, although the precise implications for capacity are contingent on the combination of media being used. For example, in the case of telemedicine applications, very high quality video links will be needed, in turn placing a high bandwidth requirement on the system. Video-conferencing is beginning to be used in public service arenas too. For example, in *Project LAMBDA* in the north of Scotland, a video-conferencing link sits on the multimedia terminals and provides interactive capability for discussions

Table 5.1   Bandwidth requirements of different services

Information source	Bandwidth required
Digital telephone/fax	64 kbps
Videotex	15 kbps
Videophone	64 or 128 kbps
Videoconference	128–960 kbps
Video on demand	2 mbps
High-definition TV	140.8–560 mbps

Source: Compiled from House of Commons (1993–4a).

Table 5.2 Transmission times for telematics applications of typical size on networks of different bandwidths

	9.6 kbps	64 kbps	2 mbps	20 mbps
Colour fax	9 min	1 min	3 s	0.3 s
Video conference	3 min	23 s	0.8 s	0

between public service officials and consumers who live in remote geographical areas. Similarly, where local cable television is being used as part of an interactive relationship with citizen and voter panels, such as those to which we referred in Chapter 4, the technological requirements also include high bandwidth.

This analysis is illustrated in Table 5.1, which shows that whereas videotext information services require comparatively modest bandwidth in telecommunications circuits, once we move on to digital telephony and video requirements bandwidth need rises sharply. Table 5.2 takes this analysis further still by offering a view of the relationship between telecommunications bandwidth on the one hand and the speed of transmission of applications on the other. If speed, picture quality and the cost of video transmission are important then the higher is the bandwidth required. To achieve a video–conferencing service which has an unstuttered picture quality approximating to that of TV requires a bandwidth of more than 2 megabits per second, a standard far higher than can be provided in the late 1990s over much of the UK's public telecommunications infrastructure. Finally, Table 5.3 shows the significance of different transmission systems to the delivery of bandwidth. Whereas copper wire – the vast majority of the UK's telephone network is a copper wire network – will deliver high bandwidth over very short distances, optical fibres retain very high bandwidth capabilities over any distance.

It follows from this analysis that an underlying and dramatic issue facing government is whether the principle of universalism in public services can be maintained given both the shift of interest to electronic service delivery among public service providers and the problems of telecommunications infrastructure provision. Information age scenarios appear to presume that telecommunications infrastructures will be sufficient, in capacity, quality, geographical spread and cost, for the full exploitation of ICTs and information systems in enhancing relationships between customer, citizen and the state. As yet, such an

Table 5.3 Bandwidths of different sorts of cable

Cable	Over 1 km	Over 3 km	Over 10 km
Copper	6 mbps	3 mbps	0.5 mbps
Cable TV (coaxial)	1,000 mbps	150 mbps	25 mbps
Optical fibre	10,000 mbps +	10,000 mbps +	10,000 mbps +

Source: Compiled from House of Commons (1993–4a).

assumption cannot be plausibly made, for innovations around the use of ICTs in governance clearly have different minimal infrastructural requirements, ranging from modest line speeds and switching capacity through to broadband, multi-service, two-way networks with line speeds in excess of 20 megabits per second. This crucial issue raises a number of questions. Should the government rest broadly content that a strategy for telecommunications provision based around the regula-tory stimulation of both 'competition and choice' is the right one? Or should the government be broadening the emphasis of regulation to embrace explicitly a higher order or more differentiated universal service obligation (USO) than that which presently applies? Do public service obligations force on to the superhigh-ways agenda the need to consider the case for the universal availability of high bandwidth telecommunications, specifically for public service use?

Telecommunications and social exclusion

These questions are made more significant by the fact that, as we began to trace above, even basic telephony is by no means universally consumed in the UK. Although the competitive regime which has been in place since 1981 has substantially increased the proportion of households which are attached to the telephone network, there remains a significant number of households which are not. While about 10 per cent of UK homes are without telephony (OFTEL 1994b), a figure which is high by international comparison, only about one-third of that 10 per cent can be explained by a combination of conscious choice to remain 'unphoned', and frictional reasons; that is, people moving between homes. The remaining two-thirds apparently want telephony but cannot afford to be connected. Only when many of these low-income households take up telephone line rental will the UK be at the levels of domestic telephone penetration of the USA (94 per cent) and Australia (95 per cent), for example.

Moreover, these UK-wide figures mask considerable differences in re-gional and local penetration rates for telephony (OFTEL 1994b; Marvin 1994; Graham and Marvin 1996; Graham et al. 1996). There are many small pockets in the UK where telephone penetration is well below 50 per cent and, equally, there is an increasing number of other areas where it is well in excess of 100 per cent, accounted for by households with more than one line rental. Here lies a paradox for public service delivery in the information age: that the areas in which the uptake of telephony is lowest may well be areas where the need for consumption of public services is most intensive, and where the much vaunted benefits which might derive from electronic consumption of both services and citizenship opportunities might be supposed to be the greatest.

Other available data on telecommunications expose a further dimension to this form of social exclusion. In 1995, BT published details of its UK-wide disconnections from its network for the first three quarters of 1995. These data, brought forward in Table 5.4, show both the large number of total disconnec-tions in any single quarter, and the net disconnections following reconnections, allowing for those who have subsequently settled their debt.

Table 5.4 Quarterly disconnection statistics, BT (first three quarters 1995)

	Total disconnections	Net disconnections*
First quarter	208,929	75,641
Second quarter	194,396	70,438
Third quarter	207,045	90,599

*Net disconnections exclude those customers who are subsequently reconnected following payment of their outstanding bill
Source: Compiled from OFTEL (1995b).

Here is the delineation of a major issue for government in the information age, given the norms of inclusion and ease of access which have prevailed in public service organizations as the twin foundations of equitable service provision. Relatively large numbers of 'unphoned' households, and even larger numbers of unphoned individuals, in society bring government organizations face to face with the problem of exclusion. Sections of the population for whose welfare governments have historically had a prime concern may, in effect, be excluded from service provisions as governments seek to do more and more of their business electronically.

Infrastructure provision and electronic service provision: the case of Scotland

We turn in the final substantive part of this chapter to look at the development of telecommunications infrastructures in one part of the UK, Scotland. We do so in order to illustrate some of the dilemmas for telecommunications provision and consumption which are to be faced as we move further into the information age. These dilemmas help to spell out the problems which exist for the realization of the supposed social, economic and political advantages to be gained in society through the widespread adoption of ICTs.

In the broadest of terms, a number of recent studies related to both telecommunications infrastructure provision and public service development and innovation in Scotland give rise to considerable reservations about the adequacy of present telecommunications policy in the provision of an infrastructure which will serve as a universalist underpinning for electronically enhanced public services (Taylor et al. 1993a, b, 1995a; Taylor 1994; Taylor and Webster 1996). Immediately below we look at the impact on the Scottish public switched telecommunications networks of the public policy of liberalized provision.

The development of the hard-wired telecommunications infrastructure in Scotland, from which the country's superhighway will be formed, is emerging from four sources. Three of these – infrastructure development by the 'old' duopoly providers, BT and Mercury; developments emerging from other more recently licensed operators such as Scotland's two electricity companies; and the laying down of cable by companies franchised and regulated to provide a combination of cable television and local telephony services – have a commercial basis to their investment decisions. The fourth source of telecommunications infrastructure in Scotland has its origins in a unique venture in the UK context: the laying down, in the period from 1989, of digital telecommunications network in the north of the country. This integrated services digital network (ISDN) is the consequence of a joint venture between BT and the economic and social development agency in this part of Scotland, *Highlands and Islands Enterprise*. It is a venture based, in principle, upon a supply-led and universalist concept of infrastructure development, a concept which is at odds with the demand-led nature of mainstream UK telecommunications policy since the early 1980s, and not one, therefore, directly inspired by commercial considerations (Taylor and Williams 1990).

Looking at these developments more closely, four key points emerge from this work which are of relevance to the various discussions of this chapter. First, both BT and MCL have built optic fibre networks linking their main switches in Scotland, thereby giving each company the basis for effective competition with the other in the main business centres of the country. Elsewhere in Scotland (including, surprisingly, parts of the Highlands and Islands, as we show below), telecommunications infrastructure provision is uneven. Mercury has scarcely developed its network in Scotland beyond the main centres, and BT's network enhancement programme is based upon forecast demand rather than universalist principles, thus leaving its programme of network upgrade as patchy. Moreover, while BT's network in Scotland is scheduled to be 'modernized' by about the turn of the millennium, that modernization programme is of a quality which will leave much of the country – in geographical rather than in population terms – with relatively low-grade 'pseudo-digital' switches that will permit most but not all network telephone services (Taylor 1994). Additionally, the modernization programme will leave Scotland with a predominantly copper wire transmission system whose bandwidth capabilities, as we have seen, remain uncertain. Without further advances in data compression techniques, this system will not carry the multimedia, interactive applications which the heady visions of the information age are offering up. Issues related to telecommunications infrastructure enhancement are further confused because of the installation by large companies and public service organizations of their own private networks. By developing their own private networks and meeting their own telecommunications needs largely outside the public network, these organizations are, in effect, by-passing local public infrastructures. They are thereby slowing their 'exhaustion rate'. This process, in turn, allows the main telecommunications providers, particularly BT, to defer aspects of their modernization upgrades.

Second, the Highlands and Islands Initiative, by which that large northern and western tract of Scotland was to be upgraded to full digital standards, is resulting in sub-optimal implementation. This project, which began fully in 1990, was to deliver an upgraded system to ISDN standards in the north and the islands, with the aim that all digital network services were to be available to businesses, homes and public service organizations in the area, on demand. The project further implied that, regardless of specific demand for ISDN services, the whole area would benefit from a fully modernized infrastructure. In the event the upgrade has been slow and, in the specific case of the north-west mainland of Scotland, has hardly occurred at all. Thus some small communities remain on analogue telecommunications despite the enormous publicity which this initiative has received, and despite the assumptions of ubiquity which the initiative carried with it.

This brief evaluation of the ISDN initiative is given further significance once we examine an example of electronic public service innovation which the Highland Regional Council, now The Highland Council, began in the early 1990s. This innovation, the *LAMBDA* project, was an ambitious attempt to use telecommunications and multimedia systems to bring public services to people in remote communities, in ways more immediate than has traditionally been the case. Terminals were located in six (later to be seven) communities, with each of those terminals supporting access to information about a range of public services, as well as supporting other activities such as remote interviewing of social welfare claimants through a video-conferencing facility. One of the major barriers to the widespread roll-out of the system has been the telecommunications infrastructure, however. Thus, despite the project team earmarking specific communities for *LAMBDA* terminals, in some instances it has not been possible to place one in those communities because of the lack of appropriate telecommunications infrastructure. The upgrade to ISDN standards which would largely support the services of *LAMBDA* has in some places failed to be implemented by BT.

Technically *LAMBDA* has been successful, having fulfilled the ambitions of its designers. It has, however, exposed two major problems with contemporary telecommunications infrastructures and policy. It is clear that multimedia systems such as these which demand high bandwidth cannot be wholly supported by enhanced telecommunications infrastructures, even where those infrastructures have been enhanced to ISDN standards. Thus ISDN cannot support the highest quality video-conferencing links, for example. In an age where public authorities will increasingly strive for better quality services by providing them electronically, *LAMBDA* reveals the extent of the infrastructure issue for the highest quality delivery of such projects. *LAMBDA* is also useful in showing the patchiness of infrastructure upgrading in the UK. For although the area in which it is being implemented has been the subject of a much vaunted upgrade, it is still less than a universally enhanced system.

Third, the Scottish case is useful in exposing the situation in respect of the development of cable infrastructures in the UK. Fourteen cable franchises have been awarded in Scotland to date, eleven of which are 'active'. Of these active franchises six are offering telephony as well as cable television and one offers only telephony (CCA 1995; Monopolies and Mergers Commission 1995). Each of the franchise areas is one of the more heavily populated areas of

Scotland, leaving the remainder of the country uncabled. These features of the roll-out of cable – the slow development of some franchises, geographical patchiness of provision and unevenness in respect of telephony – are replicated in all parts of the UK. Cable TV infrastructures, while providing for some extension of telecommunications provision, are not, therefore, resulting in an alternative infrastructure for the support of universal service.

Fourth, it is clear from our work that telecommunications competition in Scotland is happening as yet in only a few places; that is, in the main centres for business and residential customers. The core city areas have become the competitive arena, with the outer parts of the main cities and the rural areas untouched by competitive presence. For the largest geographical swathes of Scotland, BT remains *de facto* the only viable supplier of services and is, therefore, in a monopolistic position. Linked in our work to this theme of competitive presence is awareness of telecommunications developments among potential customers. We have found that awareness levels rise where there is competition or where there has been a significant public investment in infrastructure development such as in the Highlands and Islands. Furthermore, we have shown empirically that public service innovations occur most strongly in these areas of the country marked by competitive presence or by public service infrastructure enhancements. Where neither of these conditions exists, then innovation in electronic public services is at its weakest (Taylor *et al.* 1995).

Conclusions: policy implications

In this chapter we have pointed up the centrality of modern telecommunications infrastructures to the changing business of government. It is clear from our analysis that telecommunications will play a major role in the fulfilment of information age visions of public services. Two important debates, one on the provision of superhighways, the other on the reinvention of government, must therefore be regarded as being ineluctably entwined. Public policy for telecommunications is of increasing significance for the gamut of public policy which leads to the provision and delivery of public services. It is also clear that the demand for high bandwidth telecommunications among public service providers will become stronger, especially as more interactive multimedia systems are included in the strategic plans of public bodies. Thus, from a public services perspective, that aspect of the telecommunications policy debate which is concerned with the changing definitions of universal service is of acute concern. Public services carry their own responsibilities for universal provision, and have, therefore, developed around them a set of assumptions about what these responsibilities mean. What this chapter has uncovered, therefore, are the implications of a possible disjuncture between the normative basis of public services, on the one hand, and liberalized telecommunications, on the other. This is a disjuncture which has practical importance for government, in two main ways. In the first place, without the telecommunications infrastructure and its growing technical capacity, the options for providing and delivering electronic services will remain severely limited. In the second place, the problem is not simply one of infrastructure. As we have also seen, a significant minority of citizens and customers of government organizations have yet to bring even the simplest form of telecommunications, telephony, into their homes. Even if the information superhighway were to become a geographically ubiquitous feature of life in Britain, there remain major issues of social policy, specifically issues about telecommunications uptake, issues of awareness, training and affordability, that must be addressed if it is to be turned into a universally accessible utility. Without this access, governments will be frustrated in their attempts to deliver information age services and some forms of electronic democracy will remain in the realm of utopia.

These issues need to be addressed at a number of levels. At the macro-level, UK government policy for telecommunications has become increasingly reliant upon the role and thinking of the regulatory authority which was brought into existence in the 1980s. In its first ten years, OFTEL's energy was more or less entirely consumed by the management of competition and the creation of consumer choices. Only in the mid-1990s, as the competitive environment in telecommunications matured, has the regulator begun centrally to address issues of universal provision. As we saw above, educational establishments may well be the target for enhanced provision; a new independently managed universal service fund may be established. Furthermore, through the removal of price restraints on higher volume telecommunications business in June 1996, the regulator has, in effect, introduced a new regime of price control which is designed to produce real price reductions for lower volume users during the next few years. It might, therefore, be anticipated that more of the 'unphoned' will choose to bring a telephone into their homes as a consequence of this price reduction.

Second, however, we would argue that a further measure might sensibly be investigated by both the regulatory authority for telecommunications and public authorities. That is, the special requirements for universalism which are embedded in public services should be exploited by both sides of this equation, so that more universalistic telecommunications provision can be supported. Public bodies represent a large potential market for widespread, high-quality telecommunications. Moreover, it is a market which is recognized by both the US and European strategic plans, as well as implicitly by the UK government's proposals, to be crucially important in the building of the information society. On the one hand, the very size of this market could help to establish the critical mass of activity that would provide an irresistible momentum behind the superhighway. On the other, the development of social, civic and democratic applications could provide the normative legitimation for this high-tech future. For both these reasons it is, therefore, in the mutual interests of telecommunications operators, corporate business and public service bodies alike that this demand be encouraged, articulated and recognized.

Third, it follows from such an interpretation that telecommunications infrastructure will begin to occupy a more central role in the information and IT strategies of public authorities, particularly at the local and regional levels where the impact of the new geography of telecommunications will be most significant. As we began to see at the end of Chapter 4, there has been some, rather limited, interest in the concept of the 'wired city' in the UK. Despite this endorsement, we also argued that, in contrast to European and American thinking, there has been a more or less exclusive focus on the economic development aspects of the concept, at the expense of public service or tele-democratic initiatives. This focus reflects greater awareness of the economic and social implications of the geography of telecommunications for the *production* of goods and services than of the equally significant social, economic and political implications associated with *consumption* of public services. It is this disparity which this chapter has sought to redress.

While public authorities might be expected to have a pre-eminent interest in developing infrastructures for the delivery of services to the public, one major political problem in articulating this interest in either a politically or an economically forceful way resides in the fragmentation of policy interest in information age public services (Bellamy and Horrocks 1995a). Moreover, although CCTA has an interest in government beyond Whitehall, its papers on public services applications of the superhighway were focused almost exclusively on central government, a focus which was largely replicated in the 1996 Green Paper, *government.direct* (Office of Public Service 1996b). At local level, the policy interest of the elected local authority is compounded by that of many other stakeholders, including health authorities, schools, further and higher education establishments, economic development and training agencies, such as TECs, and the erstwhile public utilities, all of which are in the hands of separate managements. The Foundation for IT in Local Government (FITLOG), has argued strongly that 'it is because of the range and number of interested parties that [a communications] initiative needs to be recognized by central government. A cohesive national communications strategy such as that being explored overseas should be seen to be a key component for the UK economy' (FITLOG 1994: 25). As we write, however, the prospects for such a strategy appear to be slim.

6

Understanding the information polity

Today's and tomorrow's choices are shaped by the past. And the past can only be made intelligible as a story of institutional evolution.
(North 1990: vii)

Introduction

It seems to be a facet of the human condition that major technological advances are heralded as signalling important opportunities for reshaping our lives, including our ways of organizing, working and governing. Technology provides endless opportunities for hubris, for an overweening arrogance about human capability for establishing ever increasing control over natural forces. The technologies of the information age are certainly no exception, with their apparently full-scale assault upon the natural laws which have governed the significance of time and space in human affairs.

As we write this book, almost at the end of the second millennium, information and communications technologies seem to be so much a part of life that the future is impossible to conceive without them. The capabilities which they bestow upon us as employers, workers and consumers have become so taken for granted that these same capabilities seem likely to become equally embedded in our roles as politicians, bureaucrats and citizens. The communication of information is the bloodstream of government. This stream flows, in part at least, through ICTs, as they both widen and increase in number the arteries of government.

Governments engage with new technologies in a variety of ways. They exploit them most obviously in the conduct of their own business, as employers of labour, as producers of public services and as providers and regulators of many of the facilities through which democratic politics is conducted. Governments also make policy with and for other important stakeholders in the information age. They may bring forward broad policy initiatives, such as the EU's Information Society programme; promote information-age projects, such as technology-oriented research; and establish regulatory frameworks, such as that which is currently administered in the UK by OFTEL. In all these ways, prevailing cultural attitudes to the possibilities offered by technologies are shaping processes and relationships within and around governance.

The significance for government of ICTs, both actual and potential, is at last becoming more clearly recognized. Over the past few decades, the social scientific study of the 'information age' has been largely concentrated on the 'information economy' and 'information society', resulting in a powerful socio-economic focus which, for example, dominated the ESRC's Programme on Information and Communication Technology (PICT). More recently, we have drawn attention to the need for systematic investigation of the significance of changing information and communication capabilities for government, using a parallel concept, the 'information polity' (Taylor and Williams 1990, 1991a; Bellamy and Taylor 1992; Taylor 1992). That is, we have advocated the need for a new heuristic framework for exploring and analysing change in and around government, including innovations centred on information and communication and their relationships to changing structures, processes and values (Bellamy and Taylor 1994a, b; 1996). It is our view that such a framework should form the theoretical basis of the study of the information polity and it is, therefore, to the building of such a framework that we turn in this final chapter.

Delineating an information polity

Our quest to understand the 'information polity' has yielded three possible approaches. The first two replicate dominant, though ultimately technicist, approaches to mapping and analysing the 'information economy' and the 'information society'. We will consider them here in outline, before rejecting them in favour of the third.

Mapping and measuring technological diffusion

The first approach is one which offers an understanding of the information polity in terms of the diffusion of ICTs, a process which we began to discuss in Chapter 1. This approach focuses on measuring the uptake of new technologies by governmental organizations and mapping the extent and distribution of technological innovation in relation to a range of managerial, operational or political functions. It yields analysis of the different patterns of technology adoption as a platform for exploring the significance of the expanding use of technologies in government. For example, the Society for Information Technology Management (SOCITM) undertakes an annual survey based very much on this approach. It counts the uptake of specific forms of IT and applications software in local authorities and gathers evidence, for example, on the size, shape and strategies of IT departments. SOCITM's survey provides some of the most valuable information on technology diffusion, forming a useful grounding for other research. However, this is, at root, an approach which is technology-led. It is so for many good reasons, not least the identification for public bodies of benchmarks and trends against which they are able to assess their own performance. It is also an approach which has enormous utility for the ICT industry, enabling it to understand the directions in which valuable markets for its products and services are being developed. It is much less helpful when it is also used to generate explanations of change: when, for example, it encourages simple-minded extrapolations to be made from quantitative data on the uptake of new technologies to assumptions about the qualitative impact of those technologies on government.

Analysing the business logic of ICTs

A second approach to understanding and delineating the information polity is one which we explored in Chapter 2, and has its origins in the substantial literature on the 'information economy'. Like the first, this approach places primary emphasis upon technological innovation and is particularly focused on its implications for the cost structures of business, and therefore for business organization and strategy. This emphasis derives from the assumption that the configuration of business organizations, the nature of inter-firm relationships and the focus of business strategies will all change radically under the weight of the economic 'logic' of technological innovation. Thus, as the Schumpeterian 'gale of creative destruction' blows on the business of government, so it will bring in its wake new organizational forms, new ways of delivering services and new ways of relating to suppliers and consumers. Indeed, as the business logic of new technologies comes to be better understood, so radical opportunities for reshaping the machinery of government and re-engineering its processes will be more strongly brought forward.

Table 6.1 captures this Schumpeterian perspective on the role of technology in determining change. It sets out the three approaches to the business logic of new ICTs and locates each one as coming to the fore in a specific period of time. That is, Table 6.1 reflects the shifting emphasis from *automation*, through *informatization* and, thence, to the *business transformation* stage in exploiting ICTs.

The evolution of the managerialist agenda in British government lends itself well to this kind of analysis. We argued in Chapters 2 and 3 that the new public management (NPM) in general, and the new consumerism in particular, can be seen as reflecting the changing business logic associated with ICTs. This is a logic which supports the emergence of loose–tight, networked, organizational forms, new hands-off techniques of managerial control and new ways of organizing relationships between government, its contractors, suppliers and customers (Bellamy and Taylor 1994a, b, c). Likewise, new information-intensive service delivery arrangements such as 'one-stop shops' and

le 6.1 Trajectories of change in technology and business

1970s	1970s to 1980s	1980s to 1990s
~~ :ion	Informatization	Transformation
Replacement of labour by machine	Development of value-added information resources	
	Changing ways of thinking/analysing	Changing ways of doing
Economies of scale	Economies of scope	Economies of scale and scope
Agglomerated industry structure		More fragmented industry structure
Centralized organizational hierarchies		Challenges to organizational boundaries, both internal and external
Traditional cultures/norms		New strategic and operational norms; change of culture

'information points' provide good illustrations of the ways in which technology-supported reforms reflect the new economies of scope to be gained from more integrated approaches to the production of services, while also permitting greater focus on the needs of different client groups or geographical areas. In this light, NPM appears as a specific stage in the process by which the information and communications capabilities associated with ICTs at first supported and reinforced, and then came to challenge, the hierarchical control and command techniques, the monolithic organizational forms and the functional division of work which dominated public administration in the late industrial era. Table 6.2 captures this disjuncture between the principles by which the 'old' public administration has been organized and those which appear to be demanded by the business logic of technological innovation, a logic which can best be illustrated from the doctrines of NPM.

An institutionalist approach to information and communication

As we have made clear throughout this book, we wish to move on from these first two approaches, partly to escape from their incorrigible technicism, and partly because of their lack of engagement with the complexities of the political and social world in which technologies are being adopted. For example, we would be deeply uneasy about an approach to the information polity which failed to engage, as we have tried to do, with the ambiguous but significant political issues implicit in the disjuncture that is captured in Table 6.2. Furthermore, it is important to see these issues as deriving from, and being interpreted

Table 6.2   Information age disjunctures in the principles of management in government

Traditional principles of 'old' public administration	Emergent principles of the 'new' public management
1 Uniformity of provision: *the administrative or equity principle*	Targeted provision in search of economy, efficiency and effectiveness: *the business principle*
2 Hierarchical structure in bureaucratic organization: *the top-down control principle*	Loose–tight structures in enabling public service: *the network management principle*
3 Division of work: *the dominance of the functional principle*	The convergence of services: the growing significance of *the integrative principle*
4 Paternalistic relationships to clients etc.: *the professional principle*	Responsive relationships to customers and citizens: *the 'whole-person' principle*

Source: Adapted from Taylor (1992).

and resolved within, specific social contexts. Thus, we argued above that the perceived business logic of the information age implies new kinds of trade-offs between values such as universalism and selectivity, equity and efficiency, and privacy and transparency. However, the nature and the implications of the trade-offs which actually occur can be fully understood only by reference to the political imperatives, business values and organizational cultures from which they arise. For example, we have argued that the increased surveillance capabilities which are commonly associated with ICTs can be interpreted more plausibly as an outcome of managerially driven attempts to take the costs out of public services, by making much more efficient use of customer information, than as an ineluctable manifestation of the Orwellian properties of ICTs. Moreover, pressures to secure new kinds of economies of scope reflect a deep-rooted cultural assumption in government, the assumption that IT must be justified primarily as a production technology. Government has therefore been suffused with an automation approach to exploiting new technology and is, in consequence, relatively blind to other possibilities which are equally commonly ascribed to new ICTs.

What we have also seen throughout this book is that this shaping of information age capabilities is not to be interpreted simply as a process of free and conscious choice in the exploitation of what are essentially neutral technologies. In other words, in arguing that technology is socially shaped, we are not adopting a perspective akin to that which might be labelled 'organizational choice' (Scarbrough and Corbett 1992). We do not see technologies as infinitely malleable and portable artefacts which can be bent at will to specific purposes. On the contrary, we have argued that new ICTs are themselves suffused with specific sets of informational and communications capabilities. While these capabilities lend themselves to ambiguous outcomes, the fundamental social and political choices that they present and reflect are shaped by the social processes in which they are embedded. These are processes which occur, moreover, within specific institutional settings. In practice, therefore, the same kinds of technologies tend to produce a consistent pattern of outcomes within the same (kinds of) institutions, a phenomenon which may easily be mistaken for technological determinism. For example, at the highest macro-level, trade-offs between the threats and opportunities associated with the information age are, in practice, being significantly, consistently and probably irreversibly influenced by the specific regulatory and competitive regimes under which national superhighways are being constructed. Similarly, at the micro-level, the contemporary development of public information systems in the UK is not only shaping and constraining opportunities for new kinds of democratic processes, but is doing so on the basis of longstanding cultural assumptions within government about the management of public access to information in democratic politics. If, as seems probable, these processes act together to embed and institutionalize a distinction between the information rich and poor, this patterning of inequality and social exclusion may amount to one that then seems to be inescapably associated with the information age. In fact, however, it is a process which is emerging from the interweaving of ideologically induced policy preferences, deeply rooted cultural assumptions and the possibilities offered by technological innovation.

A central proposition in the study of the information polity is, therefore, that we should not expect dramatic changes to occur as a direct consequence of the expanding uptake of what, at first sight, appear to be revolutionary technologies. While much academic and other informed commentary on the information age predicts dramatic 'impacts' from the diffusion of these technologies, we prefer to adopt an approach which allows us to juxtapose the potentially radical tendencies of ICTs with the inherently evolutionary and incremental nature of institutional change. For this reason we propose to develop a specific variant of the social shaping approach to technological change, namely 'institutional shaping'.

Relationships in the information polity

Our preferred approach to analysing the information polity is one which gives primacy to the notion that systems of governance can be conceived as networks of relationships that are sustained by, and reflected in, complex sets of information flows. In turn, these flows depend upon the information and communications capabilities which have become embedded in these systems. It follows that the 'information polity' is a heuristic device for analysing the ways in which the institutions of governance are shaping, and are shaped by, new information flows and new modes of communication which are commonly associated with information age technologies. We have focused in this book on three key sets of relationships which lie at the heart of the polity. These are:

- relationships within and around the machinery of government, concerned with the production of policies and services (Chapter 2);
- relationships between governmental organizations and the consumers of their services (Chapter 3);
- relationships between governmental organizations, political leaders and citizens of the state (Chapter 4).

We would argue, too, that an information polity perspective draws attention to the significance of two further sets of relationships which are mediating these relationships. The first of these is the increasingly important set of relationships between government agencies and the suppliers of information and communications technology infrastructure, equipment and services, which we discussed, in part, in Chapter 5. The second exists at the analytical rather than the empirical level, but is no less important for that. This is the relationship of existing and emerging technical infrastructures, information systems and communications networks to the polity's 'appreciative system' (Vickers 1965); that is, its readiness as an institutional order to attach value to some practices and agendas rather than to others. It is this second relationship that we will discuss at length in the present chapter.

Relationships between and within governmental organizations

The commercially inspired and essentially deterministic rhetorics of the information age suggest that ICTs induce profound changes in the management, configuration and business processes of formal organizations. What is common to many information age scenarios is the suggestion that new technologies will create new kinds of inter- and intra-organizational connections, causing information to flow across hitherto impermeable boundaries: the boundaries between functional compartments, between departments, between tiers of government, between governments and external agencies and between different national administrations. We saw that these kinds of new information flows appear to offer significant benefits. First, they offer massive economies of scope, leading to substantially reduced costs of service provision. Second, they offer the possibility of more holistic services, leading to much enhanced service quality for individual consumers. However, they also threaten to dislocate well established information-handling processes within the existing organizational domains of government, and pose severe challenges to the actors who control and depend upon those domains. Hence, it is not surprising that information-based innovations – for example, those associated with process re-engineering – frequently excite defensive strategies designed to frustrate the emergence of new information-mediated relationships. For example, research carried out on BPR-inspired change programmes in twenty-five companies in the USA found that 'many of their efforts to create information-based organizations – or even to implement significant information management initiatives – have failed or are on the path to failure. The primary reason is that the companies did not manage the politics of information' (Davenport *et al.* 1992: 53). Thus, in practice, the outcomes of change programmes, including those related to innovations around ICTs, are to be understood as being significantly shaped by actors on whose cooperation and commitment these innovations rest (Davenport 1993).

Relationships between governments and consumers of public services

These difficulties also apply to innovation in other sets of relationships. For example, the development of electronic service delivery (ESD) is, at face value, one of the most interesting areas for applying new ICTs in government. ESD appears to offer the possibility of cost-effective ways of taking forward the new consumerism in public administration, but this promise also derives from the possibility of securing new economies of scope. Likewise, holistic approaches to service delivery challenge the functional basis of public bureaucracies, by reorienting them around customer-sensitive principles, such as organization according to the client group or the neighbourhood that is being served. However, implementing these principles requires information to flow horizontally across functional compartments within the organization, just as new relationships with suppliers and customers require it to flow across external boundaries. The examples of the DSS's Operational Strategy, the NHS IM&T Strategy and CCCJS were used to show why this kind of reorientation may be easier to prescribe than to secure. We saw why factors such as the legacies of older mainframe systems, professional sensibilities about information sharing and the political significance attached to operational autonomies can all combine to inhibit the creation of new kinds of information sharing or exchange.

Relationships between governments and citizens

The same kinds of factors intervene in the process of realizing the promises commonly associated with electronic citizenship and democracy in the information polity. New ICTs apparently offer citizens access to rich information resources and interactive engagement with political debate, at least in countries where technologies such as cable TV and access to the Internet are extensively diffused. However, the creation of public information systems and electronic forums also puts considerable pressure on governmental organizations to develop new kinds of information-sharing arrangements, and to open themselves to new kinds of communication and information exchange with members of the public and external lobbies. For example, new forms of electronic democracy in British local government would require new kinds of information flows across the increasingly fragmented agencies of local governance, as well as between political, bureaucratic and community domains. However, our own recent work on the diffusion of ICTs into UK local government, for example, suggests that the nature of long-established relationships between officials and politicians is not being fundamentally challenged (Taylor *et al*. 1995a). Likewise, we have seen in this book how the Conservative Government's Open Government Initiative in UK central government was developed in ways that reflect and accommodate deeply embedded cultural assumptions about the control of public information and its dissemination to citizens.

Relationships between governments and the equipment industry

As well as being highly constrained by existing institutional arrangements, the new information flows on which information age relationships depend are also being mediated by governments' increasing dependence on the rapidly developing industrial complex which supplies equipment, infrastructure and other high-tech services. Moreover, the relationships which this dependency spawns are becoming more complex because of the contemporary agenda of liberalization in public services. For example, IT became the most commonly cited function mentioned in departmental plans drawn up under the market-testing initiative in the early 1990s (HM Treasury 1991; Office of Public Service and Science 1992). By 1995–6, over 30 per cent of the total Whitehall IT spend was disbursed on externally provided IT services, including training, consultancy, hardware, software and facilities management (Kable 1995). Within that total, the value of facilities management, the contracting out on a long-term basis of a specific operation, installation or function, rose from £30.5 million in 1993–4 to £210.7 million in 1995–6 (Kable 1995). IT has also been the subject of some of the largest external contracts awarded to the private sector. For example, in 1995, the IT Services Agency of the DSS was externalized through a contract valued at £82 million a year, and in 1994, the IT function of the Inland Revenue was externalized by means of a ten-year contract worth £120 million a year, a process which was designed to create a long-term 'strategic partnership' between the Inland Revenue and the American company *Electronic Data Systems* (EDS) (Margetts 1995).

These arrangements have put the few companies that are in a position to tender realistically for contracts of this size into a strategically powerful position in relation to information age government (Margetts 1995). They also expose important issues about the control and exploitation of personal data on UK citizens which are now flowing into computer installations run by commercial companies. These flows of information raise sensitive questions about data stewardship, especially data ownership and data privacy, but they also raise questions about the nature and efficacy of control over the commercial value of customer datasets, questions which have not been publicly aired or resolved. As one well placed commentator observed in 1994, 'at present there is little apparent concern about the emerging relationships between government, the citizen, the service providers and the stewardship of information' (Muid 1994: 121), a position which contrasts starkly with that in the USA, where the conflicts of interests arising from public procurement contracts have been made the subject of explicit guidelines. These sensitivities were heightened considerably by the Social Security Administration (Fraud) Bill, which was progressing through Parliament at the time of writing (early 1997). This Bill was intended to permit specific kinds of data-matching across hitherto compartmentalized government datasets between the DSS and other government departments. Similarly, the announcement that EDS was to manage IT facilities for both the Inland Revenue and the DSS may, *de facto* rather than *de jure,* produce similar consequences. Will the public protections embedded in the separate stewardship of personal data, for which Whitehall departments have historically been responsible, be broached through the tandemized management of data by this third party organization, and are there sufficient protections to ensure that data-matching begins and ends precisely as the law allows (Smith 1997)?

The second effect of liberalization is the increasing dependency of government service providers on the regulation of the telecommunications industry, in order to secure public policy objectives for the information age. For example, we showed that the liberalized telecommunications regime in the UK, together with vast technical changes occurring in the industry, is creating severe geographical discrepancies in the provision of advanced telecommunications. Traditional conceptions of universal public service are being challenged and potentially difficult problems are being posed for those public services that wish to exploit telecommunications equitably throughout their jurisdictions. Changes such as these, towards externally managed IT facilities, and the business-driven coupling of information systems appear, then, to threaten basic public service values, such as equity, privacy and stewardship. They also show, however, how technological innovation is mediated by its exploitation to support ideologically or politically motivated changes or to produce particular sets of outcomes in specific institutional settings. It must also be pointed out that these tendencies are still in their infancy: in practice, they may prove to have a profound impact on the institutional fabric of British government, or they may be muted as they are accommodated by, and absorbed into, longer-standing ways of doing business.

Relationships between information flows and the institutional order of governance

The last of the five core relationships in the information polity is that between existing information flows and the governmental institutions within which they are embedded. Governments are users of data and information on a massive scale, and some of their computerized information systems are among the largest in the corporate sector. Furthermore, these information systems represent a relatively inflexible resource, partly because of the high investment costs associated with systems building and the similarly high costs of systems demolition and reconstruction. Moreover, the longer they have been in existence, the more encrusted systems become with earlier ways of thinking, for information which is moulded to formal information systems comes to embody operational routines and organizational values which then take on a degree of permanence and authority. Thus, far from appearing as the heralds of a high-tech future, information systems are often better seen as legacies from earlier business regimes, legacies which then become major obstacles to the delivery of new business strategies.

Institutionalism and the information polity

This analysis has served to illustrate a number of important ways in which the information flows associated with the information age are, in practice, en-meshed in, and constrained by, the complex relationships which exist in and around governance. Indeed, this survey of the key sets of relationships in the information polity has brought us to a point where information and its communication are moving to the centre of our enquiry. In so doing it has also underlined two important facets of our understanding of the information polity. First, it reduces to sterility the antonymical discourse between utopian and dystopian approaches to understanding ICTs, because it reinforces the point that there are no ineluctable consequences for good or ill flowing from technological innovation. Second, our focus upon information and communication prompts us to ask what are the main influences which come to shape the nature, flow and interpretation of information, its communication and its interaction with the changing relationships of governance. It is in providing a way of addressing this question that the value of institutional analysis will become most evident.

Douglass North's (1990) *leitmotif* for institutionalism, with which we headed this chapter, captures the essential character of this approach, one which brings out its major emphasis upon stability and orderliness in social, political and economic affairs. An institution is best understood as a set of formal and informal rules, norms, expectations and conventions which govern human behaviour, maintaining the regular routines through which society is ordered. Institutions provide, therefore, for continuity and predictability in everyday life, setting frameworks for action, inaction and innovation. Thus institutions are not to be understood simply in terms of formal organizational structures, though they may validate organizational boundaries and jurisdictions. Indeed, a formal organiza-tion may accommodate a number of institutionalized systems, such as those which govern the behaviour and strategies of actors occupying various occupa-tional or functional roles. Institutions may, by the same token, stretch well beyond the boundaries of formal organizations. A bundle of organizations may become meshed together in a set of ordered, routinized relationships which are governed by well established norms and conventional procedures. It is in this sense, for example, that Lowndes has referred to more or less stable 'policy communities' in governance as 'disaggregated institutions' (Lowndes 1996).

By maintaining and legitimating the normative frameworks within which actions occur, institutions provide a predictable environment for the exercise of bounded rationality. Institutions are, in effect, a 'set of readinesses to distinguish some aspects of a situation rather than others and to classify and value these in this way rather than that' (Vickers 1965: 67). Put another way, institutions close the 'competence–decision gap' (Dosi *et al.* 1988). In times of uncertainties in the environment of organizations, such as those which currently characterize public administrations, they assist and influence decision-makers by providing tried and tested ways of doing things, enabling them, through a combination of tacit knowledge (Best 1990) and implicit references to past actions, to reduce the costs of information gathering and processing which would necessarily be incurred in the pursuit of high levels of rationality and predictability.

In short, institutions assist in the development and maintenance of three vital characteristics of stable, complex organizations or networks. In the first place they establish the routines and repertoires (Nelson and Winter 1982), the recognized ways of doing and perceiving things, by which behaviour is governed and decision-making facilitated. Second, an institutionalized environment is characterized by the existence of long-established 'epistemic communities', composed, for example, of professional or occupational groups, whose members rely on common funds of knowledge, memory and skills. The existence of epistemic communities is signalled, therefore, by the existence of Kuhnian paradigmatists who guard, protect and promote specific interpretations of the organizational world. Third, institutions support 'actor networks' (Callon 1987). That is, they reflect and embed routines and procedures which recognize and govern relations between different epistemic communities, allowing the emergence of arrangements by which different groups of actors, relying on different epistemic systems, can make their mark on technical innovation and development. For example, the design and construction of an information system assumes a mutual understanding about the roles, expertise and domains of hardware engineers, software engineers, systems analysts, project managers and users. This understanding not only permits the project to be undertaken, but, even more importantly for the present analysis, establishes and limits the scope for each set of actors to embed into the system their own assumptions about the social purpose for which it is being constructed.

Three short cases will serve to illustrate the power of institutions to constrain and shape innovations in the processing of information in institutionalized relationships within and around government.

Case 1: Constraining innovation in administrative procedures

The following story, taken from an academic article, serves to illustrate the forces for orderliness and continuity contained in established administrative practices when these practices are confronted by an innovative ICT application whose business logic suggests substantial changes.

When in April 1995 the Minister for the Office of Public Service and Science (OPSS) publicly announced his electronic mail address, a journalist sent perhaps the first electronic mail message to a UK Minister from a member of the public. At a PICT/ESRC conference on Information Technology and Social Change two months later, he asked the head of the CCTA, Roy Dibble, why he had not had a reply. Now that citizens were talking to governments when were governments going to talk to citizens? Roy Dibble replied that the journalist's questions were currently sitting on his desk. When the Minister received the electronic message it had been printed off and sent to Roy Dibble by post. One of his staff had written to the relevant agency heads with a request for information; their staff would prepare this information and send it back to Roy Dibble's office where it would be collated and returned to the Minister's office. He will check the information and one of his staff would type it on to electronic mail and transmit it to the journalist. This evidence of how new methods of communication can flounder when having to interface with existing administrative operations is not isolated; an employee of a Next Steps Agency observed in 1995 that as a matter of procedure all electronic messages sent to the agency were printed off and filed.

(Margetts 1995: 92)

Opening up opportunities for citizens to e-mail government directly has been identified in the literature on electronic democracy as one of the more powerful ways in which interactive relationships can be established between government and citizens. However, this case clearly illustrates the forces arraigned on the side of continuity and gradual evolution, rather than on the side of more fundamental change. It shows how information age communications can be tamed and muted as they are assimilated into civil servants' well established methods for dealing with external inquiries.

Case 2: Inhibiting innovation in relations between departments and contractors

In proposing a new IT procurement model in a recent article in the *Journal of the Parliamentary IT Committee* (Mills 1996), the author of our second extract, underlines the inhibiting effects on innovation stemming from the existing institutionalized arrangements for government procurement. These arrangements he refers to as the 'project model' because they typically involve a process of once-and-for-all tendering for discrete IT projects. His central proposal is that procurement should be governed by a new model which would be more sensitive to the evolutionary development of information systems. Thus, rather than treating the customer and supplier relationship as an arm's length one, the new model would recognize the benefits of teamworking between the parties and the sharing of risks associated with procurement. It would also permit more recognition of the suppliers' responsibilities towards users of systems and would acknowledge the programmatic aspects of government information systems, by placing emphasis upon continuity and inter-operability between systems developments.

What is important for our argument is less the merits of these proposals and more the force of the author's assumptions about the resistance which his proposals will meet from insiders in the Whitehall IT community. It is interesting, moreover, to note that these assumptions derive from what is, in effect, an institutionalist critique.

> The project model attracts a near automatic respect amongst specialist groups involved with procurement and purchasing. For the administrator and the financier, the model ties in with funding and approvals procedures. For the accountant, the model underpins cost benefit analysis and provides milestones against which progress can be measured and stage payments calculated. For the engineer, the model offers a logical baseline for the systematic implementation of work . . . This conventional model represents a set of strongly-held beliefs and attitudes accepted without question by important groups associated with procurement. It occupies a salient position in management education and training . . . An alternative and more powerful model, better suited to the needs of information system and service procurement, may therefore be treated not on its merits, but with prejudice.
>
> (Mills 1996: 167–8)

Case 3: Shaping innovation in information systems: the case of the criminal justice system

Institutions may not only inhibit innovation, as in the case above but, as many well documented cases have shown (for example, MacKenzie and Wajcman 1985), they may shape those innovations which do occur. In making this point, MacKenzie has argued that actors' expectations of the technological future are part of what makes a particular future, rather than other possible futures, 'real'. Thus:

> a technological trajectory is an institution. Like any institution it is sustained not by any internal logic or through intrinsic superiority to other institutions, but because of the interests that develop in its continuance and the belief that it will continue. Its continuance becomes embedded in actors' frameworks of calculation and routine behaviour, and it continues because it is thus embedded.
>
> (MacKenzie 1996: 58)

In looking at the adoption and application of ICTs in governance structures, and at their potential for both process and service innovation, we should therefore understand the importance of actor networks, each with its own framework of routines, in forming the social context within which ICTs are being procured and applied. In particular, we must analyse how the expectations and assumptions which are succoured by these networks influence the innovation process.

The UK criminal justice system (CJS) illustrates well the interaction of epistemic communities and actor networks in governmental institutions. As we saw in Chapter 2, the notion of a criminal justice 'system' captures the existence of longstanding, institutionalized relationships between autonomous, but contingent, public services. During the past ten years, each of these services has reviewed its national information systems and has brought forward plans for new strategic systems. Some of these systems are now fully implemented or, at least, well advanced, and others are developing more slowly or have been abandoned. Each service has also brought the expectations and assumptions of important sets of actors, including managers, professionals (of different kinds), consultants and IT suppliers, to bear upon the specification of its information and communication needs. These specifications have, therefore, been derived partly from existing operational routines and values, and partly from expectations about the benefits to be gained from new opportunities for efficiency savings or service improvements. In consequence, each service has declared itself willing to innovate in the way it exploits information, which might include exchanging information with other CJS agencies. Nevertheless, the institutional setting is both restricting the extent and shaping the nature of innovation. In the first place, many of the expectations of the benefits to be gained from developing new information systems undoubtedly derived from dominant images of the technological future propagated by IT professionals and the IT industry. Second, however, the 'project procurement model' and, even more importantly, the methods used within government for capital project appraisal have driven business managers to focus on the immediate costs and benefits accruing to their own individual service within the CJS (Bellamy and Taylor 1996). Together with the interests of existing IT suppliers in maintaining existing systems platforms, and the reluctance of professionals to open up client information to other CJS services, this focus has severely restricted the willingness and capacity available to engage in more fundamental re-engineering of information flows. This is especially the case where these flows would involve establishing the routine sharing of information, or the establishment of common procurement arrangements, across tiers of government or between public services.

Theorizing the information polity

To this point in this chapter we have set out a number of ways of understanding what might be meant by the 'information polity'. In so doing we have stressed that, as with any social scientific enquiry, there are different ways of seeing and understanding, and that our preferred perspective is one which moves away from the techno-economic paradigm which has been so dominant in so much of the literature. Furthermore, we do not propose to establish a perspective on the information polity which amounts to no more than the new public management with wires and computers added. As we have said, we see complexities in the nature of change with which an analysis that is based upon a 'business logic' cannot adequately deal. We have, therefore, brought forward in preference a range of examples which illustrate the sensitivities surrounding information-based change in the institutions of governance. Our illustrations also bring out the organizational politics which are made manifest by the challenges that institutional change might bring. However, we recognize that illustrating the prevalence of 'information politics' in government is not the same as explaining it. Indeed, developing an adequate explanation depends on achieving a deeper understanding of why information and the technologies which convey it have become important sources of power, and are therefore important stimuli for strategic behaviour in and around the institutions of governance.

The politics of information

The political significance of information can be analysed at three levels. That is, information can be viewed first as a political resource; as an element in embedding, and therefore routinizing, the 'rules' of the political game; and as an element in the 'mobilization of bias' within institutional structures. These three levels correspond broadly with those of the well established resource-dependency framework used in political studies for analysing complex organizational relationships (e.g. Rhodes 1981), though, in two important respects, this analysis departs from that framework. First, as might be expected in a book on this subject, it places *information* at the centre of analysis, in place of an emphasis on resources such as money, political authority or knowledge, which more typically come to the fore in other accounts (e.g Benson 1975). Our analysis identifies information as the primary resource, for information provides the means of controlling and signalling the possession of all other resources. Second, it acknowledges that the full political significance of information cannot be understood simply by focusing on its self-evident properties as a means to an end in decision-making or as a commodity being exchanged. Information takes on a tangible form in the files and documents made available in information systems and, in so doing, it captures and gives form and force to specific ways of interpreting and giving meaning to the world. Communicated information is, therefore, more than a simple reflection of an apparently objective reality: it is also formative of that reality. The discourses, the idioms, the signs, the forms into which information is put are thereby constitutive of power. Information is a critical element in creating and maintaining the institutional order which structures complex organizational relationships. The analysis of these relationships should recognize this role, a point which will become more pertinent as we look, in turn, at why information is significant at each of these three levels on which institutions may be analysed.

Information as a political resource
The first, most obvious, level of analysis deals with information in its most material form, conceiving it as a basic political resource which enables tasks to be undertaken, decisions to be made or outcomes to be calculated. Thus, needing information held by others in order to achieve objectives is an important source of dependency, while holding information needed by others in their pursuit of goals is a source of power. According to this kind of analysis, therefore, informational asymmetries, the unequal possession by relating actors of information resources, lie at the heart of organizational power relationships, giving rise to opportunism and other patterns of behaviour designed to produce enhancements in control and reductions in dependency.

Moreover, as we began to explore above, information is unlike other resources which are exchanged in a relationship in two important respects. First, control over its form, specification and interpretation can be as important as control over physical access. For example, if government documents were to become widely available on the Internet, opacity of language or complexity in the presentation of data could each be as serious a barrier to their effective use by citizens as the failure of the latter to acquire a modem and PC. Second, semantic as well as physical control can be used to restrict access to other politically important resources: for example, accounting systems restrict the means of controlling money to those people who understand their conventions. Thus, 'information particularism', 'the tendency in complex organizations for small groups or units to lay claim to information and define it in terms that make sense to them' (Davenport 1994: 123), can take on strategic importance not only in protecting the freedom of such units to deal with their tasks in the most congenial way, but also in establishing their influence and indispensability within the wider organization.

Information as embedding the 'rules of the game'
The second level of analysis of the politics of information refers to the ways in which both the specification of information resources and the patterning of information flows reflect and represent the procedural rules and normative conventions of governance. Thus they give tangible form and force to the expectations that control behaviour and define relationships. For example, we saw in Chapter 2 how attempts to establish new kinds of management information systems in the wake of the Financial Management Initiative exposed the clash between traditional understandings of public accountability and the demands of new forms of business management in government. Traditional accounting systems have become a major source of inflexibility, inhibiting the emerging managerialist agenda. To take another example, teledemocratic systems, were they to be introduced, would be imbued with a significance that would go far beyond the establishment of the formal procedural changes they would bring in their train. Rather, they would legitimate or, conversely, profoundly challenge important sets of assumptions about the conventions embedded in the relationships between political representatives, government and citizens.

Information and institutional bias

Our discussion of these first two levels of analysis serves to underline the semantic significance of information in organizational politics. It is not enough to possess it: it matters whether, and by whom, it can be understood. It matters considerably, therefore, how it is formatted, presented and communicated. We follow Machlup (1983), who explores the significance of information as a phenomenon which is inseparable from communication and argues that:

● Information cannot exist independently of a communications or storage medium. Hence its form is inextricably connected with the demands of the technology being utilized, whether that be smoke signal, morse code message, written memorandum transmitted through an official hierarchy or computer network.
● Information can be communicated, stored or transacted only if it can be formed in such a way that it is amenable to being conveyed on a communications medium. This formation has technical elements, ensuring that it can be effectively transmitted, and semantic elements, ensuring that its users and recipients can interpret it effectively.
● Information is communicable, storable or transactable in so far as there is a (more or less) shared interpretation of its meaning between originator, mediator, receiver and user. Thus, the stronger and more consensual the institutional structures within which communication and information processing occurs, the greater the facility for 'accurate' communication and interpretation.

A number of interrelated points flow from these propositions. First, it is clear that analysis of the information polity must take due account both of the properties inherent in the relevant technologies and, in particular, of the inextricable relationship of these properties to the ways in which information is formed, conveyed and used. Second, it follows that the notion of information-mediated government implies analysis of routinized social relationships, between information originators, mediators, receivers and users, which allow information to be transacted and thus to take material form. Third, since information has no way of acting on the world except through a meaning which is institutionally constructed, its transaction in government or business is comprehensible only if we go beyond analysis of the formal purpose, pattern and content of information flows, to take account also of the institutional context which determines the way in which information is interpreted and valued. Hence, information exchange and exploitation must be set within the wider economic, cultural and political 'biases' in social institutions through which interpretations of its meaning are mobilized, maintained and advanced.

We are now at the point from which we can see the significance of the third level at which the political significance of information can be analysed. We have written of the reflexive qualities of ICTs, by which we mean that information conveyed by ICTs has an iterative relationship with its institutional setting. It is not only formed and given meaning by that setting, it also reflects back upon it. In particular, the forms into which information is put are themselves not only symbols of institutional identity, but also continually constituting and reconstituting its political order. In these kinds of way, ICTs and the information they convey are to be understood as active elements in the definition, reproduction and reshaping of institutional politics and power.

It also follows from what we have said that information is unlikely to carry fully agreed meanings or value beyond the specific institutional structures from which it is generated. The precise meanings and value attached to information derive from a number of sources, but most powerfully from the discourses of 'epistemic communities'. Once this point is accepted it becomes unsurprising, for example, that systems failure appears to be less a consequence of technological problems and more to do with the organizational politics of systems implementation. We can expect, therefore, that a dominant feature of an information polity will be the presence of political struggles over the definition and management of information, struggles that will centre on its ownership and control. It is for this reason that we now propose the concept of 'information domain' as central to the analysis of the politics of information in the information polity.

Information domains

The concept of an 'information domain' derives by analogy from the concept of the 'organization domain' (Thompson 1967). The concept of organizational domain was used to denote the sphere of influence over which the organization could claim legitimate control and, at the same time, served to clarify the point that organizations are enmeshed in a set of domain interdependencies, both internally and externally, as they seek the resources to achieve their goals. The concept of 'domain' is especially pertinent for the analysis of the politics of information in the information polity, for what is common to many empirical accounts of changes in the relationships in the polity, including NPM-inspired change in government, is the reporting of conflicts which emanate, in effect, from the existence of 'information domains'.

The organization's domain serves to guarantee a measure of independent activity and, in the context of the wider set of network relationships within which a single organization exists, domains also offer participants a degree of predictability and certainty in the management of their goal-seeking strategies. This is especially so where there is a mutual recognition of domains within a network. As Thompson says:

> Domain consensus defines a set of expectations both for members of an organization and for others with whom they may interact, about what the organization will and will not do. It provides, although imperfectly, an image of the organization's role in a larger system, which in turn serves as a guide for the ordering of action in certain directions and not in others.
>
> (Thompson 1967: 29)

By analogy with organizational domain, we can define an 'information domain' as a recognized sphere of influence, ownership and control over information, its specification, format, exploitation and interpretation. Information domains are given empirical expression in sets of information holdings, which may be clerical or electronic, over which dominant actors enjoy significant physical and semantic control. In turn, these actors may be understood as belonging to epistemic communities which provide the knowledge base which, in turn, shapes and validates the meanings and significance attached to particular kinds of information. Information holdings, therefore, reflect the (often) unspoken, but dominant, assumptions within information domains, about the kind of data that should be collected, the form in which they should be held, the uses to which they should be put and the interpretations which they can be made to yield. An information domain can therefore be said to exist where significant control over access to informational holdings has been established, so that information can be withheld or presented only on terms and in a form negotiated by dominant actors. So, for example, a medical department may constitute an 'information domain' within a hospital, where that department has an established right to keep separate patient records, where patient information is organized and presented according to its own classification of maladies and where direct, unsupervised access is allowed only to medical specialists or to staff working under their supervision. In turn, medical staff can be seen as belonging to the epistemic community, a community constituted from their particular speciality, which itself acquires a high degree of influence over the presentation and interpretation of information generated within that domain.

Thus, the existence of an 'information domain' is signalled by:

- a break in flows of information;
- compartmentalization of information resources;
- idiosyncrasy of information specification;
- the hegemony of specific epistemic discourses which shape information and validate particular kinds of interpretation.

It is in the nature of information domains that they at once determine, reflect and reinforce the structure of the critical sets of information resources. The specific domain consensus that prevails at any time gives expression to their power by the recognized influence which they establish over information specifications, information resources and information flows. Information systems act, therefore, both as the mirror in which that power is reflected and as an arena in which it is made manifest. It follows that the processes by which domain consensus is maintained and challenged are crucial to the construction and reconstruction of information systems in government and are, therefore, central to structuring the politics with which this process is imbued.

Empirical research will yield much more knowledge about how and when information domains are formed, as well as about the specific conditions under which domain consensus can be maintained. For the time being we hypothesize that the configuration of information domains reflects the interaction of four factors and thereby of four types of network. These four factors, together with their associated networks, are as follows.

- Formal organizational jurisdictions: reflecting the outcome of the politics of the allocation of functions in government, including legislative processes, budget-shaping and bureau-shaping strategies of the network composed of the *political executive* and their immediate advisors.
- Changing public policies: reflecting the trade-offs between prevailing ideologies, on the one hand, and interests, institutional values and operating requirements, on the other, as they are interpreted through a particular species of network, the *policy community*.
- Dominant professional, technological and managerial paradigms: reflecting the relative power of the *epistemic communities and networks* in asserting and protecting their operational assumptions, preferences and values.
- The trajectory of information and communications technologies at crucial points of organizational history: reflecting the paradigms and power of specific *actor networks* which shape and control technological trajectories and innovations.

Analysing information politics

This approach to understanding the significance of information in complex institutional settings offers several distinct benefits. In the first place, it clarifies and renders more operationally useful, for purposes of both academic research and policy analysis, the concept of 'organizational domain'. 'Organizational domain' has been helpful in developing an understanding of organizational politics, but the unit of analysis, the organizational domain, is ultimately imprecise. What unit of analysis constitutes an organizational domain, and why? Is it a department, a division, a group of workers, for example? 'Information domain' offers the specificity which 'organizational domain' lacks because it avoids a conventional focus on formal organizational structure and achieves analytical precision by reference to institutionalized processes of information generation, holding, use, interpretation and exchange.

This approach allows us to propose certain refinements of existing frameworks for analysing complex organizational relationships. First, we have shown why information should be recognized as much more than an ordinary political resource. If it is the case that a major imperative for actors in networks is to reduce dependency and uncertainty, then information is a particularly powerful resource: indeed, it may be the *key* resource which unlocks and makes manageable and tangible other political resources. By this analysis, information appears as a paramount instrument of political control. Second, information can be expected to become the more sensitive and salient in contemporary government, as the rhetoric of the information age challenges the taken-for-granted nature of its information platforms. For example, if a major political purpose behind reinvention strategies is to break up existing, producer-dominated hierarchies in favour of looser networks of purchasers and providers, contractors and suppliers, then we can expect a profound impact in terms of the increased risks and uncertainties borne by governmental organizations. In turn, there would a sharp escalation in the costs and problems involved in managing those risks and bounding those uncertainties. It follows, therefore, that the analysis of information age networks should not focus simply on the definition, flow, distribution and control of information in government, but also on its special relationship to the strategic behaviour of actors in complex networks as they seek to manage resources and uncertainties in the changing systems of governance. Third, given Machlup's argument that information cannot be divorced from the medium on which it is conveyed, we must also recognize that these strategies may increasingly centre on the development and design of electronic networks and information systems. As Mulgan has written, 'networks are created not just to communicate but also to gain position, to out-communicate' (Mulgan 1991: 21). Moreover, as they also come to embed the changing rules of the game, and reflect the biases which are institutionalized and reinstitutionalized in systems of governance, information systems become important arenas in which the nature and significance of institutional changes are exposed and challenged. It is for this reason that they offer a particularly fruitful field for academic research. Fourth, this approach draws particular attention to two specific kinds of networks, epistemic communities and actor networks, that should be given more prominence in the study of complex organizational relationships. We would expect the role and influence of both epistemic communities and actor networks to become more salient as the new public management, and other emergent organizational and management scenarios such as facilities management of information resources, challenge the legitimacy of existing organizational domains.

Plus ça change . . .

A final benefit to be gained from this approach to understanding the information polity is that it lays open as highly problematic the notion that there is a historical shift occurring which will bring forward a distinctive form of government for the information age. The principles of information age management in government, set out in Table 6.2, imply a substantial and comprehensive redesign of information resources and information flows, the scale and complexity of which is difficult for most of us fully to comprehend. As we have already seen, they require: massive reorientation of the information and intelligence of public service organizations to the point of contact with customers; extensive lateral integration of customer records and administrative codes across existing functional, professional and departmental boundaries; and major changes in the topology of management, accounting and executive information systems. That is, the doctrines associated with the NPM, as well as those implied by ambitious reinvention strategies, are predicated on the highly questionable assumption that information *can* be made to flow throughout the system of governance in ways which challenge fundamentally the integrity of many of its information domains.

The managerial disjuncture captured in Table 6.2 appears all the more profound once we understand how deeply embedded into government are the information domains associated with the 'old' public administration. We have argued elsewhere that the bureaucratic dysfunctions commonly associated with public administration arise from institutional factors, which, in consequence, are not easily changed at will. These dysfunctions, such as rigidity, red tape and functional segmentation, can be explained in large part by the interaction of the normative values of public administration – especially upward accountability associated with parliamentary scrutiny, equity, stewardship and responsibility – and the informational sclerosis arising from clerically managed, paper-based files (Bellamy and Taylor 1992). For example, complex bureaucracies have typically segmented their records into holdings located within different functional commands, where information is generated, managed and processed. Coupled with the demands of upward accountability, this compartmentalization of information resources has led to vertically segmented organizations displaying a strong emphasis on the upward and downward, rather than the lateral, flow of information. The resulting inflexibility of information flows has meant that, to date, government organizations have found it difficult to escape from domination by functional, producer-driven, bureaucracies.

Furthermore, we have pointed in this book to the enormous weight of inertia and resistance inhibiting the reorientation of government towards information-age scenarios. Apart from the huge costs which have already been sunk over the years into the myriad information systems of government, there is the hugely complex, some say impossible, technical task of rewiring government to connect the multitude of bureaucratic codes and transaction files which have been built into these systems. Furthermore, information systems have spawned their own actor networks: the congeries of project managers, IT specialists, external contractors and equipment manufacturers which have acquired stakes not only in particular technological solutions but in the managerial and organizational paradigms that these systems represent. Moreover, lying behind these IT-oriented networks are the epistemic communities which shape the information holdings contained and reflected within the information domains of government.

As we would expect, the vertical, functional structuration which is reflected in information systems has ramifications throughout the institutions of government. For example, it has become almost a truism to point to the high degree of vertical segmentation between policy sectors, and the substantial barriers to effective horizontal coordination which exist throughout all tiers of UK government. Even academic commentators find it difficult to escape from a mindset which is preoccupied with vertical accountability and control. As we have remarked elsewhere, most academic analysis of institutional change associated with the Next Steps project in central government has been restricted by a dominant hierarchical paradigm which has centred on relationships between agencies, ministers and Parliament (Bellamy and Taylor 1992). In contrast, academics have made relatively little attempt to apply alternative institutional models, or to consider their behavioural or organizational dynamics. Consequently, scant attention has been paid to the increasing importance of complex lateral relationships between agencies and other kinds of business units, suppliers, contractors and consumers (Bellamy 1994).

However, it is also the case that arraigned against this analytical conservatism are enormously potent forces propagating the heady notion that we are entering an information age. While some suppliers and IT professionals may be locked into ageing technologies or inflexible systems, the high-technology industry which is concerned with developing and marketing the converging technologies of computing, telecommunications and broadcasting stands to reap huge profits from persuading businesses, governments and citizens, alike, of the imminence of the global information superhighway and the emergence of the information society. Furthermore, the persuasive images of the information age have found powerful reflectors in the heroic visions brought forward by both academic and popular writers and in high-level strategies brought forward by governments. It must be assumed that the industry has succeeded in shaping expectations of a high-tech future from which governments will not be immune. The concept of an 'information polity' is vital, therefore, in offering a framework for analysing the processes of change and continuity in an era which has already been marked out as an 'information age'.

Despite the powerful hyperbole which surrounds the notion of an information age, heroic scenarios for reinventing government through the application of ICTs are fundamentally misleading. The institutions of governance will mould and fashion the revolutionary potential of ICTs into an evolutionary reality. A polity is, essentially, a settled ordering of politics and government. As it evolves into an information polity, it may be expected to do so in ways which are generally inclined to replicate and reinforce, and only sometimes to rupture or depart from, existing practices and patterns of behaviour. Thus the explanatory power of the 'information polity' is embodied in its essentially homeostatic quality. The heady images which are so often associated with ICTs, together with the technologically determinist expectations that they will transform the nature of relationships in and around governance, are balanced by the relative insusceptibility to change of the normative and assumptive worlds which suffuse political institutions. The information polity is, in consequence, an arena which will display the same kinds of political compromises and policy confusions that characterize other important arenas of society. For all these reasons, the intoxicating visions of government in the information age should be allowed to dissipate in the thin air from whence they came.

Appendix 1

Glossary of acronyms

ACPO	The Association of Chief Police Officers
ADP	Automatic data processing
CAT	Community access terminal
CCCJS	The Project known as Triple CJS, or the Coordination of Computerization in the Criminal Justice System
CJN	The Criminal Justice Network, a private network used in the criminal justice system
CJS	The criminal justice system
EDI	Electronic data interchange
EFTPOS	Electronic funds transfer at the point of sale
ELS	The Inland Revenue's Electronic Lodgment Service, used for direct filing of tax returns
EPIS	Electronic public information system
ESD	The company known as Electronic Data Services
ETM	Electronic town meeting
EVH	Electronic village hall
FMI	The Financial Management Initiative (launched in British central government in 1982)
G-7	The G-7 Group of Industrialized Nations
GII	Global information infrastructure
GIS	The (British) Government's Information Service
GPS	Global positioning system
HOLMES	The Home Office Large Major Enquiry System

html	hypertext markup language, used to link documents over the World Wide Web
IBIS	The Benefits Agency's Integrated Benefits Information System
ICT	Information and communication technology
ID	Identity (as in 'identity card')
IS	Information system
ISDN	Integrated services digital network
JANET	The Joint Academic Network
KBS	Knowledge-based system
LASCAD	The London Ambulance Service Computer Aided Dispatch system
MAFF	The Ministry of Agriculture, Fisheries and Food
MCL	The company known as Mercury Communications Ltd
MINERVA	Multiple Input Network for Evaluating Reactions, Voters and Attitudes. An American electronic democracy project in the 1970s
NAFIS	The National Automated Fingerprint Identification System
NII	The [US] National Information Infrastructure
NPR	The US Federal Government's National Performance Review, launched in 1993
NPTN	The National Public Telecomputing Network, a US not-for-profit organization
NSFnet	The US scientific and academic network
NSPIS	The National Strategy for Police Information Systems, published in 1994
OFTEL	The office of the telecommunications regulator
PC	Personal computer
PEN	The Public Electronic Network set up in the mid 1980s in the city of Santa Monica, California
PES	The Public Expenditure Survey
PICT	The Economic and Social Research Council's former Programme on Information and Communication Technology
PNN	The Police National Network, a private network used by English police forces
PSO	The public service orientation, a doctrine used in public management in the 1980s
RPI	Retail price index
SOCITM	The Society for Information Technology Management
USO	The universal service obligation, a doctrine used in telecommunications policy

Appendix 2

Electronic sources of information about governing in the information age

The following Web sites contain information relevant to the subject matter of this book. Many of the official documents cited in the references can also be found by accessing these sites.

http:///www.open.gov.uk/
The UK Government Information Service

http://www.open.gov.uk/govoline/golintro.htm
G-7 Government On-line Project

http://www.open.gov.uk/search/search.htm
MUSCAT search facility to government papers

http://www.tagish.co.uk/nip/
UK National Inventory Project

http://www.open.gov.uk/citu/cituhome.html
The British Government Central IT Unit

http://www/open.gov.uk/cogs/coglist.htm
British government open collaborative groups on the Internet

http://www.number-10.gov.uk/
No. 10 Downing Street

http://www/number-10.gov.uk/depts/index.html
UK government departments

http://www.parliament.uk
Parliament: the House of Commons, the House of Lords and parliamentary publications

http://www.soton.ac.uk/~nukop/
The New United Kingdom Official Publications Online (NUKOP Online) main index (maintained by the University of Southampton)

http://www.kable.co.uk/	Signposts to Government (maintained by Kable)
http://tagish.co.uk/tagish/links/localgov.htm	Directory of UK local authorities on the Web (maintained by Tagish)
http://www.oftel.gov.uk	OFTEL
http://www.tagish.co.uk/nip/nip/localg.htm	UK National Inventory Project – Local Government
http://www.ispo.cec.be/	European Commission Information Society Project Office
http://www.ispo.cec.be/infoforum/isf.html	European Information Society Forum
http://www.ispo.cec.be/g7/g7main.html	G-7 Information Society Conference
http://www.edc.org.uk/telecities/	The European Telecities Project
http://www.civic.net:240/	American Center for Civic Networking
http://apt.org/apt/	Alliance for Public Technology
http://www.cdt.org/	Center for Technology and Democracy
http://ofcn.org/networks/By-state.txt.html	Directory of Free-nets and community networks, worldwide
http://www.senate.gov/	US Senate
http://www.whitehouse.gov/	The White House (USA), including federal government pages
http://nii.nist.gov/nii/niiinfo.html	Papers relating to the American National Information Infrastructure
http://www.npr.gov/	Papers relating to the American federal government National Performance Review
http://www.ncb.gov.sg/ncb/it2000.asp	Papers of the National Computer Board of Singapore (IT 2000 documents)
http://www.mpt.go.jp/	Papers of the Japanese Ministry of Posts and Telecommunications on the Information Society
http://www.glocom.ac.jp/	Papers of the Japanese Ministry of International Trade and Industry Programme for Advanced Information Infrastructure
http://www.nla.gov.au/lis/govnii.html	Papers of the Australian Government Policy and the Information Superhighway
http://www.finance.gov.au	Papers of the Australian Ministry of Finance

http://www.x.info.ic.gc.ca/info-highway/	Papers of the Canadian Information Highway Advisory Council
http://www.tbs-sct.gc.ca/info-highway/	Papers of the Treasury Board of Canada on government reform

References

ASTEC (1994) *The networked nation.* Canberra: Australian Science and Technology Council.

Abramson, J.B., Arterton, F.C. and Orren, G.R. (1988) *The electronic commonwealth. The impact of new media technologies on democratic politics.* New York: Basic Books.

Adonis, A. and Mulgan, G. (1994) 'Back to Greece: the scope for direct democracy', *Demos,* 3: 2–9.

Alliance for Public Technology (1993) *Connecting each to all.* Washington, DC: APT.

Angell, I. (1995) 'Goodbye to nation. Hello the world', *Parliamentary Brief,* 3(7): 39–40.

Arterton, F.C. (1987) *Can technology protect democracy?* Washington, DC: Roosevelt Centre for American Policy Studies and Sage.

Arthur Andersen (1994) *Predictable patterns. Navigating the continuum from protected monoploy to market competition.* Los Angeles, CA: Arthur Andersen & Co.

Audit Commission (1986) *Computing in local government.* Bristol: Audit Commission

Audit Commission (1992) *Citizen's Charter performance indicators.* London: Audit Commission.

Audit Commission (1995) *Talk back. Local authority communications with citizens. National report.* Bristol: Audit Commission.

Bangemann, M. (1994) *Europe and the global information society. Recommendations to the European Council.* Brussels: European Commission.

Bangemann, M. (1995) *Policies for a European information society.* Charles Read Lecture, 1995, given under the auspices of ESCR/PICT.

Barber, B.R. (1984) *Strong democracy. Participatory politics for a new age.* Berkeley, CA: University of California Press.

Barker, J. and Downing, H. (1985) 'Word processing and the transformation of patriarchal relations of control in the office', in D. MacKenzie and J. Wajcman (eds) *The social shaping of technology.* Milton Keynes: Open University Press.

Bartlett, W. (1991) 'Quasi-markets and contracts: a markets and hierarchies perspective on NHS reforms', *Public Money and Management*, 11: 52–61.

Beamish, A. (1995) 'Communities on-line: community-based community networks', unpublished MA Thesis, Massachusetts Institute of Technology.

Becker, T. (1981) 'Teledemocracy. Bringing power back to the people', *The Futurist*, December: 6–9.

Becker, T. (1993) 'Teledemocracy: gathering momentum in state and local governance', *Spectrum: the Journal of State Government*, 66, 14–20.

Bell, D. (1973) *The coming of post-industrial society. A venture in social forecasting*. New York: Basic Books.

Bellamy, C. (1994) 'Managing strategic resources in a Next Steps department: information agendas and information systems in DSS', in B.J. O'Toole and G. Jordan (eds) *Next Steps: improving management in government?* Aldershot: Dartmouth Publishing Co.

Bellamy, C. (1996) 'Transforming social security benefits administration for the twenty-first century: towards one-stop services and the client group principle', *Public Administration* 74: 159–79.

Bellamy, C., Horrocks, I. and Hambley, N. (1996) *Community governance in the information society*. Unpublished report prepared for the Foundation for Information Technology in Local Government, Nottingham Trent University.

Bellamy, C., Horrocks, I. and Webb, J. (1995a) 'Exchanging information with the public. From one stop shops to community information systems', *Local Government Studies*, 21(1): 11–30.

Bellamy, C., Horrocks, I., and Webb, J. (1995b) 'Community information systems: strengthening local democracy?' in W.B.H. Van de Donk, I.Th.M. Snellen and P.W. Tops (eds) *Orwell in Athens. A perspective on informatization and democracy*. Amsterdam: IOS Press.

Bellamy, C. and Taylor, J.A. (1992) 'Informatisation and new public management. An alternative agenda for public administration', *Public Policy and Administration*, 7: 29–41.

Bellamy, C. and Taylor, J.A. (1994a) 'New public management and the information polity. Towards theoretical development', Paper given to European Consortium of Political Research Joint Sessions, Madrid.

Bellamy, C. and Taylor, J.A. (1994b) 'Introduction. Exploiting IT in public administration: towards the information polity', *Public Administration*, 72: 1–12.

Bellamy, C. and Taylor, J.A. (1994c) 'Reinventing government in the information age', *Public Money and Management*, 14(3): 59–62.

Bellamy, C. and Taylor, J.A. (1996) 'New information and communications technologies and institutional change: the case of the UK criminal justice system', *International Journal of Public Sector Management*, 9(4): 51–69.

Bellamy, C., Taylor, J.A. and McLean, D. (1993) *The changing business of government in the information age*. Proceedings of a workshop organized for OPSS. London: ESRC/Programme on Information and Communication Technology and CCTA.

Bench-Capon, T. (ed.) (1991) *Knowledge-based systems and legal applications*. London: Academic Press.

Benefits Agency (1992) *One stop. Benefits Agency service delivery*. Leeds: Benefits Agency.

Benefits Agency (1993a) *One stop. Report on consultations*. Leeds: Benefits Agency.

Benefits Agency (1993b) *Towards 2000: one stop service for BA customers*. Leeds: Benefits Agency.

Benefits Agency (1993c) *Towards 2000: customer service definitions*. Leeds: Benefits Agency.

Beniger, J.R. (1986) *The control revolution*. Cambridge, MA: Harvard University Press.

Benjamin, R., Rockart, J., Scott Morton, M. and Wyman, J. (1984) 'Information technology. A strategic opportunity', *Sloan Management Review*, Spring: 3–10.

Benn, T. (1980) *The right to know: the case for a freedom of information law to safeguard our basic liberties*. Nottingham: Institute of Workers' Control.

Benson, J.K. (1975) 'The interorganizational network as political economy', *Administrative Science Quarterly*, 20(2): 229–49.

Benton Foundation (n.d.) *Telecommunications and democracy*. Communications Policy Briefing no. 4. Washington, DC: Benton Foundation. Available at http://www.benton.org/.

Best, M. (1990) *The new competition. Institutions of industrial restructuring*. Cambridge: Polity Press.

Beynon-Davies, R. (1995) 'IS failure and risk assessment: the case of the London ambulance service computer-aided dispatch system', *Proceedings of the Third European Conference on Information Systems*, 2: 1153–70.

Blackburn, P., Coombs, R. and Green, K. (1985) *Technology, economic growth and the labour process*. Basingstoke: Macmillan.

Braverman, H. (1974) *Labour and monopoly capital: the degradation of work in the twentieth century*. New York: Monthly Review Press.

Bridgeman Report (1932) *Report of the Commission of Inquiry on the Post Office*, Cmnd 4149. London: HMSO.

Budge, I. (1996) *The new challenge of direct democracy*. Oxford: Polity Press.

Burns, D., Hambleton, R. and Hoggett, P. (1994) *The politics of decentralisation*. Basingstoke: Macmillan.

CCA (1995) *Cable competition: where is cable in the UK?* London: Cable Communications Association.

CCTA (1990) *Information technology in central government. Changes and trends*. London: HMSO.

CCTA, The Government Centre for Information Systems (1994a) *Information superhighways. Opportunities for public service applications*. London: CCTA.

CCTA, The Government Centre for Information Systems (1994b) *BPR in the public sector. An overview of business process re-engineering*. London: HMSO.

CCTA, The Government Centre for Information Systems (1995a) *Report on information superhighways*. Norwich: CCTA.

CCTA, The Government Centre for Information Systems (1995b) *Information superhighways. An update on opportunities for public sector applications*. Norwich: CCTA.

CCTA, The Government Centre for Information Systems (1995c) *Making the best use of the Internet*. Norwich: CCTA.

Cabinet Office (1982) *Efficiency and effectiveness in the Civil Service*, Cmnd 8616. London: HMSO.

Cabinet Office and HM Treasury (1983) *Financial management in government departments*, Cmnd 9158. London: HMSO.

Calabrese, A. and Borchert, M. (1996) 'Prospects for electronic democracy in the United States. Rethinking communication and social policy', *Media, Culture and Society*, 18(2): 249–68.

Callon, M. (1987) 'Society in the making. The study of technology as a tool for sociological analysis', in W. Bijker (ed) *The social construction of technological systems*. Boston: MIT Press.

Carter Report (1977) *Report of the Post Office Review Committee*, Cmnd 6850. London: HMSO.

Carter, D. (n.d.) ' "Digital democracy" or "information aristocracy": economy re-generation and the information economy', Discussion Paper, Department of Economic Development, Manchester City Council.

Carter, N. (1989) 'Performance indicators: "backseat driving" or "hands off" control?' *Policy and Politics*, 17: 131–8.

Castells, M. (1989) *The informational city*. Oxford: Basil Blackwell.

Castells, M. (1996) *The rise of the network society. Economy, society and culture I*. Oxford: Blackwell.

Cawson, A., Morgan, K., Webber, D., Holmes, P. and Stevens, V. (1990) *Hostile brothers. Competition and closure in the European electronics industry*. Oxford: Clarendon Press.

Child, J. (1987) 'Information technology, organization and the response to strategic challenges', *California Management Review*, 30 (Fall): 33–50.

Child, J. and Loveridge, R. (1990) *Information technology in European services. Towards a microelectronic future*. Oxford: Blackwell.

Civil Service Department (1981) *Efficiency in the Civil Service*, Cmnd 8293. London: HMSO.

Civille, R., Fidelman, M. and Altobello, J. (1993) *A national strategy for civic networking*. Washington, DC: Center for Civic Networking.

Clarke, M. and Stewart, J. (1985) *Local government and the public service orientation. Or does a public service provide for the public?* Luton: Local Government Training Board.

Clarke, M. and Stewart, J. (1986a) *The public service orientation. Developing the approach*. Luton: Local Government Training Board.

Clarke, M. and Stewart, J. (1986b) 'Local government and the public service orientation', *Local Government Studies*, 12: 1–8.

Cochrane, A. (1994) *Whatever happened to local government?* Buckingham: Open University Press.

Cochrane, P. (1994) 'Copper mind-sets', *British Telecommunications Engineering*, April: 10–11.

Collingridge, D. and Margetts, H. (1994) 'Can government information systems be inflexible technology? The Operational Strategy re-visited', *Public Administration*, 72: 55–72.

Coombs, R. (1992) *Organizational politics and the strategic use of information technology*, PICT Policy Research Paper No. 20. Newcastle: ESRC, Programme on Information and Communication Technology.

Corrigan, P. (1996) *No more big brother*, Fabian Pamphlet 578. London: Fabian Society.

Crick, B. (1964) *In defence of politics*. Harmondsworth: Pelican Books.

Danziger, J., Dutton, W., Kling, R. and Kraemer, K. (1982) *Computers and politics*. New York: Columbia University Press.

Davenport, T.H. (1993) *Process innovation. Re-engineering work through information technology*. Boston, MA: Harvard Business School Press.

Davenport, T.H. (1994) 'Saving IT's soul. Human-centred information management', *Harvard Business Review*, March–April: 119–31.

Davenport, T.H., Eccles, R.G. and Prusak, L. (1992) 'Information politics', *Sloan Management Review*, Fall: 53–65.

Davidow, W.H. and Malone, M.S. (1992) *The virtual corporation*. New York: HarperCollins.

Davies, A. (1994) *Telecommunications and politics. The decentralised alternative*. London: Pinter.

Dawson, P., Buckland, S. and Gilbert N. (1990) 'Expert systems and the public provision of welfare benefit advice', *Policy and Politics*, 18(1): 43–54.

Department for Education and Employment (1995) *Education superhighways for education. The way forward*. London: HMSO.

Department of Health (1995) *Code of practice on openness in the NHS*. London: Department of Health.

Department of Health and Social Security (1985) *The reform of social security*, Cmnd 9517–9519. London: HMSO.

Department of Social Security (1990) *The logical office: report on the relocation of work project*. Unpublished.

Department of Social Security and HM Treasury (1994) *Social Security departmental report. The government's expenditure plans 1994–95 to 1996–97*, Cm 2513. London: HMSO.

Department of Trade and Industry (1991) *Competition and choice: telecommunications policy for the 1990s*, Cm 1461. London: HMSO.

Department of Trade and Industry (1994) *Creating the superhighways of the future: developing broadband communications in the UK*, Cm 2734. London: HMSO

Department of Trade and Industry (1996) *Development of the information society. An international analysis*. London: HMSO

Depla, P. (1995) 'Technology and the renewal of local democracy: Dutch experiences after 1990', paper given to the UK Study Group on Information, Communication and New Technology in Public Administration, De Montfort University, June.

Dizard, W. (1989) *The coming information age* (3rd edn). London: Longman.

Doctor, R.D. (1994) 'Seeking equity in the National Information Infrastructure', *Internet Research*, 4(3): 9–22.

Donk, W.B.H.J. Van de and Tops, P.W. (1992) 'Informatization and democracy: Orwell or Athens. A review of the literature', *Informatization and the Public Sector*, 2: 169–96.

Donk, W.B.H.J. Van de, Snellen, I.Th.M. and Tops, P.W. (1995) *Orwell in Athens. A perspective on informatization and democracy*. Amsterdam: IOS Press.

Dosi, F., Freeman, C., Nelson, R., Silverberg, G. and Soete, L. (1988) *Technical change and economic theory*. London: Pinter.

Doulton, A. (1993) *Exchanging information with the public. EIP Report 1992 and case studies*. Oxford: Dragonflair and CDW & Associates.

Doulton, A. (1994) *Government and community information services. EIP report, 1994*. Oxford: Dragonflair and CDW & Associates.

Dunleavy, P. (1994) 'The globalization of public services production: can government be "best in world"?' *Public Policy and Administration*, 9(2): 36–64.

Dutton, W.H. (1992) 'Political science research on teledemocracy', *Social Science Computer Review*, 10: 505–21.

Dutton, W.H. (1994) 'Lessons from public and nonprofit services', in F. Williams and J. Pavlik (eds), *The people's right to know: media, democracy and the information highway*. Hillsdale, NJ: Lawrence Erlbaum Associates.

Dutton, W.H. (ed.) (1996a) *Information and communications technologies: visions and realities* Oxford: Oxford University Press.

Dutton, W.H. (1996b) 'Network rules of order: regulating speech in public electronic fora', *Media, Culture and Society*, 18: 269–90.

Dutton, W.H., Blumler, J.G. and Kraemer, K.L. (eds) (1987) *Wired cities: shaping the future of communications*. Los Angeles: Annenberg School of Communications.

Dutton, W.H., Guthrie, K.K., O'Connell, J. and Wyer, J. (1991) *State and local government innovations in electronic services: the case in the Western and Northeastern United States*, a report to the Office of Technology, US Congress. Los Angeles: Annenberg School of Communications.

Dutton, W.H., Blumler, J., Garnham, N., Mansell, R., Cornford, J. and Poltu, M. (1994) *The information superhighway. Britain's response*, PICT Policy Research Paper 29. Uxbridge: ESRC/PICT.

Dutton, W.H., Blumler, J., Garnham, N., Mansell, R., Cornford, J. and Peltu, M. (1996) 'The politics of information and communication policy: the information superhighway', in W.H. Dutton (ed.) *Information and communication technologies: visions and realities*. Oxford: Oxford University Press.

Dybkjær, L. and Christensen, S. (1994) *Info-Soc 2000*. Copenhagen: Ministry of Research and Information Technology.

The Economist (1995) 'The future of democracy, and democracy and technology', *The Economist*, 17 June: 15–16 and 21–3.

Edwards, A. (1995) 'Informatization and views of democracy', in W.B.H.J. Van de Donk, I.Th.M. Snellen and P.W. Tops (eds) *Orwell in Athens. A perspective on informatization and democracy*. Amsterdam: IOS Press.

Efficiency Unit (1995) *Resource management systems*. London: HMSO.

Elam, M. (1990) 'Puzzling out the post-Fordist debate. Technology, markets and institutions', *Economic and Industrial Democracy*, 11: 9–37.

Ernst, H. and Jaeger, C. (eds) (1989) *Information society and spatial structure*. London, Belhaven.

Etzioni, A. (1972) 'Minerva. An electronic town hall', *Policy Sciences*, 3: 457–74.

Etzioni, A. (1993) *The spirit of community*. New York: Crown Publishers Inc.

Eulau, H. (1977) *Technology and civility: the skill revolution in politics*, publication no. 167. Stanford, CA: Hoover Institution, Stanford University.

European Commission (1993) *Growth, competitiveness and employment. The challenges and ways forward into the twenty-first century*, White Paper. Brussels: European Commission.

European Commission (1994a) *Europe's way to the information society. An action plan*. Brussels: European Commission.

European Commission (1994b) *The IDA programme*, available at http://www.ispo/ida.

European Commission (1994c) *Vers une economie Européenne dynamique*, Green Paper. Brussels: European Commission.

European Commission (1995a) *G-7 Ministerial Conference on the Information Society: theme paper*. Brussels: European Commission.

European Commission (1995b) *G-7 Ministerial Conference on the Information Society: chair's conclusions*. Brussels: European Commission.

European Commission (1995c) *G-7 Information Society Conference pilot projects: executive summaries*. Brussels: European Commission.

Fallon, I. (1993) *The paper chase: ten years of change at DSS*. London: HarperCollins.

Fenchurch, R.A. (1994) 'Network wonderland', *Demos*, 4: 11.

Fishkin, J. (1991) *Democracy and deliberation: new directions for democratic reform*. New Haven, CT: Yale University Press.

Fishkin, J.S. (1992) 'Talk of the tube. How to get teledemocracy right', *American Prospect*, 11(Fall): 46–52.

FITLOG (1994) *In touch: using technology to communicate with the public*. Bristol: Foundation for IT in Local Government.

Foreman-Peck, J. and Millward, R. (1994) *Public and private ownership of British industry 1820–1990*. Oxford: Clarendon Press.

Fox, C. and Miller, H. (1995) *Postmodern public administration: towards discourse*. Thousand Oaks, CA: Sage.

Freeman, C. (1984) *The economics of innovation*. Harmondsworth: Penguin.

Frissen, P.H.A. (1992a) 'Informatization in public administration', *International Review of Administrative Sciences*, 58: 307–10.

Frissen, P.H.A. (1992b) 'Informatization in public administration. Research directions', Paper given to UK National Study Group on Information, Communication and New Technology in Public Administration, London, March.

Fulton Committee Report (1968) *The Civil Service*, Cmnd 3638. London: HMSO.

G-7 Government On-line Project (1995) Publicity document available at http://www.open.gov.uk.

Gans, H.J. (1994) 'The electronic shut-ins. Some social flaws of the information super-highway', *Media Studies Journal*, 8: 123–7.

Garrett, J. (1980) *Managing the Civil Service*. London: Heinemann.

Gibbs, D. and Leach, B. (1992) 'Telematics and local economic development: the Manchester Host computer network', paper presented to the PICT National Conference, Newport, Wales, March.

Gingrich, N. (1994) *Speeches*, available at http://dolphin.gulf.net/Gingrich/.

Giordano, L. (1993) *Beyond Taylorism*. London: Macmillan.

Glover, C. and O'Dwyer, K. (1990) 'Using IT to support administrative moderniza-tion', in P. Frissen and I. Snellen (eds), *Informatization strategies in public administra-tion*. Amsterdam: Elsevier Science Publishers.

Goldman, H. (1986) *Co-ordination of computerization of the criminal justice system*. London: Home Office, unpublished.

Gore, A. (1991) 'Infrastructure for the global village', *Scientific American*, 265 (September): 108–11.

Gore, A. (1993) *Creating a government that works better and costs less*. New York and Harmondsworth: Plume Books and Penguin.

Graham, G. (1994) *Free-nets and the politics of community in electronic networks*, available at net-happenings@net.internic.is.

Graham, S. (1991) *Best practice in developing community teleservice centres*. Manchester: University of Manchester.

Graham, S., Cornford, J. and Marvin, S. (1996) 'The socio-economic benefits of a universal telephone network', *Telecommunications Policy*, 20(1): 3–10.

Graham, S. and Marvin, S. (1996) *Telecommunications and the city: electronic spaces, urban places*. London: Routledge.

Greer, P. (1994) *Transforming central government: the Next Steps initiative*. Buckingham: Open University Press.

Grint, K. and Willcocks, L. (1995) 'Business process re-engineering in theory and practice. Business paradise regained?' *New Technology, Work and Employment*, 10(2): 99–109.

Gulick, L. (1937) Notes on a theory of organization', in L. Gulick and L. Urwick (eds) *Papers on the Science of Administration*. New York: Institute of Public Administration.

Guthrie, K.K. and Dutton, W.H. (1992) 'The politics of citizen access technology. The development of public information utilities in four cities', *Policy Studies Journal*, 20(4): 574–97.

Gyford, J. (1985) *The politics of local socialism*. London: George Allen and Unwin.

HM Treasury (1986) *Multi-departmental review of budgeting*. London: HM Treasury.

HM Treasury (1991) *Competing for quality*, Cm 1730. London: HMSO.

Hambleton, R. (1988) 'Consumerism, decentralization and local democracy', *Public Administration*, 66(2): 125–47.

Hambleton, R., Hoggett, P. and Tolan, F. (1989) 'The decentralisation of public services. A research agenda', *Local Government Studies*, 15 (January-February): 39–56.

Hammer, M. (1990) 'Reengineering work. Don't automate, obliterate', *Harvard Business Review*, July–August: 104–12.

Hammer, M. and Champy, J. (1993) *Re-engineering the corporation*. New York: HarperCollins.

Hawker, I., Tandon, V., Cotter, D. and Hill, A. (1994) 'New network infrastructures for the 21st century', *British Telecommunications Engineering*, July: 103–110.

Henderson, A.M.C. (1993) 'Informatization of the delivery and administration of social security. Developments and issues in the Australian DSS', paper given to ESRC Study Group on Information, Communication and New Technologies, London.

Hepworth, M. (1989) *The geography of the information economy*. London: Belhaven.

Hepworth, M. (1992) 'The municipal information economy?' *Local Government Studies*, 18(3): 148–57.

Hoggett, P. and Hambleton, R. (1988) *Decentralization and democracy. Localising public services*. Bristol: School for Advanced Urban Studies, University of Bristol.

Holman, K. (1994) *Plan large, deliver small. Balanced decentralisation in the county councils*. London: Association of County Councils.

Home Office (1993) *Police reform: a police service for the twenty-first century*, Cm 2281. London: HMSO.

Home Office Science and Technology Group (1994) *The national strategy for police information systems*. London: Home Office.

Home Office (1995a) *Annual report 1995. The government's expenditure plans 1995–96 to 1997–98 for the Home Office and Charity Commission*, Cm 2808. London: HMSO.

Home Office (1995b) *Identity cards. A consultation document*, Cm 2879. London: HMSO.

Home Office (1996) *Annual report 1996. The government's expenditure plans 1996–97 to 1998–99*, Cm 3208. London: HMSO.

Hood, C. (1991) 'A public management for all seasons', *Public Administration*, 69: 3–19.

House of Commons (1921–2) *Report of the House of Commons Select Committee on the Telephone Service*, HC 121. London: HMSO.

House of Commons (1976–7) *Eleventh report from the Expenditure Committee on the Civil Service*, HC 535-I. London: HMSO.

House of Commons (1981–2) *Third report from the Treasury and Civil Service Committee on Efficiency and Effectiveness in the Civil Service*, HC 236. London: HMSO.

House of Commons (1983–4) *Minutes of evidence taken before the Public Accounts Committee, 28 March, 1984*, HC 361. London: HMSO.

House of Commons (1988–9) *Report from the Trade and Industry Committee on information technology*, HC 338. London: HMSO.

House of Commons (1993–4a) *Third report from the Trade and Industry Committee on optical fibre networks*, HC 285-I. London: HMSO.

House of Commons (1993–4b) *Third report from the Trade and Industry Committee on optical fibre networks, memoranda of evidence*, HC 285-II. London: HMSO.

House of Commons (1995–6) *First report of the Information Committee on electronic publication of House of Commons documents*, HC 328. London: HMSO.

Humbert, M. Meijer, J., Nieuwehuis, M. and Schouten, R. (1992) *Government service centres: final report*. The Hague: B and A Policy Group on behalf of the Ministry of Home Affairs.

Information Highway Advisory Council of Canada (1995) *Connection, community, content. The challenge of the information highway.* Ottawa: Ministry of Industry.

Information Infrastructure Task Force (1993) *The National Information Infrastructure. Agenda for action.* Washington, DC: US Government Printing Office.

Information Society Forum (1995) *Theme paper.* Brussels: European Commission.

Information Society Forum (1996) *Networks for people and their communities. Making the most of the information society in the European Union,* first annual report to the European Commission from the Information Society Forum. Brussels: European Commission.

Information Technology Advisory Panel (1983) *Making a business of information.* London: HMSO.

Information Technology Review Group (1995) *Clients first. The challenge for government from information technology.* Canberra: Ministry of Finance. The references in this book are to the on-line version downloaded from the Ministry's Web site.

Inland Revenue (1994) *Electronic lodgement service. Consultative document.* London: Inland Revenue Change Management Divison.

Inland Revenue (1995) *Electronic lodgement service. Second consultative document.* London: Inland Revenue.

Jarillo, J.C. (1993) *Strategic networks. Creating the borderless organization.* Oxford: Butterworth–Heinemann.

Jones, M. (1994) Don't emancipate, exaggerate: rhetoric, reality and reengineering, in R. Baskerville *et al.* (eds) *Transforming organizations with information technology.* Amsterdam: North-Holland.

Jones, S.G. (ed.) (1995) *Cybersociety. Computer-mediated communication and community.* Thousand Oaks, CA: Sage.

Jøsevold, R. (1994) 'Improving public services through intergovernmental cross-level and cross-professional organization, paper given to the Nordic Network on One-Stop Shops, University of Bristol.

Kable (1995) *Civil Service IT market profile 1995–6.* London: Kable.

Keane, J. (1988) *Democracy and civil liberty.* London: Verso.

Keen, J. (1994a) *Information management in health services.* Milton Keynes: Open University Press.

Keen, J. (1994b) 'An information strategy for the NHS?' *Public Administration,* 72: 33–53.

Kerry, R. and Harrop, M. (n.d.) *The G-7 Government On-line Initiative,* available at http://www.open.gov.uk/.

Kemp, P. and Walker, D. (1996) *A better machine. Government for the twenty-first century.* London: European Policy Forum.

LGUA (1996) *Your local authority in the information society.* London: Local Government Users Association.

The Labour Party (1995) *Communicating Britain's future.* London: The Labour Party.

Laudon, K. (1977) *Communications technology and democratic participation.* New York: Praeger.

Leach, S., Stewart, J. and Walsh, K. (1994) *The changing organisation and management of local government.* Basingstoke: Macmillan.

Lipietz, A. (1987) *Mirages and miracles.* London: Verso.

Lipnack, J. and Stamps J. (1993) *The teamnet factor: Bringing the power of boundary crossing into the heart of your business.* Vermont: Oliver Wight Publications.

Lowndes, V. (1996) 'Varieties of new institutionalism: a critical appraisal', *Public Administration,* 74: 181–97.

Lynn, P. (1992) *Public perceptions of local government: its finances and services*. London: HMSO.

Lyon, D. (1988) *The information society: issues and illusions*. Cambridge: Polity Press.

Lyon, D. (1994) *The electronic eye. The rise of surveillance society*. Cambridge: Polity Press.

Lyytinen, K. and Hirscheim, R. (1987) 'Information systems failures. A survey and classification of the empirical literature', *Oxford Surveys in Information Technology*, 14: 257–309.

MacKenzie, D. (1996) *Knowing machines: essays on technical change*. London: MIT Press.

MacKenzie, D. and Wajcman, J. (eds) (1985) *The social shaping of technology. How the refrigerator got its hum*. Milton Keynes: Open University Press.

McLean, I. (1989) *Democracy and new technology*. Cambridge: Polity Press.

Macpherson, C. B. (1973) *Democratic theory. Essays in retrieval*. Oxford: Clarendon Press.

Machlup, F. (1983) 'Semantic quirks in studies of information', in F. Machlup and U. Mansfield (eds), *The study of information: interdisciplinary messages*. New York: John Wiley.

Manchester City Council (1991) *Manchester. The information city*. Manchester: Manchester City Council.

Mansell, R. (1993) *The new telecommunications. A political economy of network evolution*. London: Sage.

Margetts, H. (1991) 'The computerization of social security. The way forward or a step backward?' *Public Administration*, 69: 325–34.

Margetts, H. (1995) 'The automated state', *Public Policy and Administration*, 10(2): 88–103.

Martin, J. (1978) *The wired society*. Englewood Cliffs, NJ: Prentice Hall.

Marvin, S. (1994) 'Accessibility to utility networks. Local policy issues', *Local Government Studies*, 20: 437–57.

Masuda, Y. (1990) *Managing in the information society. Releasing synergy Japanese style*. Oxford: Basil Blackwell.

Matthews, R.S. (1979) 'Accountable management in the Department of Health and Social Security', *Management in Government*, 34: 125–32.

Metcalfe, L. and Richards, S. (1987) *Improving public management*. London: Sage and European Institute of Public Administration.

Miles, I. (1996) 'The information society: competing perspectives on the social and economic implications of ICTs', in W.H. Dutton (ed.) *Information and communication technologies: visions and realities*. Oxford: Oxford University Press.

Miller, D. (1989) *Market, state and community. Theoretical foundations of market socialism*. Oxford: Oxford University Press.

Miller, D. (1995) 'Citizenship and pluralism', *Political Studies*, 43: 432–50.

Mills, M. (1996) 'Changing the project culture for procurement', *Information Technology and Public Policy*, 14(3): 167–9.

Ministry of Reconstruction (1918) *Report of the Machinery of Government Committee*, the Haldane Report, Cmd 9230. London: HMSO.

Mitchell, J. (1979) *The politics of secrecy. The case for a freedom of information law*. London: National Council for Civil Liberties.

Monopolies and Mergers Commission (1995) *Telephone number portability*. London: HMSO.

Mueller, M. (1993) 'Universal service in telephone history. A reconstruction', *Telecommunications Policy*, July: 352–69.

Muid, C. (1994) 'Information systems and new public management. A view from the centre', *Public Administration*, 72: 113–25.

Mulgan, G. (1991) *Communication and control: networks and the new economics of communications*. Cambridge: Polity Press.

Naisbitt, J. (1984) *Megatrends. Ten new directions transforming our lives*. London: Macdonald.

NCC (1996) *The information society. Getting it right for consumers*. London: National Consumer Council.

NHS Management Executive (1992) *IM&T strategy overview*. London: Information Management Group, NHSME.

National Audit Office (1986) *The Financial Management Initiative*. London: HMSO.

National Audit Office (1991) *Office automation in government departments*. London: HMSO.

National Computer Board of Singapore (1995) *IT 2000. Visions of an intelligent island*. Singapore: National Computer Board.

National Telecommunications and Information Administration (1991) *The NTIA infrastructure report. Telecommunications in the age of information*. Washington, DC: US Government Printing Office.

Negroponte, N. (1995) *Being digital*. London: Hodder and Stoughton.

Nelson, R. and Winter, S. (1982) *An evolutionary theory of economic change*. New Haven, CT: Belknap.

Newman, K. (1986) *The selling of BT*. London: Holt, Rinehart and Winston.

Nora, S. and Minc, A. (1980) *The computerization of society. A report to the President of France*. Cambridge, MA: MIT Press.

North, D. (1990) *Institutions, institutional change and economic performance*. Cambridge: Cambridge University Press.

OECD (1992) *Information technology in government. Management challenges*. Paris: Organization for Economic Co-operation and Development.

OECD (1995) *Telecommunication infrastructure. The benefits of competition*. Information and communications policy paper no. 35. Paris: Organization for Economic Co-operation and Development.

OFTEL (1994a) *Households without a telephone*. London: OFTEL.

OFTEL (1994b) *A framework for effective competition. A consultative document on interconnection and related issues*. London: HMSO.

OFTEL (1995a) *Effective competition: framework for action. A statement on the future of interconnection*. London: OFTEL.

OFTEL (1995b) *Universal telecommunications services. A consultative document on universal service in the UK from 1997*. London: OFTEL.

Office of Public Service and Science, Citizen's Charter Unit (1992) *The Citizen's Charter first report. 1992*, Cm 2101. London: HMSO.

Office of Public Service and Science, Citizen's Charter Unit (1993) *Open government*, Cm 2290. London: HMSO.

Office of Public Service and Science, Citizen's Charter Unit (1994a) *Open government. Code of practice on access to government information*. London: HMSO.

Office of Public Service and Science (1994b) *The Civil Service. Continuity and change*, Cm 2627. London: HMSO.

Office of Public Service and Science (1995) *The Civil Service. Taking forward continuity and change*, Cm 2748. London: HMSO.

Office of Public Service, Citizen's Charter Unit (1996a) *Open government. Code of practice on access to government information. 1995 Report*. London: HMSO.

Office of Public Service, Central IT Unit (1996b) *government.direct. A prospectus for the electronic delivery of government services*, Cm 3438. London: HMSO

Office of the Vice President (1993a) *From red tape to results. Creating a government that works better and costs less*, report of the National Performance Review. Washington, DC: US Government Printing Office.

Office of the Vice President (1993b) *Reengineering government through IT*, accompanying report to the National Performance Review. Washington, DC: Government Printing Office.

Oliver, I. (1996) *Police, government and accountability* (2nd edn). Basingstoke: Macmillan.

Osborne, D. and Gaebler, T. (1992) *Reinventing government. How the entrepreneurial spirit is transforming the public sector.* Reading, MA: Addison Wesley.

Palfreman, J. and Swade, D. (1991) *The dream machine. Exploring the computer age.* London: BBC Publications.

Peltu, M., MacKenzie, D., Shapiro, S. and Dutton, W. H. (1996) 'Computer power and human limits', in W.H. Dutton (ed.) *Information and communication technologies: visions and realities.* Oxford: Oxford University Press.

Percy-Smith, J. (1995) *Digital democracy. Information and communication technologies in local politics.* London: Commission for Local Democracy.

Peters, T. and Waterman, R.H. (1982) *In search of excellence: lessons from America's best-run companies.* New York: Harper and Row.

Phillips, A. (1994) *Local democracy. The terms of the debate.* London: Commission for Local Democracy.

Piore, M. and Sabel, C. (1984) *The second industrial divide. Possibilities for prosperity.* New York: Basic Books.

Pirie, M. (1991) *The Citizens' Charter.* London: Adam Smith Institute.

Pitt, D.C. (1980) *The telecommunications function in the British Post Office. A case study of bureaucratic adaption.* Farnborough: Saxon House.

Plant, R. (1990) 'Citizenship and rights', in R. Plant and N. Barry, *Citizenship and rights in Thatcher's Britain. Two views.* London: Institute of Economic Affairs.

Pollitt, C. (1993) *Managerialism and the public services* (2nd edn). Oxford: Blackwell.

Ponting, C. (1989) *Secrecy in Britain.* Oxford: Basil Blackwell.

Quinn, J.B. (1992) *Intelligent enterprise. A new paradigm for a new era.* Berkeley: University of California Press.

Raab, C., Bellamy, C., Taylor, J., Dutton, W.H. and Peltu, M. (1996) 'The information polity: electronic democracy, privacy and surveillance', in W.H. Dutton (ed.) *Information and communication technologies: visions and realities.* Oxford: Oxford University Press.

Ranson, S. and Stewart, J. (1989) 'Citizenship and government: the challenge for management in the public domain', *Political Studies*, 37: 5–24.

Ranson, S. and Stewart, J. (1994) *Management for the public domain: enabling the learning society.* Basingstoke: St Martin's Press.

Rawlings, C., Temple, M. and Thrasher, M. (1994) *Community identity and participation in local democracy.* London: Commission for Local Democracy.

Rheingold, H. (1993) *The virtual community in a computerized world.* London: Secker and Warburg.

Rhodes, R. (1981) *Control and power in central–local relations.* Aldershot: Gower.

Richardson, J. and Cram, L. (1992) *Citizenship and local democracy. A European perspective.* Luton: Local Government Management Board.

Ridge, M. (1994) 'Towards a European nervous system. The role of the European Union', *Public Administration*, 72: 127–34.

Rogers, E.M., Collins-Jarvis, L. and Schmitz, J. (1994) 'The PEN Project in Santa Monica. Interactive communication, equality and political action' *Journal of the American Society for Information Science*, 45: 401–10.

Rose, H. (1988) 'Constructing organisational forms for flexible computing', in D. Boddy, J. McCalman and D. Buchanan (eds) *The new management challenge*. London: Croom Helm.

SOCITM (1988, 1994, 1995, 1996) *IT trends in local government*. Northampton: Society of Information Technology Management.

Sackman, H. and Boehm, B. (1972) *Planning community information utilities*. Montvale, NJ: AFIPS Press.

Sackman, H. and Nie, N. (eds) (1970) *The information utility and social choice*. Montvale, NJ: AFIPS Press.

Sawhney, H. (1994) 'Universal service. Prosaic motives and great ideals', *Journal of Broadcasting and Electronic Media*, 38(Fall): 375–95.

Sawhney, H. (1996) 'Information superhighway. Metaphors as midwives', *Media, Culture and Society*, 18: 291–314.

Scarbrough H. and Corbett, J.M. (1992) *Technology and organization. Power, meaning and design*. London: Routledge.

Schalken, C.A.T. and Tops, P.W. (1995) 'Democracy and virtual communities. An empirical exploration of the Amsterdam digital city', in W. van de Donk, I. Snellen and P. Tops (eds) *Orwell in Athens. A perspective on informatization and democracy*. Amsterdam: IOS Press.

Scott Morton, M. (ed.) (1991) *The corporation of the 90s. Information technology and organizational transformation*. Oxford: Oxford University Press.

Self, P. (1977) *Administrative theories and politics: an inquiry into the structure and processes of modern government*. London: George Allen and Unwin.

Self, P. (1985) *Political theories of modern government*. London: George Allen and Unwin.

Smith, S. (1997) 'Orwell and good?' *Computer Weekly*, 23 January: 38.

South West Thames Regional Health Authority (1993) *Report of the inquiry into the London Ambulance Service*. London: South West Thames Regional HA.

Stewart, J. (1993) 'The limitations of government by contract', *Public Money and Management*, 13(3) 7–12.

Stewart, J. and Clarke, M. (1987) 'The public service orientation. Issues and dilemmas', *Public Administration*, 65: 161–77.

Stewart, J. and Stoker, G. (1995) 'Fifteen years of local government restructuring 1979–94. An evaluation', in J. Stewart and G. Stoker (eds) *Local government in the 1990s*. Basingstoke: Macmillan.

Stoker, G. (1988) *The politics of local government*. Basingstoke: Macmillan Educational.

Stoker, G. (1994) *The role and purpose of local government*. London: Commission for Local Democracy.

Stonier, T. (1983) *The wealth of information. A profile of the post-industrial economy*. London: Methuen.

Swinden, K. and Heath, W. (1994) *Wired Whitehall 1999*. London: Kable.

Taylor, J.A (1992) 'Information networking in government', *International Review of Administrative Sciences*, 69: 375–89.

Taylor, J.A. (1994) 'Telecommunications infrastructure and public policy development. Evidence and inference', *Informatization and the Public Sector*, 3(1): 63–73.

Taylor, J.A. (1995) 'Don't obliterate, informate! BPR for the information age', *New Technology, Work and Employment*, 10: 83–8.

Taylor, J.A., Bardzki, B. and Wilson, C. (1995a) 'Laying down the infrastructure for innovations in teledemocracy. The case of Scotland', in W. van de Donk, I. Snellen and P. Tops (eds) *Orwell in Athens. A perspective on informatization and democracy*. Amsterdam: IOS Press.

Taylor, J.A., Bardzki, B. and Wilson, C. (1995b) 'Superhighways and public services. Is information age government viable?' paper presented to the conference on the governance of cyber-space, University of Teesside.

Taylor, J.A., Bellamy, C., Raab, C., Dutton, W. H. and Peltu, M. (1996) 'Innovation in public service delivery', in W.H. Dutton (ed.) *Information and communication technologies: visions and realities.* Oxford: Oxford University Press.

Taylor, J.A. and Webster, C.W.R. (1996) 'Universalism, public services and citizenship in the information age'. *Information Infrastructure and Policy*, 5(3): 217–233.

Taylor, J.A. and Williams, H. (1988) *Organizational evolution. Policy development and changing capabilities in British Telecommunications plc and its antecedents*, unpublished report. Newcastle: Centre for Urban and Regional Development Studies, University of Newcastle.

Taylor, J.A. and Williams, H. (1989) 'Telematics, organisation, and the local government mission', *Local Government Studies*, 15(3): 75–93.

Taylor, J.A. and Williams, H. (1990) 'Themes and issues in an information polity', *Journal of Information Technology*, 5: 151–60.

Taylor, J.A. and Williams, H. (1991a) 'Public administration and the information polity', *Public Administration*, 69: 171–90.

Taylor, J.A. and Williams, H. (1991b) 'The networked firm', in Williams, B.C. and Spaull, B. (eds) *Information technology and accounting. The impact of information technology.* London: Chapman and Hall.

Taylor, J.A. and Williams, H. (1992) 'Police management, office automation and organizational change', *New Technology, Work and Employment*, 7(1): 44–53.

Taylor, J.A. and Williams, H. (1994) 'The "transformation game". Information systems and process innovation in organizations', *New Technology, Work and Employment*, 9: 54–65.

Taylor, J.A. and Williams, H. (1995) 'Superhighways or superlow-ways', *Flux. The International Journal on Telecommunications*, 19: 45–54.

Taylor, J.A., Williams, H. and McLeod, B. (1993a) 'Telecommunications in Scotland: auditing the issues', *Quarterly Economic Commentary*, 18(3): 66–74.

Taylor, J.A., Williams, H. and McLeod, B. (1993b) 'Telecommunications in Scotland: detailing the issues', *Quarterly Economic Commentary*, 18(4): 67–75.

Taylor Walsh, R. (1993) 'Development of a community information service. The National Capital Area Public Access Network (CapAcess) – a work in progress', *Internet Research*, 3: 41–59.

Telecommunications Council (Japan) (1994) *Reforms towards the intellectually creative society.* Tokyo: MPT.

Thompson, J. (1967) *Organizations in action.* New York: McGraw-Hill.

Toffler, A. (1980) *The third wave.* New York: William Morrow.

Toffler, A. (1990) *Power shift.* New York: Bantam Books.

Treasury Board of Canada (1995) *Blue print for renewing government services using information technology.* Ottawa: Treasury Board of Canada. The references in this book are to the on-line version from the Treasury Board's Web site.

US Congress Office of Technology Assessment (1993) *Making government work: electronic delivery of federal services.* Washington, DC: US Government Printing Office.

Valdar, A., Newman, D., Wood, R. and Greenop, D. (1992), 'A vision of the future network', *British Telecommunications Engineering*, 11(3): 142–52.

Varn, R.J. (1992) *A national information and service delivery system.* Washington, DC: National Governors' Association.

Venkatraman, N. (1991) 'IT-induced business reconfiguration', in M. Scott Morton (ed.) *The corporation of the 90s. Information technology and organizational transformation.* Oxford: Oxford University Press.

Vickers, G. (1965) *The art of judgement. A study of policy making.* London: Chapman and Hall.

Vickers, J. and Yarrow, G. (1985) *Privatization and the natural monopolies.* London: Public Policy Centre.

Waldegrave, W. (1993) 'The reality of reform and accountability in today's public service', lecture given to the Public Finance Foundation, reprinted in N. Flynn (ed.) (1994) *Change in the Civil Service. A Public Finance Foundation reader.* London: The Chartered Institute of Public Finance and Accountancy.

Walsh, K. (1995) *Public services and market mechanisms. Competition, contracting and the new public management.* Basingstoke: Macmillan.

Webster, J. (1996) *Shaping women's work. Gender, employment and information technology.* Harlow: Longman.

Weston, J. (1994) 'Old freedoms and new technologies. The evolution of community networking', paper given to the Free Speech and Privacy in the Information Age Symposium, University of Waterloo, Canada, November 1994, available from the Teledemocracy Programme of NPTN at http://www.nptn.org.80/cyber.serv/tdp.

Williams, F. (1991) *The coming of the new telecommunications structure for the information age.* New York: Free Press.

Willcocks, L. (1994) 'Managing information systems in UK public administration. Issues and prospects', *Public Administration*, 72: 13–32.

Wilson, D. (ed.) (1984) *The secrets file. The case for freedom of information in Britain today.* London: Heinemann.

Winner, L. (1993) 'Beyond inter-passive media', *Technology Review*, August–September: 69.

Yates, J.-A. (1989) *Control through communications.* Baltimore: Johns Hopkins University Press.

Zuboff, S. (1988) *In the age of the smart machine. The future of work and power.* Oxford: Heinemann.

Index

THE WHITEHALL READER
THE UK's ADMINISTRATIVE MACHINE IN ACTION

Peter Barberis

The UK's permanent bureaucracy of senior civil servants is concentrated in Whitehall, and never before has Whitehall and the work of mandarins been the subject of so much public interest and controversy. This volume presents a rounded picture of some of the most important issues and recent developments. It covers the structure and workings of the Whitehall machine; Whitehall's interactions with other agents such as Parliament, organized interests and the general public; the relationships between mandarins and ministers; managerial reforms and their implications; and the ethics of officialdom, including questions of loyalty and neutrality. It reflects a wide range of perception and opinion, expressed in the words of academics, politicians, civil servants and other informed observers. This it does through a series of excerpts from books, articles, official documents and other sources, some of which are not otherwise readily available.

Its key features include:
- a general introductory essay
- over forty excerpts, organized thematically into sections
- each section introduced by a brief commentary
- concluding annotated bibliography.

For the first time in many years, students will have access, in one volume, to some of the most accomplished and up-to-date writings, offering varied and penetrating insights into the 'official' world of Whitehall.

Contents

Introductory essay: Whitehall since the Fulton Report – The Whitehall machine: structure and process – Civil servants and ministers: power, influence and public policy – Loyalties, responsibilities and ethics – Reforming Whitehall I: hopes, visions and landmarks – Reforming Whitehall II: the critics have their say – Civil servants, Parliament and the public – Bibliography – Index.

304pp   0 335 19311 0 (Paperback)   0 335 19312 9 (Hardback)

THE STATE UNDER STRESS
CAN THE HOLLOW STATE BE GOOD GOVERNMENT?

Christopher D. Foster and Francis J. Plowden

This is a comprehensive account of the changes that have taken place in British government in recent years – since 1979 but, more especially, since 1988. It argues that (and explains why) there has been a general decline in competence and ability to deliver good government. Ministers are increasingly overloaded, their longstanding relationships with civil servants have altered and the power of Parliament has declined. And the machinery of government has been transformed, at one level, by changes in the use of Cabinet and at another by privatization, contractorization and the creation of executive agencies. Any new government will find government transformed to a point where most memories of how it used to work in the 1970s are irrelevant. *The State Under Stress* argues that, while the clock cannot be turned back, urgent reforms are needed if democracy is not to be further undermined.

Contents
The causes of fiscal crisis – The politics of fiscal crisis – New public management examined – Separating provision from production – Complete separation: social objectives and regulation of privatization – Impermanent separation: contractorization – Decentralization: empowering local communities – The agency: incomplete separation – Ministers and agencies: separation as metaphor? – The role of minister – What future for politics? – Conclusion – References – Index.

288pp   0 335 19713 2 (Paperback)   0 335 19714 0 (Hardback)

MAKING SOCIAL POLICY
THE MECHANISMS OF GOVERNMENT AND POLITICS, AND HOW TO
INVESTIGATE THEM

Peter Levin

Making Social Policy is a new and original textbook on policy making in British central government. Starting from first principles, it examines policy making through concepts drawn not from academic theories and interpretations but directly from the experiences and perceptions of the politicians, officials and others involved in the decision-making process. Peter Levin sets out a range of techniques for doing this, and applies them to five case studies of policy making by the Thatcher and Major governments. He elegantly brings out the various *mechanisms* at work, including the strategies deployed by the various participants. These case studies, which bring together material from a variety of sources, cover:

- housing and education policy
- social security reform
- the poll tax
- the annual public expenditure cycle
- Europe: the Social Charter and the protection of women workers

Making Social Policy is also about *how to study* policy making. It shows you how to recognize a policy when you see one, and how to make your own analysis of the mechanisms by which government produces and adopts policy proposals, and by which legislative and other measures subsequently come about. Peter Levin also demonstrates how many theoretical perspectives employed by academic writers comprehensively fail to capture the reality of what actually takes place.

Making Social Policy is essentially reading for students of social policy, politics, government, and public administration.

Contents
Introduction – The policy-making machinery – 'Policy' and 'social policy' – Approaches and methods – Formulating intentions: housing and education in the Conservative 1987 election manifesto – The dependence of the Prime Minister: the 'poll tax' saga – Consultation and pressure: reforming social security in the mid-1980s – The Treasury versus the spending departments: the annual spending round – European social policy and the UK: the Social Charter and the protection of women workers – Conclusion: the mechanisms of policy making – Notes and references – Index.

288pp   0 335 19084 7 (Paperback)   0 335 19085 5 (Hardback)